Political Benefits

Political Benefits

Empirical Studies of
American Public Programs

Edited by
Barry S. Rundquist
University of Illinois
at Chicago Circle

LexingtonBooks
D.C. Heath and Company
Lexington, Massachusetts
Toronto

For
Carolyn, Johanna, and Alicia

Library of Congress Cataloging in Publication Data

Main entry under title:
    Political benefits.

    1. Economic assistance, Domestic—United States—Addresses, essays,
lectures. 2. Grants-in-aid—United States—Addresses, essays, lectures. 3. Policy
sciences—Addresses, essays, lectures. I. Rundquist, Barry.
HC110.P63P64   361.6'13'0973   78-19542
ISBN 0-669-02509-7

Published simultaneously in Canada.

Printed in the United States of America.

International Standard Book Number: 0-669-02509-7

Library of Congress Catalog Card Number: 78-19542

Contents

List of Figures

List of Tables

Preface

This book is about the distribution of political benefits by American governments. Its purpose is to make available a set of empirical investigations concerning the nature of political benefits in American public programs. In this preface I introduce the problem with which these studies are concerned, the more general program of research in which they partake, and the specific subject of each of the chapters.

Problem

The district of the chairman of a House standing committee receives a federal project. A majority of states are made eligible for a program that only a few selected states need. Congressman X votes for a community health program that will benefit Congressman Y's district in return for Congressman Y's support of a tax provision that will benefit businesses in X's own district. A bureau's activities are funded at a higher than necessary level because they benefit the constituencies of certain key legislators. Federal funds are given to local governments to carry out national goals rather than being administered more efficiently by federal officials.

These are examples of a phenomenon, the "political benefit," that occurs, or is alleged to occur, repeatedly in American public programs. A political benefit may be defined as a subset of "programmatic benefits." Thus, if a programmatic benefit is any increase in utility that a unit—that is, an individual or group—derives from a given governmental activity, a political benefit is the amount of that increase that results from a policy maker's influence. Thus, the distinguishing characteristics of political benefits are that they benefit some policy maker, or the people a policy maker wants to benefit, and that they are either directly or indirectly caused by that policy maker. Political benefits are important because they may affect the content and impact of public programs. They are problematical because the most basic things about them are as yet not well understood. For example, how prevalent are political benefits in public programs? What form do they assume? Do they only occur under some conditions? Do different programs have different amounts of political benefits? What other factors affect the content of programs and how do they relate to the political influences on programs?

The initial attraction of the study of political benefits for political scientists is that it allows them to combine their concern for why policy takes the form it does with their longstanding interest in how policy decisions are made. The concept of political benefits treats the programs that a government delivers as the result of the process in which they are formulated and implemented. Since in American government policy-making processes are often formally complex and informally pluralistic, the political benefits in a program are seen as registering the cumulative or net impact of political influences operating within and between many different subprocesses. Thus, by determining the beneficiaries of a program, one can evaluate who has the most influence in the policy-making process and which subprocesses (for example, authorization and implementation) are more important than other subprocesses. In contrast, much research on policy processes has focused on particular subprocesses, such as agenda setting, deliberation, coalition formation, implementation, and evaluation, in isolation from other subprocesses and their results.

There are, unfortunately, many obstacles to doing meaningful research on political benefits. Lowi and others have provided some general hypotheses about who benefits from different kinds of programs.[1] But, because policy makers may inflate and/or conceal the extent to which they have succeeded or failed in affecting policy decisions, depending on interviews—the favored strategy for testing such hypotheses during the 1960s and 1970s—is an unreliable device for testing political-benefits hypotheses. To surmount this problem, researchers have begun to combine analyses of aggregate data on programmatic activities with their interviews, participant observation, and speculation.[2] In effect, their work constitutes a systematic, albeit still fledgling, program of basic policy research.

The initial empirical studies of political benefits produced a hodgepodge of conflicting findings. Whether or not one found support for a political-benefits hypothesis seemed to depend as much on the methods employed and the programs examined as on the characteristics of the policy makers. But these studies did raise some serious doubts about whether public programs are indeed shaped so as to benefit powerful policy makers, and whether certain policy makers and policy processes that are hypothesized to be important are important after all. The chapters in this volume explore the substantive and methodological issues raised by previous studies.

Research Program

A research program may be thought of as a set of investigations that are related by the nature of their underlying assumptions about the phenomenon being investigated.[3] Essentially, political-benefits researchers start by assuming that, under some conditions, some policy maker will use some process (such as bargaining or commanding) to influence some other policy makers in order to affect the distribution of programmatic activities among some units, so that units they favor benefit in some way. Then political-benefits research addresses five questions that follow from this general assumption.

1. What individuals or groups in society benefit from policy makers' influence?
2. What forms do political benefits take?
3. What policy makers are especially proficient in generating political benefits?
4. What strategies do policy makers employ in obtaining political benefits?
5. What are the conditions that facilitate or impede policy makers' efforts to produce political benefits?

Regarding the first question, researchers may, for example, try to determine whether policy makers benefit certain geographically discrete electoral constituencies, as the various electoral-responsiveness theories would seem to imply;[4] groups that support their party with money and votes, regardless of where the groups are located; or business and corporate interests at the expense of other groups. Theory, conjecture, and anecdote suggest that these and other units are sometimes candidates for political benefits. But it remains unclear whether particular units actually receive these benefits, and whether some receive more than others. And, of course, unless the appropriate units are specified, conclusions regarding the scope of the political benefits in a program, and which policy makers are more successful in producing them, may be spurious. For example, if one examines the distribution of programmatic activities among geographic constituencies, but policy makers actually distribute them to benefit businessmen regardless of where they reside, one might wrongly conclude that a program lacks political benefits.

Consider the second question. Although political benefits can be defined in the abstract as the improvements in personal utility that individuals or groups of individuals experience as a result of a policy maker's influence on a policy decision, what this definition denotes in the real world is unclear. For example, if a unit receives more of a programmatic activity relative to what it experienced before the program went into effect, does it benefit more than it would from alternative programs, or more than do other units? Does the programmatic activity that includes the benefit consist of money, staff, discretion, a ratio of expenditures received to taxes paid, government-related employment, the existence of positive program activity of any kind (such as some military construction as opposed to none or to closing the base), or simply impressions of people composing the unit that they are benefited? Moreover, is this quantity a *political* benefit if a policy maker announces that he caused it, if other policy makers say he caused it, if he was the official who decided how program activities were to be distributed, or if he participated in a political process (such as logrolling or bargaining) that resulted in programmatic activity in a unit he favored? As in the specification of political units, the way one chooses to answer these questions can easily lead one to ignore political benefits when they are present in a program, and/or to observe them when they are not.

The third question concerns which policy makers in American government are likely to have the greatest influence on policy decisions and hence on the distribution of political benefits. For example, the relative influence of the following actors is in doubt: (1) legislators, executives, bureaucrats, and judges; (2) elected and nonelected decision makers; (3) federal, state, and local officials; (4) authorizers and appropriators; and (5) those who form the initial decisions about how particular policies will be formulated (the rule makers) and those who make subsequent decisions within the context of those rules.

In regard to the last two questions, about strategies and processes, it remains unclear whether policies are approved because minorities of legislators want them and logroll with others to get them enacted, or because the constitutionally specified number of legislators (or more) want them approved. Also problematical is the extent to which interinstitutional policy cooperation reflects consensus, indifference, or compromise; whether large and small programs are produced in different ways; how the presence or absence of budget ceilings affects the passage of positive (progovernment intervention) or negative (antigovernment intervention) policy preferences; and whether formal and informal decision-making rules embody a bias against certain kinds of policy settlement (for example, compromises with bureaucrats).[5]

The Studies

At present we are a long way from being able to provide definitive answers to these questions. The chapters in this volume, however, represent major steps toward answering them. To begin with, they move beyond the analysis of single programs to comparisons among a variety of programs. For example, the papers examine such expenditure programs as economic development grants; pensions; the National Endowments for the Arts and Humanities; health-care grants and water-pollution construction grants; tax programs, such as the oil depletion allowance and the federal income tax; aggregate spending by the Departments of Agriculture, Defense, Health, Education, and Welfare, Urban Development, and the Interior, and the Office of Economic Opportunity and the Veterans Administration; and even total federal aid to the states. Such a wide range of programs is useful if we are to begin to consider the scope of political benefits and the conditions under which they occur.

Most of the chapters are concerned with the proper measurement of the concept of political benefits. Gone are the days of measuring such benefits as, for example, the average amount of program expenditures in the states or congressional districts of Democratic or Republican legislators at one point in time. Some of the authors treat benefits as year-to-year changes in expenditures or numbers of grants; as partial effects of political factors, controlling for a range of variables that are treated as exogenous influences; as people's perceptions that they benefit from certain programs; and as the difference between current profit margins and the profit margins that would occur in the absence of the program.

The authors also share a concern with the theory of how political benefits are produced. Early studies in this genre tended to examine hypotheses suggested by politicians and journalists. The present works draw more heavily on the theories of economists and political scientists.

Finally, although most of the authors are concerned with the distribution of political benefits among geographic units, such as states and congressional districts, some of them treat the distribution of programmatic benefits among nongeographic units, such as occupational groups—farmers, for instance—and industries.

Taken together, these studies provide important additional clues regarding the overall scope and nature of political benefits, and indicate some routes for further research. The chapters are presented in the following order:

1. Bruce Ray analyzes the extent to which districts represented on the congressional committees authorizing and funding seven different federal departments receive larger year-to-year increases in spending than do other districts. He finds little support for the hypotheses that they do.

2. J. Norman Reid summarizes his analysis of factors affecting the distribution of health grants among the states. Among the variables he considers are the local demand for the program, representation on congressional committees, whether the state supported the incumbent president, the political value of the program, and whether the distribution of grants was determined by formula or by administrative discretion. This study suggests that officials may choose not to influence certain programs if, for example, they are politically insignificant back home. Or they may not have discretion to affect the distribution of activities in certain programs. But if programs are politically desirable, officials seem capable of influencing the authorization phase of formula-grant programs and/or the funding phase of project-grant programs, so that their constituencies benefit somewhat.

3. Theodore Anagnoson's chapter concerns the extent to which the distribution of Economic Development Grants among congressional districts reflects universalism ("to each according to need") or the operation of the distributive theory ("to each according to the power of its congressman"). He cautions that political benefits need not favor occupants of committees, bureaus, party leadership, or other key governmental positions.

Rather, the policy-making process may be structured so that many decision makers are able to obtain projects for favored sectors of society, and this results in a more universalistic than distributive allocation of programmatic benefits.

4. Ralph Carlton, Timothy Russell, and Richard Winters report their analysis of changes in distribution of funds in the rapidly growing National Endowments for the Arts and Humanities. They show that, at least in the case of the National Endowments for the Arts, funds were initially distributed to benefit the states of the congressmen in the coalition who supported this legislation. But after the Arts Endowment was better established, its funds became more evenly distributed among states.

5. Richard Sylves examines the effect of partisan, intergovernmental and need considerations in the distribution of pure-water construction grants in New York State. He concludes that the distribution of water-pollution projects reflects a combination of efficiency and political considerations—the latter benefiting Republican state senatorial districts.

6. Heywood Sanders examines the use of Civil War pensions in generating electoral support for the Republican Party in the period preceding the 1896 electoral realignment. This study illustrates the way in which apparently innocuous formula programs may contain massive political benefits, but only if a mediating political organization—in this case, the Grand Army of the Republic—mobilizes its members to take advantage of them.

7. Susan B. Hansen reports on a time-series analysis of public opinion regarding the federal income tax since World War II. Her tentative conclusion is that the more people perceive that they benefit from federal spending programs, the more they are willing to accept a tax increase.

8. John Echols compares the geographical distribution of spending and federal aid in the United States with practices in several other countries. He demonstrates that the United States is unique in the world in its expenditure and aid patterns, and argues that the often-observed tendency for social-welfare spending by state governments to reflect the state's economic wealth is in large part due to a failure of the federal government to give greater amounts of aid to poorer states.

9. Jon Bond describes his analysis of the effect of oil depletion allowances on oil exploration and industry profits from 1900 to 1974. He shows that the programmatic benefit to the oil companies from the oil depletion allowance took the form of larger profits than the companies would have earned in the absence of this tax program.

10. In the concluding chapter I review some of the findings of this research and discuss the theory of political benefits.

Notes

1. See, for example, Theodore J. Lowi, "American Business and Public Policy, Case Studies and Political Theory," *World Politics* 16 (July

1964):667-715; and William A. Niskanen, Jr., *Bureaucracy and Representative Government* (Chicago: Aldine, 1971).

2. See, for example, John A. Ferejohn, *Pork Barrel Politics* (Stanford, Calif.: Stanford University Press, 1974); and Barry S. Rundquist and John A. Ferejohn, "Observations on a Distributive Theory of Policy Making: Two American Expenditure Programs Compared," in Craig Liske, John McCamant, and William Lehr, *Comparative Public Policy* (New York: John Wiley and Sons, 1975).

In addition to the various papers on committee-centered influences on the geographic distribution of federal expenditures (which are amply cited in the various chapters included herein), other studies of political benefits include some of the studies of state and urban policy making and comparative government. For example, comparative state analyses which hypothesize that Democratic party control produces higher levels of welfare spending, and cross-national studies which hypothesize partisan effects on inflation and employment rates, may be interpretable as political-benefits studies. See, for example, Edward Tufte, *Political Control of the Economy* (Princeton, N.J.: Princeton University Press, 1978).

3. See the discussion of Imre Lakatos' view of research programs in Terence Ball, "From Paradigms to Research Programs: Toward a Post-Kuhnian Political Science," *American Journal of Political Science* 20 (February 1976):151-177.

4. Much of the research so far focuses on geographic constituencies, but as the inclusion of the papers by Jon Bond and Susan Hansen is meant to suggest, political benefits may go to other units as well.

5. For a discussion of these issues, see Barry S. Rundquist and Gerald S. Strom, "On Explaining Legislative Policy Making," in Lawrence C. Dodd and Bruce I. Oppenheimer, eds., *Congress Reconsidered*, 2nd ed. (Washington, D.C.: Congressional Quarterly, 1981).

Acknowledgments

Several of the chapters included in this volume represent a research program that dates to the late 1960s and includes many more scholars than those so-far named. Its inspiration lies in writings by Theodore Lowi, Harold Lasswell, E.E. Schattschneider, Charles Lindblom, Anthony Downs, Roland Pennock, Brian Barry, and others. Discussions with John Ferejohn, Larry Rose, Richard Winters, Barry Ames, and Raymond Wolfinger generated some of the first empirical studies of political benefits. Several graduate students at the University of Illinois, especially Jon Bond, Cary Covington, Donald Emerich, Richard Fleisher, David Griffith, Norman Reid, Gerald Strom, and Richard Sylves, continued this research and contributed a number of the ideas (as well as several of the chapters) included in this volume. And a number of other students and colleagues, both in Illinois and around the country, have offered constructive criticism of and encouragement for these studies. Of course, the authors and myself are responsible for our errors. Finally, I am grateful to Stuart Nagel for helping me to find a publisher, to Andrea Friedman for help with editing several papers, to the Department of Political Science at the University of Illinois and the School of Government at American University for typing assistance, and to Kathy Benn at Lexington for patient but persistent shepherding of the whole project.

1

Congressional Promotion of District Interests: Does Power on the Hill Really Make a Difference?

Bruce A. Ray

Introduction

While the 435 members of the U.S. House of Representatives comprise an American elite, they are not all of equal stature. Some are more powerful than others. Factors such as election or appointment to a leadership position, the accrual of seniority, close relations with the President and/or other officials in the executive branch, and membership in the majority (controlling) party may all serve to differentiate the powerful representatives from their less well-placed colleagues. The committee and subcommittee structure of Congress also helps in the creation of elites within the elite.

To a large extent policy questions that fall within the jurisdiction of a particular elite are decided by the members of that elite. Those who have the power, dictate the outcomes. They are "winners." But what do they win? The benefits accruing from policy choices are frequently incalculable, intangible, and/or indivisible. The specific programs enacted to implement these chosen policies, on the other hand, frequently entail the distribution of rewards which *are* calculable, tangible and divisible—military bases, sewage treatment plants, construction contracts, crop subsidies, transfer payments, and so on. If jurisdictional elites determine broad policy questions, but fail to secure resulting program benefits for their home districts, it becomes questionable what they have won. Today, constituents depend upon their congressmen for the provision of these benefits to a greater extent than ever before (Fiorina, 1977). Furthermore, congressmen depend on constituent gratitude for these services as a major contribution to their continued electoral security (Mayhew, 1974).

Thus, we should expect congressmen to be at least as concerned with the distribution of system rewards as they are with policy resolution. Fiorina (1977) argues that these direct constituent benefits should be of even greater

I wish to thank William Claggett, Lawrence Flood, Barry S. Rundquist, and Kenneth Shepsle for comments on earlier versions of this manuscript. Financial support for the data collection was provided by the National Science Foundation and the Graduate School of Washington University, St. Louis.

importance to congressmen. The natural assumption, therefore, is that members of the jurisdictional elites, who have the power to shape national policy, also occupy the influential institutional positions whose powers may be used to dictate the distribution of specific program benefits. The corollary assumption, which is really a testable hypothesis, is that these members do use their potent positions to determine reward distribution in a manner most suited to their individual needs. That is, they maximize federal spending within their constituencies.

Evidence for the Hypothesis

Most evidence cited in support of this corollary assumption is anecdotal. When Carl Vinson and Richard Russell chaired, respectively, the House and Senate Armed Services Committees, the Pentagon moved a substantial portion of its operations to Georgia. The rise of Mendel Rivers to prominence on the House Armed Services Committee corresponded very closely with the increasing concern of the Department of Defense for the economic well-being of the First District of South Carolina (Pearson and Anderson, 1968, pp. 267-268). Not only military expenditures have been affected in this manner. The late Senator Robert Kerr (D., Okla.) used his position as chairman of the Senate committee overseeing the space program to channel NASA contracts to Oklahoma companies. As the second-ranking Democrat on the Finance Committee he also protected the interests of Oklahoma oilmen—including himself, as partner in Kerr-McGee (Barone et al. 1972). He even left a permanent tribute to himself and his power in the form of the McClellan-Kerr Navigation System, which, via an extensive canal system, makes Tulsa, Oklahoma, an ocean port. Even Gerald R. Ford admitted, during his first speech to Congress as President, that as minority leader he had "sometimes voted to spend more taxpayers' money for worthy federal projects in Grand Rapids" (1974). We are left with the impression that congressmen who, by their institutional power, are blessed with the power to allocate federal benefits for the specific sustenance of their own constituents, do not hesitate to so act. The logical conclusion, all other things being equal, is that federal outlays are more likely to flow into districts of powerful congressmen than into the districts of their less well-placed colleagues. In other words, districts represented by those most powerful on the Hill should receive more than their "fair share" at the federal trough, and this excess should come at the expense of constituencies with representatives poorly positioned in the Capitol hierarchy.

Several studies have attempted tests of this thesis. Charles R. Plott (1968) questioned whether Urban Renewal Administration (URA) funds flowed disproportionately into congressional districts represented by members of the urban renewal elite; that is, those sitting on the Banking and

Currency Committee which exercised legislative jurisdiction over the URA. He discovered that, in 1964, while committee members comprised only 7.1 percent of the House, they attracted 15.7 percent of all federally funded urban renewal projects to their districts. Moreover, these projects accounted for 25.2 percent of the URA's expenditures. Plott concluded that, within their jurisdictions, members of congressional elites do shape distributional patterns for the benefit of their own constituencies.

Weldon Barton (1970) performed a similar analysis for the Armed Services elite. He reported that districts of House Armed Services Committee members were more than one and one-third times as likely to contain military installations than were those of congressmen not included in the elite (63.4 percent to 46.9 percent). Moreover, there was a similar, although smaller, disparity for the location of private defense contractors (53.7 percent to 49.0 percent).

Using 1968 data, Carol F. Goss (1972) concluded that membership in the Armed Services elite (including the House Appropriations Subcommittee on Military Construction as well as Armed Services) increased Defense Department (DOD) employment, both military and civilian, in represented constituencies. She did discover, however, that membership on the House Appropriations Subcommittee on the DOD appeared to confer no distributional advantages. Her suggestion was that these legislators, with jurisdiction over military procurement, were faced with the problem that defense contracts frequently could be handled by only a select group of firms, and were, therefore, somewhat immune to congressional tampering. Barry S. Rundquist (1973) used 1960 data to examine the distribution of prime military contracts in greater detail. Paralleling Goss, he found no disproportionate benefits in districts represented by Armed Services elites. However, John A. Ferejohn (1974), using a methodology similar to Rundquist's, did discover, for 1967, disproportionate elite benefits in the Corps of Engineers public works policy area.

Not only can similar methods used to assess congressional influence over federal benefits in different policy areas yield contrasting results, but differing methodologies applied to the same policy area may also result in contradictory conclusions. Research concentrating on the jurisdiction of the Armed Services Committee demonstrates this. For example, although from 1952-1972 states represented on the House and Senate Armed Services Committees and the relevant appropriations subcommittees averaged a gain nearly four times as large ($25.2 million versus $6.4 million) as unrepresented states for every additional one billion dollars of military procurement expenditures (Rundquist and Griffith, 1974), the gaining or losing of a seat on Armed Services by a state resulted in no significant change in the percent of prime military contracts being allocated to that state. Moreover, if there was any change, it was more likely to be in the "wrong" direction (Rundquist and Griffith, 1976).

The smallest change in the dependent variable can also result in anomalous findings. Arnold (1977, p. 26) concludes that a seat on Armed Services helps a congressman prevent the closing of military bases in his district during periods of retrenchment and, to a lesser extent, helps him secure new installations at other times. However, when attention is diverted from the bases themselves to their staffing levels, Arnold is forced to conclude (p. 32) that this same seat on Armed Services does not help representatives increase, nor even prevent decreases in, base employment. In fact, the relationship is negative. Committee members suffer more than their colleagues from changing employment levels.

The annual operating outlays of the Atomic Energy Commission (AEC)— including monies spent for plant acquisition and expansion, such as additions to capital investment, as well as those spent for operating costs incurred in both private and AEC installations—are program benefits which appear ripe for manipulation by the appropriate congressional elite, in this case the Joint Committee on Atomic Energy (JCAE), now defunct. However, in a time-series analysis of the JCAE spanning nearly two decades, Kenneth F. Cook (1976) concluded that there was "a conscious effort on the part of the AEC and of the JCAE to distribute the yearly benefit of the AEC as widely as is practicable" (Cook, 1976, p. 122). A similar point was made by Rundquist (1978). He argued that the DOD may deliberately spread its disbursements among many districts—at least a majority. This way congressional support for policies beneficial to the Defense Department may be induced.

Policy control, even in a jurisdiction with calculable, tangible, and divisible program benefits, does not automatically lead to disproportionate rewards for represented congressional districts. In some jurisdictions elites secure disproportionate benefits, and in some jurisdictions they do not. Whether this is due to differing member philosophies, different political processes within different jurisdictions, the methodology and/or data base of individual researchers, some combination of these factors, or an unknown cause is, at best, unclear. It does seem clear, however, that micro-level analyses of various federal benefits are not the proper way to proceed. If various programs are affected by congressional influence differently or not at all, it becomes important to assess the "total picture." Only a macro-level analysis can tell us whether the constituencies of congressional elites benefit more in the end. However, the results of the macro-level studies are no more immune to differing data and methods than are micro-level analyses.

This was demonstrated by two recent studies which analyzed most House committees (elites) and many different spending jurisdictions (Goss, 1975, using 1970 data; and Ritt, 1976, using 1972 data). The two studies reached opposite conclusions. Goss (1975) believes that constituencies benefit disproportionately from program implementation in the jurisdictional areas of their representatives' policy dominance (committee assignment). Among other examples, she cites disproportionate Department of Agriculture spending in the districts of House Agriculture Committee members, disproportionate DOD outlays in Armed Services districts, an overabundance of HUD expenditures in Banking and Currency constituencies, and a similar relationship between Science and Astronautics membership and NASA disbursements. Similar correspondences were discovered within the jurisdictions of many of the subcommittees of the House Appropriations Committee. For example, the districts of Public Works and AEC Subcommittee members averaged 693 percent of the House mean in AEC outlays, with similar, although not so blatant, circumstances reported for Agriculture, Military Construction, and Transportation. Leonard Ritt (1976), however, after examining virtually the same elites and jurisdictions, was unable to uncover the anticipated pattern of disproportionate rewards. He concluded that congressmen are amazingly unsuccessful at translating policy dominance into constituent benefits in their areas of specialization.

Thus, despite this multitude of studies, the basic question remains unanswered. Do constituencies represented by well-placed congressmen disproportionately benefit from the distribution of federal largesse? In the next section I will discuss why previous studies have left us with such ambiguous answers.

A Look at the Evidence

Evidence for the belief that influential congressmen get more federal benefits for their districts has been of two types: anecdotal and statistical. The anecdotal evidence, with Rivers as probably the most notorious example, has colored our thinking. As students of Lasswell we are already predisposed to believe that "the influential are those who get the most of what there is to get" (Lasswell, 1951, p. 295). The anecdotes, however, prove nothing. What of conflicting examples? In fiscal year 1970, when Rivers was at the pinnacle of his power, his district received $582.2 million in federal funds (Ray, 1977). The DOD share was $385.9 million. A few hundred miles to the northeast was the First Congressional District of Virginia, also blessed with a natural harbor, Norfolk. Represented by Thomas N. Downing (D, Va.), who was neither included in the Armed Services elite nor a senior member of the House, this constituency, in the same fiscal year, secured $898.6 million in federal expenditures, with the Defense Department contributing a hefty $604.2 million—more than the *total* spending in Rivers's district. Power is not a necessary condition to "get the most of what there is to get."

Is it a sufficient condition? I think not. Another southern area with an excellent harbor a few hundred miles to the southwest of Charleston is New

Orleans. In fiscal year 1970 the city was divided into two congressional districts. Louisiana One was represented by F. Edward Hebert (D), who sat third on the Armed Services and succeeded Rivers as chairman upon his death the following year. The Second District was served by Hale Boggs (D), the majority whip, who was named majority leader in the Ninety-second Congress. In addition, the state's senators chaired the two most important committees in the upper house—Appropriations and Finance. New Orleans's representation on the Hill was definitely well-placed, both overall and in the Armed Services elite, yet in the competition for federal funds the area did poorly. Hebert's constituents received only $525.1 million, and Boggs's a mere $368.7 million (Ray, 1977). For the DOD, the outlays in these two districts were only $143.6 million and $89.7 million, respectively. Many other counterexamples could also be cited. Thus, it is unwise to rely upon anecdotal evidence to substantiate the hypothesis that power on the Hill is always, or even usually, translated into tangible benefits in the associated congressional districts.

The more systematic data analyses are also flawed. A major problem is the lack of differentiation between "base" and "increment" in the federal spending process. Lasswell asserted that the powerful get the most of what there is to get, not that they have the most of what there is to have. Apparently, his maxim referred to the distribution of emoluments that become available during the period of power, not to the *re*distribution of previously mandated allocations. It is quite reasonable to assume that many district benefits are the fruits of congressional power bases and other factors which no longer exist. Despite the fact that in 1971 the old Armed Services king was dead and his successor crowned, it would be unreasonable to expect that, overnight, the Charleston polaris submarine base would become the New Orleans polaris submarine base. Rather, it seemed more likely that the benefits of the 2200-man squadron would continue to accrue to Rivers's old constituents no matter what congressional position the area's new representative occupied. There was little expectation that massive new military rewards would be disbursed in this locale, but the base, that is, existing federal operations, was seen, for the most part, as secure. In general, if well-placed legislators use their positions to reap dispropotionate benefits for their constituents, their attention is devoted to new system rewards, the increment, rather than toward a massive redistribution of previously conferred federal projects. This concentration on the increment is possible because, in recent history at least, the federal pie has continuously expanded. Of the authors discussed above, only Ferejohn (1974), Rundquist and Griffith (1974, 1976) and Cook (1976) examined the distribution of increments. Interestingly, although all were concerned with potentially malleable segments of the federal budget, they came to conflicting conclusions. It is, however, only these increments which should be assessed when questioning congressional success at translating power into constituent benefits.

A second methodological problem in the literature, previously cited, is the tendency to conduct micro-level analyses. Goss (1975) and Ritt (1976) were less narrow in their focus, but both inappropriately selected the base, rather than the spending increment, as the dependent variable. Macro-level analysis requires two procedures. The first of these is replicating the test across several policy areas. Only in this way can it be determined whether or not allocation patterns are similar in different jurisdictions. The second requirement is the assessment of the "total picture"—determining whether well-placed legislators benefit overall or only in narrow program areas, when compared with their less well-situated peers. For example, if Banking Committee members allocated the entire HUD budget to their districts, but received virtually no other federal benefits, would they really be winning? I doubt it, because, in the aggregate, they would probably be receiving less than most other constituencies. Doing well within a narrow jurisdiction, but poorly overall, may not be enough to satisfy constituent desires for federal benefits.

A related defect in existing literature is the absence of measurement of or controls for congressional logrolling. The assumption has been that only those members with positions on a committee or subcommittee with direct jurisdiction over a program's authorization or appropriations have influence over the distribution of rewards obligated under that program. If this is so, and if congressmen are concerned with the provision of federal benefits to their constituents, why would members seek, or even accept, assignments to committees with limited jurisdictions vis-à-vis tangible and divisible rewards, such as the House Committees on International Relations and Administration? Perhaps because of their ability to use policy jurisdiction within these domains as bargaining chips, in logrolling for distributive rewards controlled by colleagues on other panels, members do not completely shun these assignments. Wayne Hayes (D., Ohio) was reputed to have used his chairmanship of House Administration to extract many favors from his colleagues. However, no previous study has included any measures of this potential indirect influence over the geographic distribution of federal outlays. Furthermore, resources available for logrolling for constituency benefits are not limited to committee positions. Other possible power bases include close ties with the White House, and the willingness to cast a vote helpful to one's colleagues. Thus, a more precise model of the distributive process must allow for some mechanism whereby those powerful in nondistributive elites can trade for benefits in other jurisdictions by the process of logrolling. This necessitates the inclusion in the analysis of measures of institutional power other than committee membership on those panels with direct legislative jurisdiction over the spending programs in question.

Another type of error has been a general misspecification of the basic model. The question concerns causal direction of the model, and follows directly from nonrecognition of the difference between base and increment. By assumption, analyses of the relationship between congressional influence and the geographic distribution of federal spending have used congressmen as the independent, or causal, variable and district receipts as the dependent phenomenon. However, any covariance between the magnitude of federal largesse disbursed in a constituency and the institutional position occupied by that constituency's representative could easily be explained by a model specifying a reverse causal direction. In other words, congressional districts, through some unspecified process, might become involved in particular areas of federal activity. In fact, they may even become dependent upon the continuation of certain federal programs if they are to maintain their economic health and/or stability. This dependence then mandates the committee assignments that congressmen will strive to obtain. For example, in Mendel Rivers's last term in office, 35 percent of the payrolls in the First Congressional District of South Carolina came from either military installations or defense industries (Barone et al., 1972, p. 916). The district's economic well-being had become inseparably tied to the jurisdiction of the House Armed Services Committee. Following Rivers's death, his godson, Mendel Davis, was sent to Washington as his replacement. The new legislator, coming from a district with an existing interest in the military budget, sought, and eventually secured, a seat on Armed Services. The same relationship between committee assignment and disproportionately high shares of the defense budget that had existed during his predecessor's tenure was still apparent, yet the causal direction was now reversed. Few would credit Davis for the proliferation of installations. While Rivers's goal was to create and expand district interests, Davis's objective was the maintenance of an existing situation. In goals, Rivers was a *promoter* and Davis a *protector*.

Other examples of protection-oriented committee assignments abound. Boeing Aircraft was a beneficiary of extensive government contracting long before former Representative Brock Adams (D., Wash.) first arrived on the Hill. However, with this company the largest employer in his district, it is no surprise that he sought membership on the Transportation and Aeronautics Subcommittee of the House Interstate and Foreign Commerce Committee. Similarly, the decision to construct the Viking Craft in Colorado had already been made when Senator Floyd Haskell (D., Colo.) first sought membership on Aeronautics and Space Sciences. In fact, not only is it quite common for members to seek assignments for which the demographic characteristics of their districts make them "interesteds," but it is also quite common for these requests to be honored by the Committees on Committees (Bullock, 1973; Shepsle, 1978). Although Rundquist and Ferejohn (1975) discuss a recruitment hypothesis and Goss (1975) and Cook (1976) note that the causal relationship in the model is unclear, no previous study has made an attempt to develop a method of analysis which would isolate the two competing explanations.

Therefore, the conclusions drawn from the relationships between committee position and the geographic allocation of federal spending, as reported in the literature discussed above, are suspect. The possibility that the distribution of federal funds could have mandated the pattern of committee assignments was not investigated. Ray (1977, chapter 5) was able to predict 75-93 percent of freshman assignment requests to six House committees in the Ninety-second, Ninety-third, and Ninety-fourth Congresses by using the geographic distribution of federal spending in each committee's area of jurisdiction as the independent variable, while controlling for electoral insecurity and the existing committee representation of each freshman's state party delegation.[1]

It is the nonrecognition of the difference between a district's base and increment that has resulted in this model misspecification. Current congressional positions and behavior may have an impact on current and future increments, but they cannot cause the already established base. Nonetheless most of the statistical tests used have ascertained whether or not representatives have caused the current pattern of federal allocation, despite the fact that the geographic locations for many of these activities were determined prior to the election of sitting members. The problems stemming from the use of other improper methodological techniques may be equally as severe, and may also contribute to the conflicting results in existing literature. One such flaw is the tendency for studies to be micro (single-committee jurisdiction) analyses. The possibility of intercommittee logrolling has also been completely ignored. Negotiation and bargaining allow congressmen to translate influence in one jurisdiction into benefits in another. Therefore, congressional influence must be related to the total package of benefits districts receive, not merely to those system rewards under the immediate control of each constituency's representative. Ill-advised measures of federal benefits in a congressional district, such as use of the budget base or failure to differentiate between small and large federal projects (Ferejohn, 1974), as well as the reluctance to use reasonably high-powered statistical techniques such as multiple regression in the analysis, despite the availability of interval-level federal spending data, are additional methodological failings. A method for overcoming each of these problems is presented in the next section.

The Model

By using annual change in federal activity, rather than a given year's total federal funding, in a congressional district as the dependent variable, the difference between base and increment is acknowledged. Congressmen are seen as responsible, to some extent, for increases and decreases in their district's base; specifically, for changes from the level of federal funding previously enjoyed in the locale. They are not, however, seen as responsible

for the magnitude of these prior federal commitments. Use of this change
measure also alleviates the problem of a misspecified causal direction. If the
institutional positions of representatives serving in year t are independent
variables, the dependent variable is the increment (or decrement) in district funding in year $t + 1$, as compared with year t. The base distributions of year t may or may not have been a causal factor in establishing the
committee positions of year t, but it is clear that the change in district
receipts between year t and year $t + 1$ could not possibly have caused this
committee structure. If there is a causal relationship in this model, its direction must be from congressional influence to the geographic distribution of
federal spending.

The possibility of logrolling can also be incorporated into this model.
By including other indicators of institutional influence besides membership
on the committee(s) with direct legislative jurisdiction over the spending
area in question, the importance of these other power bases in obtaining
favorable distributions can also be assessed. Thus, the basic model takes the
form of the following regression equation.

$$\Delta S_t = a + b_1 X_{1t} + b_2 X_{2t} \ldots b_N X_{Nt} \tag{1.1}$$

where:

S_t = district receipts during year t;
a = increase (or decrease) in district receipts accruing for reasons
       other than congressional position; and
X = indicators of institutional influence.

Beta weights of positive slope indicate that their associated indicators of institutional influence correlated with increases in district spending and vice versa.

My change measure, ΔS_t, is the actual difference, measured in
thousands of dollars, between federal disbursements in a congressional
district during a given fiscal year and federal outlays in that area during the
previous fiscal year. If federal spending increased in this constituency, this
figure is positive; otherwise, it is negative. A zero change score representing
neither growth nor decline is also possible. Spending figures were obtained
from U.S. Office of Economic Opportunity (OEO)[2] publications, *Federal
Outlays in [state name]: Fiscal Year 19[xx]*, for fiscal years (FY) 1968 to
1976, inclusive. These volumes contain, for each state, county, and large
city, lists of all outlays of the executive branch of the federal government,[3]
broken down into over 1700 programs, appropriations, and federal activities. For each item and geographic area the exact dollar amount disbursed is displayed. (Although some figures are estimates, this is the most
precise federal spending data available). Unfortunately, totals are not given
for congressional districts. Therefore, it was necessary to transform the
city- and county-level data into district-level outlays. The statistical pro-

cedure used in this transformation is discussed in detail in Ray (1977) and summarized in an appendix to this analysis.

With nine years of spending data, I was able to compute measures of spending change for eight consecutive years, FY 1969-1976. In addition to collecting figures on total federal spending in congressional districts, I also computed subtotals for five departments, including Agriculture (DOA), Defense (DOD), Health, Education and Welfare (HEW), Housing and Urban Development (HUD), and Interior (DOI), one branch of the Executive Office of the President, OEO;[4] and one independent agency, Veterans Administration (VA). These were selected because of their great dissimilarity in size, clientele groups, associated bureaucracies, and public visibility. If different congressional behaviors vis-à-vis promotion of district interests are operative in different budget areas, replication of a standardized test for this variety of subsystems should uncover the disparities. For example, it is possible that some budget areas are more susceptible to logrolling, and, thus, are more likely to have their benefits distributed widely than are other policy jurisdictions. This may be due to factors of size, as it is harder for committee members with direct jurisdiction to keep a large program all to themselves; or it may be due to the need for some committees to attract floor support for their policies by permitting a more widespread distribution of outlays under their control.

Use of ΔS_t as a dependent variable could create statistical problems if ΔS_t and S_t are highly correlated. This could occur if, for example, districts with large federal spending bases (S_ts) are less likely than other constituencies to reap large increments (ΔS_ts), since they are less able to absorb additional federal projects. Alternatively, districts heavily involved in major federal activities, such as defense contracting, might have an inside track for massive increments since the foundation has already been laid. However, with an R^2 of .131, ΔS_t and S_t appear to be statistically independent of one another, and use of ΔS_t therefore poses no statistical problem.[5]

Another potential complicating factor is that so much of the current federal budget is composed of "uncontrollables." Uncontrollables are those programs which obligate the federal government to make payments to individuals or governments meeting program requirements specified by law, for which it is not necessary that obligational authority be provided in advance. Subsequently, appropriations are required, although they are essentially dictated by the legislation establishing the uncontrollable programs. Since the mandating legislation can be changed, no program is totally uncontrollable (Blechman et al. 1975). Nonetheless, uncontrollables do differ from their complement, controllables, in a fundamental way. The latter may be altered much more easily, in either the authorization or appropriations arenas, as well as in the actual spending process (Fisher, 1975).

Since controllables are more malleable, it would be expected that, if congressional influence does to some extent dictate the geographic distribution of federal outlays, the impact would be most readily observable in these programs. Therefore, uncontrollables were deleted from the analysis, and the change scores represent increments and decrements in only those programs least immune to congressional tampering; that is, controllables. The breakdown of the spending figures into over 1700 items in the OEO volumes made this deletion of uncontrollables relatively easy.

A third possible complication stems from the indivisible and "lump-sum" nature of many federal outlays. For example, consider the award of any large defense contract or public works project to a given locale. Assume, for the moment, that such awards are more likely to be made in the districts of powerful congressmen than in the constituencies of their less well-placed colleagues. It may be unreasonable, however, to expect even powerful congressmen to receive large lump-sum increments, such as new public works projects, year after year, with the less powerful being virtually ignored. In some years districts represented by powerful legislators might receive little or no increment, while others took their turn. In the limited time frame necessary in this study it might be possible to miss sporadically occurring large increments in federal outlays in the districts of the powerful, despite the fact that over the long haul these constituencies might be doing better than those represented by the less well-placed. Could this create statistical anomalies—that is, could an association between power on Capitol Hill and a skewed geographic distribution of federal spending increments be "missed" for this reason? Probably not because, if such a relationship exists, the regression techniques detailed in this section should uncover it. The tested hypothesis is not that every powerful congressman is able to infuse his district with larger than average increments each and every year. Rather, the expectation is that, if indeed there is a relationshp between power and the distribution of federal spending, it is more likely for the constituencies of powerful representatives to receive large increases than it is for other districts. Thus, in any given year, we can expect the districts of the powerful to be overrepresented among the winning constituencies. For statistical purposes, as long as the powerful do better as a class, the beta weights will be positive, and it therefore makes no difference if a particular influential congressman is unable to produce massive increments every year. If the well-positioned really do dictate spending outcomes for their personal pleasure, some, but not all, will win each year, and the lump-sum nature of many federal awards will not distort the aggregate results.

Thus, the dependent variables in this test of the ability of influential congressmen to alter the geographic distribution of federal spending in the interests of their own constituents are the actual annual increments and decrements in controllable federal outlays in congressional districts. These data are available for all congressional districts for an eight-year period. In addition to change in overall controllable spending, dependent variables measuring controllable increments in seven budget areas are available and will be analyzed separately.

Construction of independent variables representing congressional influence proved to be less complex. I chose not to define a concept as ambiguous as congressional power. Rather, I selected several common measures of institutional influence. These measures serve as indicators of the relative importance of congressmen.

The most obvious indicator is each member's committee assignment. For each of the seven budget sub-areas, membership on the major authorizing committees with direct jurisdiction was deemed to indicate potential power in the allocative process for federal benefits within that subsystem. Separately, for each of the seven areas, representatives were coded "1" if they were on an appropriate committee and "0" otherwise. The same procedure was followed for membership on the relevant Appropriations subcommittees. This is my second indicator of institutional power. The committees and subcommittees with direct influence for each of the seven areas are listed in table 1-1.

Another indicator of institutional influence is committee seniority. At least for members of the majority party, increased seniority indicates proximity to full and subcommittee chairmanships, the real seats of power. This variable was operationalized as follows.

$$\text{Seniority} = B/(N\text{-}1) \qquad\qquad (1.2)$$

where:

B = the number of members of the same party lower ranked on the committee and

N = the number of members of the same party on the committee.

Since seniority may be worth more to majority party members than to the opposition, seniority scores were computed separately for Democrats and for Republicans. Nonparty members were coded "0" on the seniority measures of the other party.

Table 1-1
Committees and Appropriations Subcommittees with Direct Jurisdiction over the Seven Budget Areas

Budget Area	Committees	Subcommittees
DOA	Agriculture	Agriculture
DOD	Armed Services	Defense; Military Construction
HEW	Education and Labor; Ways and Means	Labor, Health, Education, and Welfare
HUD	Banking and Currency	Housing, Urban Development and Veterans
DOI	Interior and Insular Affairs	Interior
OEO	Education and Labor	Lab, HEW
VA	Veterans Affairs	HUD & Veterans

There are two types of seniority important for this model—seniority on
the committee(s) with direct jurisdiction over a given subsystem, and
seniority on other House committees. The first of these measures potential
direct influence over the spending area in question. The latter measures one
of the potential resources available for logrolling: power in a jurisdiction
other than the one(s) with a direct role in the allocative process for the
spending area being examined. These external resources may be traded for
benefits internal to the spending subsystem. Logrolling is very much a part
of the American legislative process, and this variable, along with others
described below, may measure a congressman's indirect influence over the
geographic distribution of federal expenditures.

Respectively, I call these two measures in-group and out-group seniority. If a member has only in-group assignments (see table 1-1), his out-group
seniority score is zero, and vice versa. If a member had more than one out-
group seniority score, the higher value was coded; although a member may
undoubtedly use all of the resources at his command from both of his committee positions for logrolling purposes, inclusion of more than one out-
group seniority score proved to be too cumbersome a technique. Thus, with
division by jurisdiction and by party, all congressmen have four separate
seniority scores for each of the seven budget areas. Since legislators belong
to only one party, at least half of these must be zero.

The third measure of institutional power used in this inquiry is party.
Members are coded "1" if Democrats and "0" otherwise. The expectation
is that majority party members (Democrats) have greater weight in the
distributive process.

Another congressional power base is inclusion in the party leadership.
Representatives were coded "1" if leaders and "0" otherwise. Positions of
party leadership are displayed in table 1-2. It is ambiguous, however,
whether party leadership positions measure power in the same manner as do
the other indicators. Committee seniority, party affiliation, and committee
and subcommittee assignments are, in a sense, tenured power bases. Once
these are achieved, they cannot be taken from a member, except in very rare
instances. Thus, the legislator is free to use the power accruing from these
positions almost as he sees fit. If these positions provide him the methods
and power to promote the interests of his district, he is free to do so.

Party leadership positions are different. If a post is elective, the member
may be removed at the whim of the party caucus. If the post is appointive,
the representative serves only at the pleasure of the Speaker and party
leader. Therefore, it is reasonable to expect that a large proportion of a party leader's efforts and resources are expended in an effort to solidify his
own position. These same resources cannot then also be used to promote
district interests.

Table 1-2
Positions of Party Leadership

Democrats

Speaker
Majority leader
Majority whip
Deputy majority whip
Chairman of the Caucus
Secretary of the Caucus
Chairman of the National Congressional Committee
Chairman of the Steering Committee
Chairman of the Patronage Committee

Republicans

Minority leader
Minority whip
Chairman of the Conference
Secretary of the Conference
Chairman of the Policy Committee
Chairman of the Planning and Research Committee
Chairman of the National Congressional Committee
Chairman of the Committee on Committees

Although a leadership position may provide a congressman with power, he may be unable to translate this power into district benefits. In fact, with the need to expend resources maintaining his position, he may do even worse in the search for federal funds than colleagues with no power base at all.

These eight variables—membership on the committee with jurisdiction over a budget area, membership on the Appropriations subcommittee with jurisdiction over a budget area, party affiliation, party leadership, and four measures of seniority—comprise my indicators of congressional influence rooted in institutional position. In addition, each regression equation contains from nine to fourteen other independent variables. Eight of these measure possibilities for logrolling. The rest are used as controls for variations in district characteristics.

The additional logrolling variables were common to all regressions. These measure the contribution of member voting records to the geographic distribution of federal spending. Briefly, these measure the party unity and administration support of congressmen and the change over time in each of these scores, all of this done separately for Democrats and for Republicans. It was argued elsewhere (Ray, 1977) that vote trading on the House floor might be a means by which members could logroll for distributive rewards allocated in their colleagues' domains. Party unity and administration support scores were taken from the annual reports by Congressional Quarterly (CQ Almanac). The expectation is that those more loyal to their party and/or those more responsive to the administration might be rewarded with favorable distributions of federal spending. It is also conceivable that minority party members might be rewarded if they are less loyal to their own party.

One problem with this is the "bought vote" syndrome: if a legislator always votes with his party or the President no matter what, why should one bother to reward him? A better utilization of limited resources might be to spend them to entice or reward a congressman less entrenched in his voting behavior. The member who improves his voting record might receive more benefits than one who has been "right" all along. Thus, measures of change in party unity and administration support were included along with the annual scores themselves. Change scores are simply the first difference, current performance minus last year's record. The expectation is that positive change scores should correlate with increased district receipts.

Finally, selected district demographic characteristics were used to control for the need of congressional districts for certain types of federal activity, or their ability to absorb funds within these spending domains. The demographic variables and the regressions in which they are used are displayed in table 1-3. Thus, the complete regression equations contain, as independent variables, six indicators of direct institutional power; two measures of indirect institutional power (out-group seniority);[6] an additional eight variables measuring logrolling potential, derived from congressional voting records; and from one to six measures of district demographic characteristics used as control variables. The dependent variable is the dollar change (plus or minus) from the previous year in controllable federal outlays in congressional districts. Regressions are run for total federal spending, and separately for each of seven budget areas. Positive beta weights indicate that their associated independent or control variables correlated with increased district spending, negative bs indicate correlation with declines in funding levels, and coefficients of zero indicate no relationship between change in spending levels and the independent variable(s) in question. The intercept can be interpreted as the residual increase or decrease a district can expect if it is scored as zero on all independent and control variables, that is, the annual change in funding an area might expect if it had a representative with no institutional influence and no voting record, and if the constituency demonstrated no need for funding of this type based on its demographic characteristics.

In this analysis the congressional district, rather than the representative, is the unit of analysis. Thus, each constituency has scores on all variables each year, even if the seat sat vacant. In this case the measures of institutional position and voting record were coded as "0." This is appropriate because a constituency with no representative on the Hill probably has little, if any, weight in House decision making. If two or more congressmen

Table 1-3
District Characteristics Used as Control Variables

Spending Category	Control Variables
Total	Population in thousands
DOA	Percent of workforce engaged in farming Percent earning $<$ $3,000 a year
DOD	Percent of workforce engaged in manufacturing Land area
HEW	Percent black Percent Spanish University enrollment Percent earning $<$ $3,000 a year Percent over 65 Median family income
HUD	Percent central city Percent metropolitan (central city + suburbs) Percent black Percent Spanish
DOI	Land area Percent Indian
OEO	Percent black Percent Spanish Percent earning $<$ $3,000 a year
VA	Veterans (Number)

occupied the same seat during a single calendar year, the institutional positions and voting record of the member serving the greater proportion of the year were coded. Congressional characteristics, measured by calendar year, were related to fiscal-year spending figures for the accounting period beginning in the middle of the measurement year; for example, congressional positions for 1970 were used in regression equations where the dependent variables measured spending changes between fiscal 1970 and fiscal 1971 (ΔS_{70}, and so on).[7] This procedure protected the temporal relationship between the variables necessary for there to be any possibility of a causal association. In other words, institutional power and demographic characteristics are measured at a time prior to the measurement of funding increments. (Experimentation with longer lags, to allow time for bureaucratic implementation of congressional directives, yielded no significant differences in the results.)

A final technical point to make clear is that my N for all regressions is 3480. This is 435 congressional districts times eight years of data. This pooling of data is permissible because the dependent variables are not correlated from one year to the next. Independent variables also showed marked change over time.

With these data, variables, and procedures, it becomes possible to assess to what extent direct institutional power over programs and logrolling potential aid congressmen in promoting the economic interests of their districts. If power on the Hill really makes a difference in the geographic distribution of federal outlays, the beta weights attached to some or all of the measures of institutional influence used in this analysis should be positive and statistically significant. Results are presented and discussed in the following sections.

Findings

Eight regressions have been run to test the scope of successful member promotion of district interests—one regression for each of the budget sub-areas for which congressional district expenditure figures are available, and one for total federal outlays. Dependent variables are changes (from the previous year) in received controllable spending, in the aggregate and separately within each studied department and agency. Independent predictors are committee and Appropriations subcommittee assignments, in-group and out-group seniority, leadership positions, party affiliation, party loyalty, support of the President, and changes in party unity and administration support scores. The demographic control variables itemized in table 1-3 are also included in the regression equations. Table 1-4 displays the results of this analysis. The most obvious conclusion is that there is little evidence of a consistent pattern of successful district promotion rooted in institutional influence. The R-squares are minimal, many coefficients do not meet common standards for statistical significance, and the signs of the various beta weights are neither consistent across regressions nor uniformly in the anticipated directions.

There are two ways to analyze the detailed results presented in table 1-4. One is to examine patterns across regressions. The other is to describe what takes place within each studied sub-area of federal spending. Both methods will be employed.

Promotion within Budget Areas

Intraregression Analysis

One method of analyzing the results presented in table 1-4 is to discuss the situation within each of the budget areas, that is, the comparative effects of the various predictors. For this discussion, standard errors and statistical signficance will be ignored. If the reader wishes to assess the reliability of any coefficient, he may refer to the information supplied in table 1-4.

Total expenditures. Both unaccounted-for factors (the intercept) and the demographic control variable (district population) tend to decrease expected controllable receipts by a constituency. A district with 450,000 inhabitants, slightly more than average, could anticipate a decrease of $8.4 million from these sources alone. This is made up more than twice over, however, if the constituency sends a Democratic representative, that is, a member of the majority party, to Washington. On the other hand, if increases in district benefits are the primary objective, the member should, if at all possible, avoid taking a role in his party's leadership.

Accrued committee seniority also has an impact, albeit smaller. For example, the "worth" of a chairmanship is only $4 million, although increasing seniority on the other side of the aisle appears to be a detriment to promotive activities. The loss for ranking minority members, however, is, on the average, only $2 million.

For both Democrats and, especially, Republicans, party loyalty appears to be well-rewarded. One hundred percent scores can add $5 million to Democratic district receipts and funnel an additional $20 million to those in Republican hands. The expected patterns for changes in party unity do not materialize. Republicans who become more loyal to the GOP do better, as do Democrats who become less loyal to their own party.

An inconsistent pattern is revealed for presidential support and changes in presidential support, although the potential for substantial impact on district funding is there.

As in all of the regressions displayed in table 1-4, however, the vast majority of the variance in changes in controllable federal expenditures in congressional districts is left unexplained, and therefore is either totally random or random with respect to a widespread pattern of individualized congressional promotive activities rooted in institutional positions and behavior.

DOA. Although the intercept is quite small, the beta weights on the two included demographic control variables are sufficiently large to outweigh any impact the congressman might have if the district has concentrations of farmers or the poor. Significantly large concentrations of both farmers and the impoverished, however, might cancel one another out since the coefficients are of different sign. Note the unexpected negative coefficient attached to the farm proportion of the district population.

The major unanticipated results of table 1-4 occur in this regression. Assignments to both the House Agriculture Committee and the Appropriations Subcommittee on Agriculture and Related Agencies hinder the acquisition of DOA controllable funds. Furthermore, contrary to the results in most other expenditure categories, being a Democrat hurts and being a party leader helps. The Midwestern farm belt, home of most Republicans and many GOP party leaders, may explain these findings.

Although membership on the Agriculture Committee is no bargain in

Table 1-4
Institutional Power and the Geographic Distribution of Federal Spending

	Total	DOA	DOD	HEW	HUD	DOI	OEO	VA
Intercept	-3.9	-.7	-27.9	23.4	-.3	.002	-.6	.05
Independent Variables								
Committee[a]		-2.2 (2.9)	7.6 (5.9)	.2 (2.0) / .3 (2.1)	-.5 (.6)	.1 (.1)	-.1 (.2)	-.3 (.2)
Subcommittee[a]		-3.0 (3.0)	1.0 (5.8) / 5.1 (7.0)	-.5 (2.3)	.3 (.6)	.2 (.1)	-.1 (.2)	-.04 (.1)
Party[b]	19.4 (13.3)	-1.0 (5.0)	16.3 (10.7)	-9.3 (4.1)	.2 (1.1)	.1 (.1)	.3 (.3)	.6 (.3)
Leader	-9.8 (6.1)	.7 (2.3)	-4.7 (4.9)	-.2 (1.8)	-.1 (.5)	-.1 (.1)	.1 (.1)	.01 (.1)
In-group seniority								
Democrat	.04 (.05)	.02 (.05)	.06 (.1)	.001 (.03)	.01 (.01)	.001 (.001)	0+ (.003)	.01 (.003)
Republican	-.02 (.05)	.002 (.06)	-.1 (.1)	-.01 (.4)	.01 (.01)	.002 (.001)	.003 (.003)	.004 (.003)
Out-group seniority								
Democrat	-.002 (.02)	-.002 (.02)	-.004 (.04)	.001 (.02)	-.002 (.004)	0+[d] (0+)	-.001 (.001)	-0 (.001)
Republican	-.02 (.02)	-.02 (.02)	-.006 (.05)	-.01 (.02)	-.002 (.004)	-.001 (.001)	-0 (.001)	-.002 (.001)

	(1)	(2)	(3)	(4)	(5)	(6)	(7)	(8)
Party Unity								
Democrat	.05 (.07)	-.01 (.03)	.05 (.06)	0+ (.02)	.01 (.01)	.002 (.001)	.004 (.002)	.004 (.001)
Republican	.2 (.1)	.04 (.04)	-.03 (.09)	-.07 (.03)	-.02 (.01)	-.001 (.001)	-0 (.003)	.005 (.002)
Administration Support								
Democrat	-.2 (.1)	.05 (.04)	-.2 (.08)	.03 (.03)	-.004 (.01)	-.004 (.001)	-.001 (.002)	-.01 (.002)
Republican	.1 (.2)	-.01 (.06)	.2 (.1)	-.04 (.05)	.02 (.01)	.002 (.001)	.01 (.003)	.001 (.003)
Party Unity								
Democrat	-.03 (.1)	.03 (.04)	.07 (.08)	-.09 (.03)	-.04 (.01)	-.002 (.001)	-.02 (.002)	-.01 (.002)
Republican	.02 (.1)	-.09 (.05)	.1 (.1)	.02 (.04)	.01 (.01)	-.002 (.001)	-.01 (.003)	-.002 (.003)
Δ Administration Support								
Democrat	.2 (.1)	-.003 (.04)	.2 (.08)	.02 (.03)	.04 (.01)	.004 (.001)	.02 (.002)	.02 (.002)
Republican	-.4 (.1)	.07 (.05)	-.2 (.1)	.08 (.04)	-.01 (.01)	-.002 (.001)	-.01 (.003)	-.01 (.003)
Control Variables[c]								
Population	-.01 (.02)	-39.4 (22.0)					.1 (.9)	
% in Farming		11.6 (16.7)		-36.4 (25.3)				
% < $3,000								

Table 1-4 *(cont.)*

	Total	DOA	DOD	HEW	HUD	DOI	OEO	VA
% in Manufacturing			.2 (.4)					
Land Area			0+[d] (0+)			0+[d] (0+)		
% Black				1.6 (2.6)			.1 (.2)	
% Spanish				3.3 (4.7)			−.6 (.3)	
University Enrollment				.06 (.05)				
Median Family Income								
% over 65				−.1 (.07)				
% central city				−7.8 (19.3)	.6 (.3)			
% metropolitan					.001 (.004)			
% Indian						7.2 (1.4)		
Number of Veterans								0+[d] (0+)
Standard Error	61.9	23.1	49.7	18.6	5.0	.6	1.4	1.2
R^2	.007	.005	.009	.009	.019	.072	.054	.170
N	3480	3480	3480	3480	3480	3480	3480	3480

[a]See table 1-1. For the HEW regression, the Education and Labor Committee is listed first and the Ways and Means Committee second. For the DOD regression, the Defense Subcommittee is listed first and the Military Construction Subcommittee second.

[b]Democratic affiliation.

[c]See table 1-3.

[d]F-values: DOD-Area = 2.016; DOI-Area = 99.04; DOI-Out-group seniority, Dem = 0 +; and VA-Veterans = 418.655.

the competition for DOA monies, accrued seniority on that panel does off-set some of this hindrance. This is especially true for Democrats. Accrued out-group seniority does not help nonmembers acquire additional DOA dollars. This indicates that logrolling for benefits in other jurisdictions may not be practiced extensively by members of the Agriculture Committee.

Party unity can be important for Republicans in acquiring Agriculture Department outlays, although becoming more loyal to the GOP appears to result in disproportionate punishment by the controlling party. This reward for movements toward Democratic positions is also visible for members of the majority party and is the anticipated finding.

Possibly reflecting the fact that most of this study takes place during Republican presidencies, Democratic congressmen can earn rewards through high levels of administration support and are not punished severe-ly if they then choose to return to the Democratic fold. GOP members, however, can only gain by increasing their support of the president's policies.

DOD. The included demographic control variables have little impact in this regression, but the intercept is negative and of sufficiently large magnitude that most districts will experience annual decreases in Depart-ment of Defense controllable spending no matter who their congressmen are nor what they do.

As expected, the beta weights attached to membership on Armed Ser-vices and the two Appropriations subcommittees with direct jurisdiction over the DOD are positive, and two of them are quite large. The small coefficient on the Appropriations Subcommittee on the DOD parallels the findings of Goss (1972) and Rundquist (1973). Except for the huge stan-dard errors, successful promotion by powerful members would be clearly indicated in this subsystem.

A Democratic representative is also a boon to his constituents to the tune of an annual expected increase of $16.3 million. Once again, however, party leadership positions are detrimental to the economic well-being of their associated congressional districts.

The accrual of in-group seniority helps members of the controlling party but injures those in the minority. Out-group seniority is, for the most part, irrelevant. If there is widespread logrolling for DOD system rewards, it is not systematically related to committee seniority.

Party loyalty is important for Democrats eager to secure additional monies for their districts. Reflecting the earlier concern over the bought vote syndrome, increases in party unity attract even greater benefits. As ex-pected, Republicans with low party loyalty do better than their more par-tisan colleagues. A contradition, however, is that GOP members appear to be rewarded for returning to the Republican fold. The results relating to administration support are, at best, ambiguous.

HEW. A large intercept and large coefficients on control variables (not all of anticipated sign; for example, the negative, although not statistically significant, relationship between HEW funding and the percent of a district's population that is aged) can dominate determination of district increases and decreases. In other words, even controllable expenditures by the largely uncontrollable Department of Health, Education, and Welfare may be beyond the systematic control of individual congressmen attempting to use their powerful institutional positions to promote the economic interests of their districts. Committee assignment variables have little impact, and belonging to the relevant Appropriations subcommittee may even be a minor detriment. The same is true for positions of party leadership. Contrary to the results in most studied subsystems, being a Democrat has a large negative impact on district receipts.

Seniority, both in- and out-group, has a minimal effect, as does Democratic party unity. However, Republicans who often "cross the aisle" to cast their vote appear to do better than their colleagues. Unpredictably, districts represented by Democrats who, over time, become substantially more loyal to their party suffer disproportionately. Finally, in both parties, but especially in the GOP, increasing presidential support attracts additional district benefits.

HUD. Districts with substantial proportions of their residents living in census-defined central cities can expect large funding increases regardless of what positions their representatives occupy or how they vote. Although many of the coefficients on the independent predictors meet standard criteria for statistical significance, none are large enough to offset the impact of this single demographic control variable. An interesting point, however, is that the beta weight attached to membership on the House Committee on Banking, Currency and Housing (formerly Banking and Currency) is negative. This appears at odds with earlier findings reported by Plott (1968). However, neither his measurement nor his methods were as precise as those used here.

DOI. Once again, nearly all of the regression equation's predictive value is borne in the demographic control variables. Although the beta weights on the other independent predictors conform, for the most part, to expectations, none has much of an impact upon the distribution of Interior Department controllables among congressional districts.

OEO. Although large concentrations of Blacks, Spanish, and the poor can dominate predictions made by this regression, this is not necessarily the case because these effects frequently cancel one another out. This is possible because the coefficient on percent Spanish is large and of unanticipated sign. Variables measuring the positions and actions of congressmen can, therefore, have more than a marginal impact.

Although both Democratic affiliation and positions of party leadership are beneficial in the competition for federal outlays, committee-based jurisdictional authority over the OEO is not. The accrual of seniority appears irrelevant, and coefficients on other measures are ambiguous. Successful logrolling for OEO benefits is not revealed, but neither does direct jurisdiction over the program appear to have much of an impact.

VA. Once more, this is a case where virtually the entire predictive capacity of the regression equation is vested in the demographic control variable—the number of veterans residing in each congressional district. Congressmen, no matter how powerful, have only a marginal systematic impact on district allocations.

This regression by regression analysis has failed to uncover consistent patterns. Perhaps a cross-regression, variable-by-variable approach might be more revealing.

Cross-Regression Analysis

Committee Assignment. In only three of the seven subsystems is jurisdictional authority over program and project authorizations conducive to increased district benefits, and in only one of these—defense—is this impact substantial. Admittedly, three of the four negative coefficients are also minimal. However, no consistent pattern of successful district promotion by institutionally powerful members is evident.

Appropriations Subcommittee Assignment. If the coefficients for HEW and HUD were interchanged with one another, these beta weights would almost mirror those of full committee assignments. Once again, there is no basis for the macro-analyst to conclude that successful district promotion by the influential determines the geographic distribution of federal spending. This general impotence of the Appropriations Committee may relate, in part, to Richard F. Fenno's (1962) observations on common goals held by members of that prestigious body. He disclosed that in their work these representatives espoused

> a consensus that all of their House prescribed tasks can be fulfilled by superimposing upon them one, single paramount task—to guard the Federal Treasury. Committee members state their goals in essentially negative terms of guardianship—screening requests for money. Checking against ill-advised expenditures, and protecting the taxpayer dollar. . . .To the consensus on the main task of protecting the Treasury is added, therefore, a consensus on the instrumental task of cutting whatever budget estimates are submitted. (p. 311)

Apparently, this stinginess extends even to their own constituencies.

Party. In general, Democrats do better than Republicans in the competition for increased district funding. Much of this, however, appears due to substantially greater benefits in the DOD subsystem. There is also the contradictory evidence presented by spending by the Departments of Agriculture and Health, Education, and Welfare. Nonetheless, it does seem that members of the majority party may put their controlling status to good use when allocating system rewards among congressional districts.

Leadership. Districts represented by party leaders are losers in the competition for federal funds, perhaps reflecting the concerns expressed earlier. The Defense Department, which accounts for over three-fifths of all controllable expenditures, is the major contributor to this misfortune.

In-group Seniority. The more seniority Democrats accrue on a committee with jurisdiction over a spending area, the more benefits their districts receive within that subsystem. Although some of the relationships were weak, no exceptions were discovered. This appears to be a clear example of successful district promotion by the more powerful members. There is, of course, a large variance in impact. On Armed Services a chairmanship is worth $6 million more in defense spending than the lowest ranked majority party position. On Education and Labor the difference is only $24,000 in OEO expenditures. For Republicans the pattern is less clear, and most coefficients do not differ substantially from zero. This may reflect the minority party's inability to assert itself in the distributive process.

Out-group Seniority. These variables were included as one test of the extent of logrolling. That is, they measure how well seniority in other jurisdictions can be translated into system rewards in the spending area under examination. The answer appears to be "not very well." Nearly all of the beta weights are negative, and most are very near zero.

Party Unity. Except for DOA spending, highly loyal Democrats do better than Democrats more disloyal. As anticipated, just the reverse is true for the Republicans (with the exception of the DOA and the VA). An unexpected finding, however, is that, for total controllables, loyalty within both parties is apparently conducive to the reaping of rewards, with the GOP doing even better than the majority party. Ignoring this anomaly, the general conclusion is that the majority party rewards its own for good behavior and rewards those Republicans who most frequently side with the Democrats.[8] The evidence supports the conclusion that the legislator whose votes are sufficiently unconstrained that he may cast them in ways that please his colleagues is in an excellent position to promote the economic well-being of his constituents.

Changes in Party Unity. Contrary to expectations, Democrats who become more loyal to their party tend to forego district benefits (except for the DOA and DOD). Perhaps the best way to attract more rewards from the Democratic leadership is to drift out of the fold, that is, become more disloyal. The leadership may then expend energy and resources in an effort to win you back. For Republicans the pattern is inconsistent and no generalizations can be made.

Administration Support. Generally mixed results are observed for this measure, although in most spending areas highly supportive Republicans do better than their colleagues.

Changes in Administration Support. Except for the DOA (where the coefficient is quite small), Democrats earn more rewards as they become more supportive of the president's program. This confirms my expectation. However, no substantiation for the hypothesis is provided on the other side of the aisle where, in most cases, increased loyalty translates into fewer district benefits. Perhaps the Republican presidents who ruled throughout most of the studied period directed their efforts toward enticing back congressional members of their party who were moving away from support of the administration's policies.

In sum, however, there has been little evidence that systematically successful promotion of district well-being based upon influential institutional positions and voting actions is a widespread activity in Congress. Members like Rivers, Kerr and Vinson appear to be atypical. Other representatives in equally advantageous positions do not reap the same disproportionately large amounts of system rewards for their own constituencies. Every member may, at some time, be a successful district promoter. However, the net effect is then little systematic maldistribution. Neither direct jurisdictional power nor logrolling is a consistent determinant of the geographic distribution of federal monies.

Reflection-Oriented and Nonelite Promotion

Successful promotion by the congressional power elite is not an institutionalized phenomenon. This can be explained in many ways. These members may no longer have to worry about reelection; they may have turned their attention to national, rather than local, interests; they may have acquired, through experience, a keener picture of budgetary constraints; and/or they may have become more interested in questions of policy, rather than distribution (assuming, of course, that these two concepts can be separated from one another). Any, or all, of these explanations might indicate less willingness to expend energy, resources, and time on district promotion. Less powerful members, on the other hand, may still be more in tune with the desires of their constituents. They may not yet feel secure in their seats, nor have they yet acquired enough seniority to dominate national policy arenas. Admittedly, these less influential representatives may have fewer resources at their disposal. However, if their perceived need for and willingness to work toward successful district promotion is great enough, they may be better at these activities than their more senior and powerful colleagues.

In an effort to ascertain the merits of these arguments, I reran the regressions of table 1-4 in two different ways. The first of these assessed whether disinterest in reelection might prompt members to forego committing their resources to campaigns for increased district funding and instead to expend their energies in pursuit of other goals.

Reelection goals have been cited as a major motivation for the activities necessary for the promotion of district interests. Therefore, such behavior may become more prevalent as reelection time draws near. Although it is somewhat doubtful, given their short two-year lifespan, that congressmen would ever allow their attention to stray far from the needs and wants of their constituents, it may be that in election years promotional efforts accelerate, and if power on the Hill does make a difference in spending outcomes, the statistical relationships of table 1-4 might be stronger.

This is not the case. The analysis was redone for even-numbered years only. R-squares from these regressions are reported in table 1-5. Coefficients are not featured because few patterns are different from those revealed in the earlier analysis. Even when they must return to their electorate for a renewal of their mandate, the powerful members of the Capitol community do not greatly alter the geographic distribution of federal funds for their own personal convenience.

It may be, however, that senior, presumably more powerful, members may simply no longer have to or want to promote their districts' interests. Therefore, as a second reexamination of the hypothesis, I again reran the regressions of table 1-4, this time including only those districts represented by members who ranked below the median in House seniority. R-squares for these regressions are displayed in table 1-6. Once again, the vast majority of the variance in the dependent variable is left unexplained, and the coefficients which resemble those in the "parent" regressions are not shown. Low ranking members are only slightly, if at all, more successful at district promotion than their more senior colleagues. It appears that institutional position on the Hill makes little difference in determining the geographic distribution of federal spending. The powerful, on the average, get neither more nor less than less well-placed legislators.

Table 1-5
District Promotion in Election Years: R-Squares

Budget Area	R^2
Total	.013
DOA	.011
DOD	.012
HEW	.028
HUD	.047
DOI	.015
OEO	.036
VA	.099
N	1740

Alternative Explanations of the
Federal Spending Process

If not even the proximity of reelection can induce the powerful to dictate spending outcomes for personal benefit, yet one is unwilling to accept the conclusion that these members are simply disinterested in the geographic distribution of federal spending, several possible explanations come to mind. The first of these is that those presumed powerful actually have

Table 1-6
District Promotion by Nonsenior Members: R-Squares

Budget Area	R^2
Total	.017
DOA	.021
DOD	.017
HEW	.013
HUD	.026
DOI	.084
OEO	.086
VA	.178
N	1670

no more power than their more poorly positioned colleagues: they do not dictate outcomes because they *cannot* dictate outcomes. This contradicts the overwhelming mass of congressional literature and, therefore, appears unlikely.

A second possibility is that Congress is a collegial body, to the extent that it functions as a mutual protection society. In other words, a conscious effort is made to equally share the available system rewards among all members so that no representative must return to his constituents for a mandate renewal any worse off than any of his colleagues. This is possible, but appears to be an exceedingly complex system to perpetuate. Moreover, deviant cases present problems for this explanation.

A third possibility is that, when considering federal funding, representatives may not use the more-is-better-than-less decision rule ascribed to them here and elsewhere in the literature. They may not seek to maximize spending in their districts relative to other districts. Alternatively, the relevant unit of concern may not be dollars. It may be projects or jobs, for example. Ferejohn (1974), employing the former variable, and Goss (1972), employing the latter, found some evidence for the hypothesis, albeit at the micro-level. Either of these possibilities could explain the results presented here. However, neither explanation is convincing. To prefer less to more is simply not normal human behavior, and dollars, as an easily convertible medium of exchange, are not irrelevant.

Finally, powerful congressmen may be dictating outcomes, but only to the point of guaranteeing themselves sufficient funding increases for their reelection needs. Once these levels of adequacy have been reached, the provision of additional awards may be superfluous or may not compensate the congressman for the personal resources he must commit to obtain them. The powerful therefore allow these excess rewards to be distributed among the districts of their less well-placed colleagues. As long as the federal pie continues to expand at a healthy rate, there may be enough of these excess funds to result in a fairly even distribution across constituencies, with regard to institutional power. Only in times of a decreasing or slowly increasing federal pie would the true impact of congressional power be revealed. For then, after the powerful had guaranteed themselves sufficient rewards, the excess would be insufficient to make funding increments roughly equivalent across the board.

Each of these alternatives is only a theory. Empirical testing of them is strongly encouraged. Until this is done, however, I am left with essentially negative findings. Districts of the powerful, as a class, do not receive favored treatment in the federal spending process when compared with constituencies represented in Washington by poorly positioned legislators. This holds whether one defines power as direct jurisdictional influence over a program or as the possession of resources which can be traded for benefits in other members' domains.

Summary

Successful promotional activity by powerful congressmen is an inadequate explanation of the geographic distribution of federal spending. If it were an acceptable answer, districts represented by those legislators who are more powerful (either overall or in a single jurisdiction) should receive disproportionately large increases in federal funds. No such systematic pattern was discovered. In the aggregate, those with power did little better (and often did worse) than those without influence.

So how can the celebrated exploits of members like Mendel Rivers be explained? Was he truly a successful district promoter or was it merely coincidence that he sat on (and eventually chaired) the House Armed Services Committee at the same time the Pentagon was assuming responsibility for the economic well-being of the First Congressional District of South Carolina? I doubt this was an accident. Moreover, I believe that Rivers was a very successful promoter. I also believe that his institutional position was a great aid to him in his promotional activities. How can these beliefs be reconciled with the results presented in this analysis? Very easily, if one accepts the fact that a few congressmen are very successful at promotional activity, while most others are not. After all, district promotion is an individual effort. Rivers was one of the few. Perhaps he just tried harder. There is no reason to expect, however, that his predecessor, his successor, or others occupying comparatively powerful positions would also be of this ilk. That is why Rivers and a few others stand out—because they are so unusual. Successful district promotion on a widespread basis is not a common phenomenon so, when it happens, it is noticed. Obviously, generalizations about power should not be made from these examples.

The reader should not imagine, however, that I am denying that seeking benefits for one's constituents is a common practice of congressmen. All members engage in these activities at one time or another. Yet these efforts tend to be limited in scope and so widespread that the overall pattern of federal spending is not greatly or quickly distorted. Since it is not only the institutionally powerful who play this game, their districts do not benefit disproportionately, and no systematic relationship with influential congressional positions or logrolling resources exists. Therefore, the effort in this study to discover systematic relationships between the geographic distribution of federal outlays and member-related variables has failed. Rivers, as we all know, was not a typical congressman. It now appears, however, that he was not even a typical powerful congressman.

Notes

1. Agriculture, 76 percent; Armed Services, 88 percent; Education and Labor, 78 percent; Banking, 86 percent; Interior, 75 percent; and Veterans, 93 percent.

2. For fiscal 1975 and 1976 these volumes were compiled by the Community Services Administration (CSA).

3. Disbursements which, if known, would jeopardize national security are not revealed.

4. In FY 1975 and FY 1976 the CSA was substituted.

5. S_i and $\triangle S_i$ are statistically independent in the seven studied subsystems as well, R^2's are as follows: DOA, .127; DOD, .113; HEW, .263; HUD, .259; DOI, .276; OEO, .206; and VA, .301.

6. There are eight measures of institutional position in the regressions for each of the seven budget areas. For the regression on aggregate outlays, there are only four—party affiliation, party leadership, Democratic committee seniority, and Republican committee seniority. There is no distinction between in-group and out-group seniority, and committee and subcommittee assignments do not apply.

7. District demographic characteristics were measured in 1960 and 1970 (U.S. Census) and interpolated to a calendar-year basis for use in the regressions. Measurements were made at county and city levels and transformed into district-level data by the procedure described for federal spending figures in the appendix to this analysis.

8. During the period of this study, three different Presidents occupied the White House: Lyndon Johnson, Richard Nixon, and Gerald Ford. No significant differences between administrations were discovered.

References

Arnold, R. Douglas. "Congressmen, Bureaucrats and Constituency Benefits: The Case of Military Employment, 1952-1974." Paper presented at the annual meeting of the Northeastern Political Science Association, Mt. Pocono, Pa., 1977.

Barone, Michael; Grant Ujifusa; and Douglas Matthews. *The Almanac of American Politics, 1972*. Boston: Gambit, 1972.

Barton, Weldon. "The Procurement, R & D Authorization Process in the House Armed Services Committee." Paper presented at the annual meeting of the American Political Science Association, Los Angeles, 1970.

Blechman, Barry M.; Edward M. Gramlich; and Robert W. Hartman. *Setting National Priorities: The 1976 Budget*. Washington: Brookings Institution, 1975.

Bullock, Charles S. "Motivations for Congressional Committee Preferences Freshmen of the 92d Congress." Paper presented at the annual meeting of the Southwestern Political Science Association, Dallas, 1973.

Congressional Quarterly Almanac. Washington: Congressional Quarterly, 1966-1976.

Cook, Kenneth F. "The Joint Committee on Atomic Energy and Atomic Energy Policy." Unpublished Ph.D. dissertation, Washington University, 1976.

Fenno, Richard F., Jr., "The House Appropriations Committee as a Political System: The Problem of Integration." *American Political Science Review* 56 (June 1962):310-324.

Ferejohn, John A. *Pork Barrel Politics: Rivers and Harbors Legislation, 1947-1968.* Stanford: Stanford University Press, 1974.

Fiorina, Morris P. *Congress: Keystone to the Washington Establishment.* New Haven: Yale University Press, 1977.

Fisher, Louis. *Presidential Spending Power.* Princeton: Princeton University Press, 1975.

Ford, Gerald R. "Speech of August 12, 1974." Reprinted in *Congressional Quarterly Weekly Report* 32 (August 17, 1974): 2208-2212.

Goss, Carol F. "House Committee Characteristics and Distributive Politics." Paper presented at the annual meeting of the American Political Science Association, San Francisco, 1975.

———. "Military Committee Membership and Defense-Related Benefits in the House of Representatives." *Western Political Quarterly* 25 (June 1972): 215-233.

Lasswell, Harold D. "Politics: Who Gets What, When, How," in *The Political Writings of Harold D. Lasswell.* Glencoe: Free Press, 1951.

Mayhew, David R. *Congress: The Electoral Connection.* New Haven: Yale University Press, 1974.

Pearson, Drew, and Jack Anderson. *The Case Against Congress: A Compelling Indictment of Corruption on Capitol Hill.* New York: Simon and Schuster, 1968.

Plott, Charles R. "Some Organizational Influences on Urban Renewal Decisions." *American Economic Review* 58 (May 1968):306-321.

Ray, Bruce A. "Congressional Influence and the Geographic Distribution of Federal Spending." Unpublished Ph.D. dissertation, Washington University, 1977.

Ritt, Leonard G. "Committee Position, Seniority, and the Distribution of Government Expenditures." *Public Policy* 24 (Fall 1976):463-489.

Rundquist, Barry Spencer. "Congressional Influences on the Distribution of Prime Military Contracts." Unpublished Ph.D. dissertation, Stanford University, 1973.

———. "On Testing a Military Industrial Complex Theory" *American Politics Quarterly* 6 (January 1978):29-53.

Rundquist, Barry Spencer, and John A. Ferejohn. "Two American Expenditure Programs Compared." In *Comparative Public Policy*, edited by Craig Liske, John McCamant, and William Loehr. New York: Wiley, 1975:87-108.

Rundquist, Barry Spencer, and David E. Griffith. "An Interrupted Time-Series Test of the Distributive Theory of Military Policy-Making." *Western Political Quarterly* 29 (December 1976):620-626.

_____ . "The Parochial Constraint on Foreign Policymaking." *Policy Studies Journal* 3 (Winter 1974):142-146.

Shepsle, Kenneth A. *The Giant Jigsaw Puzzle: Democratic Committee Assignments in the Modern House*. Chicago: University of Chicago Press, 1978.

U.S. Bureau of the Census. *Census of Population, 1960* and . . .*1970*. Washington: Department of Commerce, 1963 and 1973.

_____ . *Congressional District Data Book, 88th Congress* and . . . *93d Congress*. Washington: Government Printing Office, 1963 and 1973.

U.S. Office of Economic Opportunity. *Federal Outlays in [state name]: Fiscal Year 19[xx]*. Washington: Government Printing Office, 1968-1977.

Appendix 1A
Computation of District Expenditures

Congressional district spending totals were compiled from county- and city-level data (OEO, 1968-1977). I assumed that outlays within each unit were allocated in a pattern approximating the population distribution. For example, if after its most recent redistricting, a constituency contained all of County A, two-thirds of County B, and 8 percent of County C, I computed its federal receipts as that which was spent in County A plus two-thirds of what was spent in County B plus 8 percent of what was disbursed in County C. Admittedly, not all parts of a geographic unit such as a county or city may benefit equally from a given federal activity, but it is hard to image an appropriation whose effects can be completely isolated. Spillover effects do occur. I have chosen to assume that these effects are distributed equally throughout a county or city when parts of this entity lie in more than one congressional district. Similarly, when a metropolitan district lies wholly within a single city, its receipts are the same proportion of that city's receipts as its population is of the city's population.

With no redistricting in the interim, successive years' spendings were computed using the same district boundaries. Measures of funding change could therefore be obtained by simple subtraction. Redistricting, however, made this procedure more complicated. In these instances, federal funding during the previous year was recomputed using the new boundaries. These figures were then used solely for purposes of subtraction, as they did not equal outlays in any existing district. The resulting amounts are the increases (or decreases) the new district secured over what was spent within the current boundaries the previous year.

District demographic variables, also collected at the county and city level, were allocated to constituencies in a manner identical to the process for spending data.

2

Politics, Program Administration, and the Distribution of Grants-In-Aid: A Theory and a Test

J. Norman Reid

Introduction

During the last several years American state and national leaders have engaged in considerable sparring over the proper division of the federal budget. Fueled by press accounts calling it the "second war between the states,"[1] both North and South have sponsored research to support their claims to larger shares of federal dollars. The fight, inevitably carried to Congress, is manifest in disputes over the allocation formulas of the larger grant programs.[2]

Interest in the distribution of federal spending has always been high, and perhaps nowhere more so than in Congress. Indeed, it is popular wisdom that a congressman's ability to "bring home the bacon" is important to ensuring long tenure in office. The proposition is seldom if ever challenged. Yet despite the certainty with which it is advanced, the thesis that "politics" lies somewhere behind the distribution of federal expenditures has been little tested and even less confirmed.

Although the distribution of federal dollars has drawn much scholarly attention over the years,[3] only a few studies, and these recent ones, have dealt with the causes of federal fund distribution. For the most part these studies have sought causal explanations within the congressional process.[4] This research has rested on several common assumptions about power within Congress: that it tends to be exercised by policy subsystems which are centered in committees and subcommittees;[5] that party leadership and seniority are important sources of power; and that congressmen who are in a position to do so will use their power to derive constituency benefits from federal spending. To date these research efforts have failed to find political and administrative factors to be either large or systematic influences on the distribution of federal funds.

As it presently exists, this body of research suffers from two primary limitations. First, with but a few exceptions, the causes of federal spending have only been sought within the congressional process. However, it is clear that other actors—the president, the bureaucracy, and, in the case of grants-in-aid, potential recipients—may be able to affect the decisional process, and it is important that they be taken into account as well.

Second, the present research has devoted little attention to the differences between programs, which may be considerable, and the ways these differences relate to the exercise of power. However, it seems reasonable that political variables may affect grants-in-aid differently than other types of federal spending. Furthermore, it is likely that some features of spending programs, such as their political value as constituency benefits or their susceptibility to discretionary distribution, may interact with political causal variables and may determine when and whether those political variables will be of importance.

What follows is an attempt to further our understanding of the political and administrative causes of distributive policies, by first elaborating some factors expected to affect those policies and then presenting a preliminary test of the model developed here. The study focuses on a particular subset of federal spending programs: federal grants-in-aid. Three sets of factors—congressional influence, presidential influence, and applicant aggressiveness—are each hypothesized to influence the way federal dollars are distributed. Both the way these factors operate and the extent of their importance are hypothesized to be conditioned by certain characteristics of the programs. In the next sections, the causal variables are discussed and a causal model is developed. Following this, the results of a test of the model, using data for five health grant programs, are reported.

Theory

The Causal Factors

Three factors, each representing a different aspect of the political and administrative process, are hypothesized to have important effects on the distribution of federal grants-in-aid. The first of these, congressional influence, is well-established in the literature.[6] As discussed earlier, this factor rests on the assumption that congressmen are interested in supporting their re-election chances by obtaining federal expenditures for their constituencies. As a result, they can be expected to act on behalf of their states and districts whenever possible.

Though ignored by most investigations, the use of presidential power to affect the distribution of funds seems equally probable. Presidents too have political objectives which may be served by the artful division of federal dollars. These include re-election and future party support, and are presumed to be adequate to motivate the use of presidential power in this fashion.

Both congressional and presidential power may reasonably affect the distribution of many types of federal expenditures.[7] By contrast, the third factor considered here, applicant aggressiveness, will only affect grants-in-aid and other types of expenditures which require some initiative to be exercised by potential recipients. This factor rests on the assumption that applicants have varying interest in receiving particular grants, and that some applicants display greater grantsmanship skills than others. Because many programs involve competitive application procedures, differences in applicant aggressiveness may affect the eventual distribution of grant funds.

While these factors are presented here as hypothesized influences on grant distribution, in fact there is substantial case study support for each of them.[8] Thus the task is not to determine *whether* these factors affect distributional policy, but to discover *when* and *how* they do so and whether they affect policy systematically or so randomly as to contribute little to the explanation of spending policies. In a later section we will develop the argument that these three causal factors do not always operate uniformly, and that their presence or absence is conditioned by certain characteristics of the grant programs themselves. Before doing so, however, let us first consider these characteristics.

Some Characteristics of Grants-in-Aid

Grants-in-aid may be conceived as varying along two dimensions—the amount of discretion exercised by program administrators in disbursing the funds, and the program's desirability as perceived by politicians and applicants.

Distributional Flexibility. Grant programs vary greatly in the amount of discretion permitted to administrators in distributing the funds. At one extreme are formula grant programs which allocate funds between jurisdictions according to a mathematical formula. Such formulas, often defined by statute, may leave administrators with very little flexibility in distributing the funds. Examples are entitlement programs such as general revenue sharing and community development block grants, which provide direct allocations to individual localities according to statutory formulas. Formula grants tend to include the larger, and often the older, programs of assistance.

Project grants, by contrast, afford program administrators greater opportunities to control both the choice of recipients and the levels of assistance. In addition to administrative discretion, the distribution of project grants is affected by the initiative of applicants, since only applicants which have requested assistance can be funded. In general, the programs offering administrators the greatest discretion tend to be smaller, and often include what are referred to as "demonstration" grants.

Among individual programs there is much diversity in the degree of flexibility permitted to administrators. As a result, grant programs are best conceived as falling along a continuum ranging from complete administrative discretion to none at all.

Desirability of Program Benefits. The benefits from grant programs also vary significantly in their desirability as perceived by potential recipients and by congressmen and presidents. Though recipients will favor any form of aid which meets their needs, the greatest enthusiasm seems likely to be generated by programs which (1) require smaller matching shares to be supplied; (2) allow greater flexibility in the kinds of resources which can be used to meet the matching requirement; (3) have larger total appropriations; and (4) impose fewer restrictions on the ways the funds may be used.[9] Applicants should be more aggressive in seeking funds from programs they perceive as most desirable.

Grants also vary in their desirability to congressmen and presidents as plums of the political process. The most politically valuable programs should be those which (1) have the most visible benefits; (2) have benefits which are the most easily divisible between geographic areas and clientele groups; (3) have the highest funding levels; and (4) require the smallest matching share by recipients. The perceived desirability of program benefits should affect the degree to which politicians are willing to influence the distribution of program funds.

The Causal Model

These two features of grant-in-aid programs—the amount of discretion exercised by administrators and the perceived desirability of the programs' benefits—are hypothesized to determine the way the three causal factors operate and the extent to which they affect the distribution of program funds.

The Effect of Program Desirability. Program desirability is expected to have rather straightforward effects on the three causal factors. Applicants are expected to be more aggressive in seeking funds under the more desirable programs; likewise, politicians are more likely to influence the distribution of funds under those programs which have the greatest political value to them. As a result, the three causal factors should have stronger effects on the distribution of the more desirable funds. Conversely, the less desirable programs should attract less attention from applicants and politicians, and the three causal factors—congressional influence, presidential influence, and state aggressiveness—should have less significant effects on these programs.

The Effect of Discretion on the Causal Factors.   The amount of discretion exercised by program administrators will also condition the effects of the three causal factors on grant distribution patterns. However, the relationship with this factor is more complex than with program desirability. First, the degree of administrative discretion is related with which of two influence channels congressmen may use to affect the distribution of funds. Where administrators exercise greater discretion, congressmen are more able to influence the distribution of funds by intervening directly in the program's administration. On the other hand, where administrators are constrained by allocation formulas, congressional influence will tend to be limited to the writing of the formula itself. The degree of administrative flexibility is expected to constrain presidential influence attempts in much the same fashion.

The position of a program on the flexibility scale may also condition the effect of state aggressiveness on the distribution of funds. In general, applicant aggressiveness should have greater effects on programs which allow administrators greater flexibility. Although states may pursue formula grants with unequal zeal or competence, these differences may not affect state funding shares under the more tightly regulated programs. Since formula allocations tend to set upper limits on the amounts each state can receive, if each state successfully applies for its entire share of funds, differences in aggressiveness will not produce any deviations from the amount allocated. Even the least aggressive state may qualify for its full allocation, and when this occurs, the more aggressive states will reap no benefit from their extra effort.[10]

On the one hand, then, program formulas will tend to determine state receipts of funds under the more tightly controlled programs (those with relatively clear and rigid formulas), with the three causal factors making little contribution to the distribution of funds. On the other hand, congressional and presidential influence and state aggressiveness are expected to have greater effects on grant distribution patterns under those programs which are susceptible to greater administrative discretion.

A Classification of Federal Grant Programs.   We may use these two dimensions—administrative discretion and program desirability—to form the basis of a classification of grant-in-aid programs, as shown in table 2-1. The four cells in the classification represent different program types; a different pattern of causation is hypothesized for each.

Pattern A: Distribution by Purpose.   The first category includes formula grant programs perceived by presidents, congressmen, and applicants as providing less desirable benefits. These include programs whose benefits tend to be both invisible and indivisible (somewhat like "public goods"),[11]

Table 2-1
Summary of Expected Relationships

	Administrative Flexibility in Distributing Grant Funds	
Desirability of Benefits	*Formula Grants*	*Project Grants*
Less desirable Invisible benefits Indivisible benefits Lower funding level Smaller federal share Greater restrictions Less matching flexibility	Pattern A Receipts tend to be controlled by formula; little effect of congressional or presidential influence; weak effect of state aggressiveness	Pattern B State aggressiveness has moderate effect on fund distribution; congressional and presidential influence have weak effects
More desirable Visible benefits Divisible benefits Higher funding level Larger federal share Fewer restrictions More matching flexibility	Pattern C Congressional influence on formula is strong but channeled through the formula; state aggressiveness effect is strong (but inhibited by formula allocations); presidential influence has weak effects; receipts will be almost wholly governed by the formula	Pattern D Congressional influence and state aggressiveness have strong effects on fund distribution; presidential influence has moderate effects

and which tend to be funded at lower levels, require a larger recipient share of costs, and involve more requirements which recipients find restrictive or burdensome.

Because political and applicant interest in these programs is likely to be low, and because program administrators have relatively little latitude in any case, the program's formula should be the major determinant of state allocations. Furthermore, congressional interest in changing the formula to alter the distribution of funds is also likely to be slight. To the extent that state aggressiveness varies, there may be a small relationship between this factor and the distribution of funds.

Pattern B: Ask and You Shall Receive. The second category also includes grants perceived to be less desirable, though in this case the programs are project grants. Although the discretion available to administrators opens the possibility for political influence and applicant aggressiveness to have a larger impact, the low desirability of the program benefits will tend to limit the impact of these factors.

Pattern C: Hidden Influence. Like Pattern A, this category includes formula grant programs. However, these programs are perceived to be more desirable. Their benefits will tend to be more visible and divisible, and hence more useful politically; the programs will tend to be funded at higher levels, require smaller recipient matching shares (or none at all), and involve fewer potentially burdensome requirements. The high desirability of these programs creates the potential for the three causal factors to have strong effects.

However, the desirability of these programs is offset by the lack of flexibility in their administration. Because of this, only a weak relationship can be expected between applicant aggressiveness and the distribution of funds, not because applicants are disinterested in the program but because they will all tend to fully utilize their allocations. Presidential influence will probably have only a slight impact on the distribution of programs funds.

By contrast, congressional influence should affect these programs. However, the limited administrative discretion should restrict congressional intervention in their administration. As a result, congressional influence regarding these programs should occur in the way the formulas are written, and we would expect the formulas to provide disproportionate benefits to the constituencies of their authors. We shall have more to say about this later.

Pattern D: Every Man for Himself.   The final set of programs includes those whose benefits are perceived as desirable and which permit administrators a large amount of discretion in disbursing the funds. In this case, none of the causal factors is constrained, and each is expected to have important effects on the pattern of fund distribution.

A Test of the Model

The Programs

The remainder of the paper presents the results of a test of the model using data for five health grant programs. The programs, authorized by various amendments to the Public Health Service Act, support a wide variety of activities and vary widely in both their political desirability and the mechanisms by which their funds are distributed; thus they provide a good sample for testing the hypotheses.

A few words about each program are in order. The "314(a)" comprehensive state health planning grant program is an example of pattern A. The program was enacted in 1966 along with a companion program of grants for areawide health planning agencies.[12] The state health planning grants, the subject of our study, were allocated according to a formula using population and per capita income, as determined by regulations, with the stipulation that no state's allocation would be less than one percent of appropriations. Funding for the program was never high, and fiscal 1973 outlays totalled only $7 million.

The second formula grant included in the study, the Hill-Burton hospital and health facilities construction grant program, is an example of pattern C. The Hill-Burton program dates from 1946 and is the oldest and best-known of the five programs.[13] The program provided formula grants to states to support local projects; the federal share of program costs ranged from one-half to two-thirds, depending on state per capita income. Funds were allocated according to population and squared per capita income, a formula which distinctly favors states with poorer populations. The formula has changed little since first adopted.

Widely regarded as a "pork barrel" program, Hill-Burton remained highly popular in Congress throughout its history. The reasons are not hard to discern. By the end of fiscal year 1971, the program had funded some 10,784 individual projects, an average of more than 447 projects during each of the preceding 24 years, or enough for one project in each congressional district and nearly nine in each state annually. The program has always received substantial appropriations, highest of the five programs, with an average of more than $150 million annually.[14] Fiscal year 1973 outlays for the program were $176.7 million.

The third program, "314(d)" comprehensive public health services formula grants, was created in 1966 by consolidating a variety of categorical grants supporting individual public health services.[15] The program's formula provides a basic allotment of $300,000 to each state; additional funds are allocated on the basis of population and population weighted by per capita income, with the resulting total adjusted so that no state will receive less than its 1967 allocation under the categorical grants the program replaced. The program, which had FY 1973 outlays of $78.4 million, falls in between patterns A and C in terms of desirability, though as discussed below the program allows greater flexibility than the other formula grants studied here.

A companion program provides project grants for public health services.[16] Intended to provide a flexible means of dealing with problems concentrated in particular states or regions, the program was also designed to highlight emergency problems and to develop and implement new approaches to public health. Like the formula grant programs, it has been funded at relatively high levels; FY 1973 outlays for the program were $107.9 million. The program is the nearest example to pattern D to be considered in this analysis.

The final program provides project grants to public and nonprofit private agencies for training, studies, and demonstrations intended to improve the quality of comprehensive health planning.[17] Never funded at a high level, the program had FY 1973 outlays of only $3.6 million. The program best fits pattern B.

The Hypotheses

The hypotheses follow directly from the model. The three causal factors, congressional influence, presidential influence, and state aggressiveness, should have smaller effects on the three formula grants than on the two project grants, where the greater administrative discretion permits freer operation to the causal factors. An exception is the Hill-Burton program, which has highly desirable program benefits and is hypothesized to be strongly affected by congressional influence on the program's formula. None of the formula grants should be much affected by presidential influence or variations in state aggressiveness. In each case, the formula should explain most of the variance in the distribution of program funds. To the extent that the formulas explain differing amounts of variance, they should control the distribution of funds most closely where they are clear and relatively rigid.

The two project grant programs, on the other hand, are hypothesized to be more strongly affected by the three causal factors. Of the two programs, the health services project grant program has the highest funding level and should be perceived as most desirable; thus it should be most strongly affected by the causal factors.

The Data

The analysis focuses on the distribution of funds during fiscal year 1973. Data for a single year provide a very narrow perspective on the distribution of funds. Because most grant funds remain available for more than one fiscal year, variations between fiscal years may occur; as a result, the distribution of expenditures in one year may differ from trends over the longer term. Yet the timing itself of grant awards is very much a matter of administrative discretion and therefore subject to political manipulation. As a result, what might be considered an error in other contexts is an important object of study here. Although the ability to generalize about other years is limited, there seems to be no reason to question the validity of the results for the period of time we have chosen to study.

Dependent Variables. The dependent variables for the study are the differences between the dollars awarded to each state (that is, new obligations) and the estimated amounts each state ought to have received. For the formula grants, this was computed by taking the difference between grant awards and estimated formula allocation shares.[18] For the two project grants, a comparable standard—state population weighted inversely for state average per capita income—was substituted. The purpose underlying this method deserves a word of explanation.

In order to show that political variables such as congressional and presidential influence affect the distribution of grants-in-aid, it is necessary to demonstrate that the funds were distributed differently than they would otherwise have been. For formula grant programs, it is easy enough to assume that in the absence of other factors the formula will entirely control the distribution of funds. Project grants, of course, lack such a criterion spelled out in advance. However, we can assume that administrators would distribute funds according to a reasonable standard in the absence of other political and administrative pressures. To the extent that this is the case, any deviation from the standard in practice may then be attributed to these political factors. For this analysis, state population weighted inversely for per capita income is used as such a standard against which to compare the distribution of project grant funds, a choice supported by the fact that each of the formula grants in this study uses a similar distributional criterion.

Congressional Influence.   In order to test the hypothesis that congressmen who are participants in a particular subgovernment will exercise disproportionate influence within that sphere, we will consider whether members of the authorizing and appropriations committees are able to direct greater shares of grant-in-aid funds to their districts. In 1972 the five health grant programs were under the jurisdiction of the Interstate and Foreign Commerce Committee in the House, and the Labor and Public Welfare Committee in the Senate. We will hypothesize that, other things being equal, the states of members serving on these authorizing committees will receive larger than expected shares of grant funds. The relationship should be even stronger for representation on the subcommittees with jurisdiction over the programs: the House Subcommittee on Public Welfare and the Senate Subcommittee on Health. Likewise we hypothesize that the members of the House and Senate Appropriations Committees and their respective Labor-HEW Subcommittees will wield disproportionate power over the distribution of funds under these programs.

Partisan Presidential Influence.   Earlier we suggested that presidents might attempt to use their influence to assure their reelection (during the first term) and build party support. Two hypotheses are tested in this analysis: that a president will direct larger shares of funds to states with governors from his own party; and that the president will steer larger benefits to states which are important in the next election. Understandably, the specific indicators chosen to represent these concepts will vary from one time period to another. The period studied here runs from July 1972 to June 1973, during which the 1972 presidential election was conducted. We expect the distribution of funds to be affected by the campaign strategy for that election, though perhaps not so much as in the preceding fiscal year.

To test the first hypothesis, we will compare the states with Republican governors in July 1972 with those represented by Democratic governors. Three indicators are used to test the second hypothesis. First, we expect states with 20 or more electoral college votes in 1972 to receive larger shares of funds than they otherwise would have.[19] Second, states carried by Nixon in 1968 should have been the beneficiaries of presidential gratitude. And finally, we expect the "swing" states, those which Nixon won or lost by narrow margins in 1968, to benefit from attempts to add them to the 1972 win column.

State Aggressiveness.   The zeal and competence with which states pursue grants may be objective characteristics, but they are difficult to measure nonetheless. This study employs a variety of indicators intended to represent several aspects of state aggressiveness.

First, Walker's state innovation scores are used on the assumption that a state's innovative tendencies may also reflect differences in the willingness of state officials to experiment.[20] Second, 1969 per capita state health spending minus federal health grants is used to indicate a state's commitment to the support of health policies; we do so on the assumption that states with larger existing commitments to health programs will desire additional funding and be less reluctant to undertake new program commitments in the area. The professionalism of state health staffs should also affect state aggressiveness. Four indicators of this concept are used here: whether the state has a personnel department of "general" scope; the proportion of state employees covered by such a department; the average earnings of state noneducation employees; and the salary of the state's chief health administrator. Finally, we hypothesize that states with Washington lobby offices will be more successful in obtaining federal grant funds.

The Results

In this section we present the results of the analysis. We begin by considering the importance of program formulas in controlling the distribution of grant funds. Following this we will analyze the relationship between the three causal factors and the distribution of health grant funds.

The Importance of Allocation Formulas.   It is an important thesis of this study that the structure of programs affects both the extent of political influence on the distribution of funds and the ways that influence can be exercised. In particular, we expect that formula grant funds will be strongly controlled by their formulas, and therefore less subject to influence by political factors than project grants, which as a consequence will be less governed by programmatic considerations. In addition, we expect most political influence on formula grants to be exercised in writing the formulas, rather than by intervening in program administration.

The data in table 2-2 support the contention that formula grants are more tightly governed by programmatic criteria than are project grants. The figures are the standard deviations of the differences between each state's percentage shares of awarded funds and estimated allocations. Lower standard deviations indicate programs which are controlled more tightly by the allocation formula. As shown in the lefthand column, the variability is highest for the two project grant programs, demonstrating that project grants are less likely to be distributed in accord with any single programmatic criterion. The figures in the righthand column are based on data from states which actually received grant awards under the three programs which had less than full participation. They are presented since a program formula cannot explain the choice of some states not to participate in a program. When only participating states are analyzed, the standard deviation for the planning grant program is sharply reduced, demonstrating that the formula controls state receipts more than under any other program. By contrast, the variation for the two project grant programs is even higher than before.

It is important that the variance is smallest for the two formula grants whose formulas are spelled out most clearly and rigidly in law. The Hill-Burton formula is defined quite precisely in the statutes, and the planning grant formula is outlined in general terms in the statutes and defined specifically in the public regulations. By contrast, the health services program formula is defined only ambiguously in either place. The implication is that loosely defined formulas allow administrators greater discretion in distributing funds, which permits greater scope for the operation of political factors. It should be clear as well that in terms of administrative flexibility the distinction between formula and project grants is one of degree rather than of kind.

Effect of the Causal Factors.   The remainder of the analysis is devoted to the three causal factors and their effects on the distribution of health grants. The relationships are tested by multiple regression analysis. The figures shown in table 2-3 are standardized regression coefficients,[21] which may be interpreted as measures of the relative effects of each variable where the others are controlled.[22] The simple correlations between the causal variables and the distribution of grants are shown in the appendix.

Congressional Representation.   Although the regression coefficients are not especially large, they do reveal some clear patterns. No single committee

Table 2-2
The Importance of Program Formulas

	Standard Deviations	
Program	All States	Participating States Only
Formula Grants		
Comprehensive health planning grants to states	1.594	.775[b]
Comprehensive health services formula grants	1.470	
Hill-Burton hospital facilities construction grants	.891	
Project Grants		
Comprehensive health planning training, studies, and demonstration project grants[a]	2.040	2.435[c]
Comprehensive health services project grants[a]	1.869	1.966[d]

Note: The figures are based on the difference between each state's percentage share of awards and allotments; n = 50 except as noted.

[a]A state's percentage share of U.S. population times the ratio of U.S. to state per capita income is used in lieu of a formula.
[b]N = 39.
[c]N = 23.
[d]N = 38.

or subcommittee appears to exercise dominant influence over the distribution of health grant funds. Rather, the regression coefficients suggest that individual committees tend to specialize in the exercise of influence. State representation on the House Appropriations Committee and subcommittee relates most strongly with benefits under the three formula grant programs, especially the Hill-Burton program, the most desirable of the three. Representation on the full House committee is positively related with benefits under the health services formula grants and, to a lesser extent, with the Hill-Burton program. As might be expected, representation on the House Labor-HEW Subcommittee is even more strongly related with benefits under the three formula grants than is representation on the full committee; this is particularly true for the Hill-Burton program. By contrast, representation on the Senate Appropriations Committee and its Labor-HEW Subcommittee is positively related with benefits under the two most desirable programs, Hill-Burton and the health services project grants.

A more pronounced tendency to specialize seems apparent for the authorizing committees. Both the House Interstate and Foreign Commerce Committee and its health subcommittee appear to affect the distribution of

Table 2-3
Effects of the Causal Factors on the Distribution of Health Grants, Fiscal Year 1973

Independent Variables	Planning Grants	Standardized Regression Coefficients			
		Health Services Formula Grants	Hill-Burton Grants	Training/ Demonstration Project Grants	Health Services Project Grants
Congressional Influence					
Appropriations Committees					
House Appropriations Committee	.03	.29	.11	-.06	.01
House Labor-HEW Subcommittee	.28	.25	.46	-.25	.00
Senate Appropriations Committee	.08	-.11	.20	-.03	.15
Senate Labor-HEW Subcommittee	-.16	-.04	.28	-.04	.16
Authorizing Committees					
House Interstate and Foreign Commerce Committee	.19	.12	.02	.32	-.04
House Public Health and Welfare Subcommittee	-.31	-.15	.21	.36	.14
Senate Labor and Public Welfare Committee	-.30	-.27	-.68	-.37	.28
Senate Health Subcommittee	-.19	-.15	-.14	-.22	.37
Aggressiveness					
Innovativeness	-.03	.11	-.11	.19	-.12
Prior health spending	-.13	.24	.00	.24	.11
Salary, chief health officer	-.56	.15	.24	.06	.12
Earnings, noneducated employees	.44	-.06	-.10	.03	-.08
Percent employees under general personnel department	-.10	.18	-.23	-.05	-.06
Presidential Influence					
Size of victory margin, 1968[a]	.25	.20	-.07	-.01	-.03
Republican governor, 1972	.16	-.41	.35	.20	.17
R^2	.53	.34	.38	.37	.18

Note: The dependent variable in each case is the difference between shares of funds awarded and allocated to each state. N = 48.

[a]Positive coefficients indicate a tendency for states where the victory margin was narrowest to receive larger shares.

benefits under the training and demonstration program; they are the only committees which appear to do so. In addition, the full committee is positively related with benefits under the planning and health services formula grants, while the subcommittee is related with benefits under the most desirable Hill-Burton and health services project grant programs. States represented on the Senate Labor and Public Welfare Committee, and especially its Subcommittee on Health, tend to benefit from the more desirable of the project grant programs, the health service project grants, while showing no positive relationship with the remaining four programs.

State Aggressiveness. On the whole, the relationships between state aggressiveness and the distribution of health grant benefits are relatively weak. However, they are generally in the expected direction, and provide some support for the model. Of the five programs, the training and demonstration grants and the health services formula grants are most strongly related to state aggressiveness, especially as measured by 1969 health spending levels and state innovativeness. Both programs are positively related with four of the five indicators. Although health services project grants were expected to be highly affected by state aggressiveness, they are positively related with only two of the five indicators—prior health spending and the chief health officer's salary.

The remaining two programs, Hill-Burton and the comprehensive health planning grants, were not expected to be much affected by state aggressiveness, an expectation which is fairly well met by the data. In only two instances do aggressiveness variables relate positively with these programs. Though in both cases the coeffecients are comparatively large, the generally negative relationships with aggressiveness indicators permit the conclusion that aggressiveness has little general effect on the distribution of funds under these two formula grant programs.

Partisan Presidential Influence. The multiple regression analysis included two variables intended to measure partisan presidential influence—gubernatorial party and the closeness of the 1968 presidential election outcome. In both cases, the most desirable programs, and especially the health services project grants, were hypothesized to be most affected by these factors. When other factors are controlled, the size of the 1968 victory margin does not relate in the expected manner. Small negative coefficients occur for the Hill-Burton and project grant programs, while there are positive relationships with the two less desirable formula grants. On the other hand, gubernatorial party appears to have some net effect on the distribution of grant funds, as moderate positive coefficients occur with the two project grant programs and two of the formula grant programs. Only the health services formula grants were directed more toward the states with Democratic governors, contrary to our hypothesis.

The Effect of Administrative Discretion

The analysis demonstrated that program formulas tend to control the distribution of grant funds, at least to the extent that the formulas are specified in ways that permit little administrative discretion. Funds under two of the formula grants were closely controlled by their formulas, while the project grant funds, when measured against a comparable programmatic standard, deviated to a much greater extent. The third formula grant, with a formula not spelled out clearly in the law, fell between the other formula grants and the project grants.

We also observed the tendency for these differences in administrative discretion to condition the impact of the causal variables on the distribution of grant funds. Given formula allocations, state aggressiveness had little effect on the most tightly controlled formula grants, Hill-Burton and comprehensive health planning grants. However, the effects of aggressiveness were evident for the three programs which permitted greater discretion. These constraints imposed by the program formulas do not appear to be absolute, however, since both congressional and presidential influence seem to affect the administration of the two most rigid formula grant programs as well as the more flexible programs. Presidential influence in particular appears to be less affected by the discretion available to administrators than by the desirability of the programs' benefits.

The significance of this is not that formula grants are impervious to political influence; rather, it is that the initial decision regarding program structure, that is, formula or discretionary distribution, will condition *how* the effect of political influence will be made, not *whether* it will be made. Where funds are to be allocated by formula, political influence may be exercised at the time the program is authorized, by writing the formula so as to achieve a preferential distribution of funds. This is illustrated by a study reported elsewhere, which found that the committee which drafted the Hill-Burton legislation in 1946 selected from among several alternatives the formula which was clearly the most beneficial to the states of its members.[23] On the other hand, where there is greater administrative flexibility in allocating the funds, as with project grants, political influence will come to bear on the administrators themselves. This form of influence—intervention in program administration—is also possible with formula grants, but to a degree that is largely limited by the rigidity of the program formula.

Program Desirability and the Distribution
of Health Grants

If administrative flexibility explains *how* influence is exercised, program desirability tends to explain *whether* it is. We hypothesized that the three causal factors would influence the distribution of funds most strongly where the progam benefits were the most desirable. The analysis provides some support for the proposition.

The evidence points to a greater amount of congressional intervention in the administration of the more desirable programs than in the less desirable ones. The most consistently high regression coefficients, shown in table 2-3, were found for the two most desirable programs. As expected, due to its desirability and the administrative flexibility, the strongest relationships were for the health services project grants. Despite a large negative relationship with state representation on the Senate Labor and Public Welfare Committee, the second most consistently supportive set of coefficients is found for the most desirable formula grant program, the Hill-Burton program. The relationships for the remaining three programs are mixed and predominantly negative, with the least evidence of congressional intervention occurring for the health planning grant program, which was judged to have the least political value. Thus, while there is little evidence of strong advantage to committee representation, such advantage as does exist involves those programs offering the highest potential payoffs.

As mentioned earlier, in addition to intervening in program administration, congressional influence can be exercised by writing formulas in a preferential manner. We may infer from the structure of the three formulas studied here that they are more likely to do so where the program benefits are more desirable. Though they may be manipulated for political reasons, allocation formulas must eventually be justified in policy terms. For this reason, formulas tend to fall into a range of reasonable alternatives, each of which distributes program funds in some relation to need. Because the concept of need is ambiguous at best, there is some variation in what can be considered reasonable. However, too much deviation from one of the more widely accepted formulas, population or population weighted by per capita income, is difficult to defend on purely programmatic grounds. As a result, the more a formula differs from these accepted formulas, the more likely that it was written with constituency benefits, rather than program goals, in mind.

None of the health formula grants use either of these widely accepted formulas. In both structure and effect, all three come closer to population weighted by per capita income than to unweighted population, and each of the formulas makes some use of weighted state population. Of the three, the formula for the planning grant program is closest to weighted population, differing only slightly by guaranteeing each state a minimum allocation. By contrast, the formulas for the more desirable programs—Hill-Burton and the health services formula grants—are fairly complex, and include such features as minimum allocations, "hold harmless" provisions, and multistage computations. Because of the difficulty of defending such complex formulas as better expressions of the need for assistance,[24] we are probably correct in concluding that greater complexity serves political objectives rather than economic ones, and that congressional interest in the design of the formulas will be highest where the programs are more politically desirable.

The evidence regarding aggressiveness and program desirability is not as conclusive. The strongest and most consistent relationships appeared for the training grants and the health services formula grants. By contrast, the relationships were weak, though generally positive, for the more desirable health services project grants, and they were largely negative for the highly desirable Hill-Burton grants. The least desirable program—the planning grants—was largely negatively related with aggressiveness indicators.

The finding for the Hill-Burton program is consistent with our expectations, since the effect of aggressiveness was expected to be constrained by the formula. Even though some states may display greater zeal and competence in seeking funding, the effect of their aggressiveness may be limited when, as with the more desirable programs, even the least aggressive states obtain their full allocations.

While the remaining three more desirable programs—the two project grants and the health services formula grants—were related positively with aggressiveness, the relationship was weakest for the most desirable project grant, a finding which is unexplained. This, together with the fact that the three programs most affected by aggressiveness also allowed the greatest administrative discretion, makes it difficult to accept the hypothesis about aggressiveness and desirability without further evidence.

The data do not support the hypothesis that presidential influence is conditioned by program desirability. Having a Republican governor correlated positively with benefits under four programs—all but the health services formula grants. The variable had its largest effect on the Hill-Burton program, even though the program's formula was expected to constrain the factor. The generally positive relationships suggest that presidential influence may have operated without reference to program desirability, at least during this year. Unexplained, however, is the large negative relationship with the health services formula grants. Size of the 1968 victory margin, taken as an indicator of 1972 electoral strategy, was positively related only with the two less desirable formula grant programs, and showed no relationship with the Hill-Burton grants or the two project grants.

The low multiple regression coefficients suggest that the stronger bivariate relationships (see the Appendix) may have been due to covariation with other variables. Since the multiple regression coefficients represent the independent effects of each variable, we conclude that there is insufficient support for the hypothesis to accept it. However, because of the strength of the simple correlations, the relationships with the gubernatorial party variable, and the case study evidence, it seems unlikely that presidential influence should be ruled out as a causal factor affecting the distribution of grants.

Summary

This study has attempted to contribute to the growing body of knowledge about the political and administrative factors affecting the formation of distributive policies by identifying some previously unstudied factors affecting those policies and by specifying some conditions under which their impact can be expected to vary.

These factors represent an attempt to capture the effects of the political and administrative processes on distributive policies, above and beyond the efforts of decision makers to form rational, issue-oriented policies. The indicators representing these factors explained between one-fifth and one-half of the variance in the dependent variables—the difference between actual health grant expenditures and proxies for such rational policies—suggesting that federal spending policies importantly serve political and organizational objectives as well as programmatic ones.

On the basis of a test using 1973 expenditures for five health grant programs, it is possible to conclude that each of the postulated causal factors—the exercise of congressional and presidential influence and the aggressiveness of grant applicants—is of some importance in determining the distribution of health grant dollars between states. Of particular interest is the finding that these factors, and especially congressional influence, are prone to having larger effects on the programs with greater political value. In addition, the structure of the programs, that is, whether they distribute funds on a formula or discretionary basis, appears to be an important determinant of the degree to which the funds are susceptible to the effects of these political and administrative variables.

Also interesting is the finding that congressional power over the distribution of benefits can be exercised at either the authorization stage—by writing preferential allocation formulas—or by influencing program administration. In some cases, congressional influence may be evident at both stages. The choice of influence channels has obvious implications for the durability of policy decisions, since clearly specified formulas may reduce, or eliminate altogether, the opportunity for subsequent congressional or presidential intervention in program administration. The apparent tendency is for formulas once enacted to remain relatively unchanged;[25] the result, for these programs at least, is that the power configurations of the past will remain relevant as explanations of the policies of the present and the future. Why Congress chooses to make some programs formula grants and others not remains unexplained. Perhaps this is a function of program desirability; if so, however, it is certainly not evident from this analysis. Another possibility, beyond the scope of this study, is that the choice of program structure reflects the state of congressional-administrative relations within the policy subsystem at the time the program is authorized. If the congressional members of the subsystem are confident of their ability to influence the program without a formula, then perhaps they will be content to permit greater administrative flexibility.

The theory as spelled out here is intended to be applicable to a broad range of spending programs. It seems reasonable to expect various degrees of presidential and congressional influence on the full scope of federal distributive policies. Clearly, however, applicant aggressiveness is more restricted, and can only be expected to apply to programs such as grants-in-aid and contracts, where a recipient's initiative might reasonably affect his chances for being funded.

There are likely some limits to the generalizability of these results, and future research might properly explore some of them. Some of the factors may well vary in importance over time; presidential influence, for instance, may be more important just before presidential elections, and it may wane near the end of a lame duck president's term. Individual presidents likewise may differ in their willingness to use presidential power for partisan advantage. It also seems likely that the importance of the causal factors may differ from one policy area to another. Some, such as health, may be perceived as being above politics, and thus may be somewhat immune from the forces which impact other policy areas. In addition, Fenno has found that congressmen who are more re-election conscious tend to seek seats on the committees with greater potential for pork barrel benefits.[26] This may well result in significant differences between committees in their willingness to use their power on behalf of their constituencies. The answers to these questions and others will help to produce a fuller understanding of the policy-making processes at the federal level.

Notes

1. "The Second War Between the States," *Business Week*, May 17, 1976, pp. 92-114. See also Joel Havemann, Rochelle L. Stanfield, and Neal R. Peirce, "Federal Spending: The North's Loss is the Sunbelt's Gain," *National Journal* 8(June 26, 1976):878-891.

2. Joel Havemann and Rochelle L. Stanfield, "A Year Later, The Frostbelt Strikes Back," *National Journal* 9(July 2, 1977):1028-1037.

3. Most studies have appeared in the economics literature and have dealt with the effects of federal spending or with questions of equity. For instance, see Roy W. Bahl and J. J. Warford, "Interstate Distribution of Benefits from the Federal Budgetary Process," *National Tax Journal* 24(June 1972):169-176; Fred K. Hines and J. Norman Reid, "Using Federal Outlays Data to Measure Program Equity: Opportunities and Limitations," *American Journal of Agricultural Economics* 59(Winter 1977):1013-1019; and Bruce C. Stuart, "The Impact of Medicaid on Interstate Income Differentials." In *Redistribution to the Rich and the Poor: The Grants Economics of Income Distribution*, edited by Kenneth E. Boulding and Martin Pfaff (Belmont: Wadsworth, 1972), pp. 149-168.

4. Leading examples are Barry S. Rundquist, "On Testing a Military-Industrial Complex Theory," *American Politics Quarterly* 6(January 1978):29-53; John Ferejohn, *Porkbarrel Politics: Rivers and Harbors Legislation, 1947-1968* (Stanford: Stanford University Press, 1974); Gerald S. Strom, "Congressional Policy Making: A Test of a Theory," *Journal of Politics* 37(August 1975):711-735; James Clotfelter, "Senate Voting and Constituency Stake in Defense Spending," *Journal of Politics* 32(November 1972): 979-983. An exception which seeks explanations outside the congressional process is Gerald S. Ferman, "A Systematic Approach to the Politics of the Distribution of Grants-in-Aid, 1960-69," paper delivered at the Midwest Political Science Association Convention, Chicago, April, 1972.

5. For examples of this literature, see J. Lieper Freeman, *Political Process: Executive Bureau-Legislative Committee Relations* (rev. ed.; New York: Random House, 1965); A. Lee Fritschler, *Smoking and Politics: Policymaking and the Federal Bureaucracy* (New York: Appleton-Century-Crofts, 1969).

6. As mentioned earlier, much of the existing literature has addressed this hypothesis. In addition to recent empirical studies, there is a good deal of case study support for the hypothesis. See, for instance, Joseph P. Harris, *Congressional Control of Administration* (Washington: The Brookings Institution, 1964), p. 90.

7. Clearly, some forms of federal spending may not be readily susceptible to influence over their geographic distribution; examples are outlays for social security or civil service retirement benefits.

8. Regarding congressional influence, see Harris, *Congressional Control*, p. 90. The use of presidential influence during the Nixon Administration is well-illustrated in congressional testimony of Frederic V. Malek. U.S. House. Committee on Government Operations. *New Federalism (Organizational and Procedural Arrangements for Federal Grant Administration)*, 93d Congress, 2nd Session (1974). The benefits of skilled grantsmanship are perhaps best illustrated by the success of New Haven,

Connecticut, in attracting urban renewal funds; see Allan R. Talbot, *The Mayor's Game: Richard Lee of New Haven and the Politics of Change* (New York: Praeger 1967), chap. 11.

9. A recent study concluded that local officials have a strong preference for flexible sources of funding, and that they will tolerate cumbersome administrative machinery and lower application success ratios in exchange for a larger voice in the use of the funds. Richard T. Pascale and George P. Barbour, Jr., *Shared Power: A Study of Four Federal Funding Systems in Appalachia* (Washington: American Enterprise Institute for Public Policy Research, 1977), p. 29.

10. This is hardly the same as saying that aggressiveness is unimportant as a causal factor in such cases, however, for aggressiveness would, in fact, contribute heavily to keeping actual receipts in line with allocations.

11. Samuelson has defined the pure public good as one "which all enjoy in common in the sense that each individual's consumption of such a good leads to no subtraction from any other individual's consumption of that good." Paul A. Samuelson, "The Pure Theory of Public Expenditures," *Review of Economics and Statistics* 36(November 1954):387. Breton has further distinguished nonprivate goods, "whose services are available in unequal amounts," from pure public goods, "whose services are available to all in equal amounts." Albert Breton, "A Theory of Government Grants," *The Canadian Journal of Economics and Political Science* 31(May 1965):177.

12. Section 314(a) of the Public Health Service Act, as added by the Comprehensive Health Planning and Public Health Services Amendments of 1966, PL 89-749 (November 3, 1966); 80 Stat. 1180; 42 USC 246(a). The areawide agencies, known as "314(b)" agencies, were supported by grants under the same legislation. Both programs were replaced by the National Health Planning and Resources Development Act of 1974, PL 93-641 (January 4, 1975); 88 Stat. 2225.

13. PL 79-725 (August 13, 1946), 60 Stat. 1040, which created Title VI of the Public Health Service Act; 42 USC 291 et seq. Following the National Health Planning and Resources Development Act of 1974, the program has been significantly cut back.

14. U.S. Department of Health, Education, and Welfare, *Hill-Burton Progress Report, July 1, 1947-June 30, 1971* (Washington: U.S. Government Printing Office, 1972), p. 9.

15. Section 314(d) of the Public Health Service Act, as amended; 42 USC 246(d).

16. Section 314(e) of the Public Health Service Act, as amended; 42 USC 246(e).

17. Section 314(c) of the Public Health Service Act, as amended; 42 USC 246 (c).

18. For further details, see John Norman Reid, "The Interstate Distribution of Federal Health Grants: An Analysis of Causal Factors" (Ph.D. dissertation, University of Illinois at Urbana, 1975), pp. 76-79.

19. A recent study concluded that the electoral college system forces "candidates—and after the election, incumbent presidents with an eye on the next election—to pay much greater attention in terms of their allocations of time, money, and other resources to the largest states." Steven J. Brams and Morton D. Davis, "The 3/2's Rule in Presidential Campaigning," *American Political Science Review* 68(March 1974):134.

20. Jack L. Walker, "The Diffusion of Innovations Among the American States," *American Political Science Review* 63(September 1969):880-899. See also his "Innovation in State Politics." In *Politics in the American States: A Comparative Analysis,* edited by Herbert Jacob and Kenneth N. Vines, 2nd ed. (Boston: Little, Brown, 1971), pp. 354-387. Gray argues that such a general dimension of progressivism does not, in fact, exist and that innovation tends to be restricted by time and issue area. See Virginia Gray, "Expenditures and Innovation as Dimensions of 'Progressivism': A Note on the American States," *American Journal of Political Science* 18(November 1974):693-699.

21. Strictly speaking, the beta weights indicate the amount of change in the dependent variable (that is, the difference between actual and expected grant awards) which is attributable to each independent variable, with the joint effects of the other independent variables controlled; the coefficients are in standard units, so that the size of the relationships is comparable between variables. See Hubert M. Blalock, Jr., *Social Statistics* (New York: McGraw-Hill, 1960), p. 345.

22. Several variables were excluded from the multivariate analysis because, when other factors were controlled, they were found to contribute little. These variables are dummy variables for states with "general" personnel departments, those with a Washington lobby office, and those carried by Nixon in 1968. We have also excluded the variable indicating states with twenty or more electoral college votes, since it is highly correlated with population and tended to produce erratic fluctuations in the remaining coefficients.

23. See Reid, *Distribution of Federal Health Grants,* pp. 86-98.

24. Elliott R. Morss, "Federal Activities and Their Regional Impact on the Quality of Life," *National Tax Journal* 24(June 1971):177-192, esp. p. 187.

25. Clara Penniman, "General Revenue Sharing and the Nonmetropolitan Small Community," in U.S. Senate, Committee on Agriculture, Nutrition, and Forestry, *National Conference on Nonmetropolitan Community Services Research,* 95th Congress, 1st Session (1977), p. 103.

26. Richard F. Fenno, Jr., *Congressmen in Committees* (Boston: Little, Brown, 1973), chapter 1.

Appendix 2A

Table 2A-1
Simple Correlations between Causal Factors and the Differences between Shares of Health Grants Awarded and Allocated, Fiscal Year 1973

	Simple Correlations				
Independent Variables	*Planning Grants*	*Health Services Formula Grants*	*Hill-Burton Grants*	*Training/Demonstration Project Grants*	*Health Services Project Grants*
Congressional Influence					
Appropriations Committees					
House Appropriations Committee	−.04	.31	.13	.07	.03
House Labor-HEW Subcommittee	.21	.13	.18	−.13	.05
Senate Appropriations Committee	.12	−.16	.04	−.10	.07
Senate Labor-HEW Subcommittee	−.04	−.06	.08	−.11	.05
Authorizing Committees					
House Interstate and Foreign Commerce Committee	−.11	.25	.03	.30	.07
House Public Health and Welfare Subcommittee	−.36	.01	.14	.21	.11
Senate Labor and Public Welfare Committee	.04	.03	−.17	.02	.31
Senate Health Subcommittee	.00	.06	−.04	.07	.30
Aggressiveness					
Innovativeness[a]	.04	.23	−.08	.34	.18
Prior health spending	−.14	.17	.04	.39	.22
Salary, chief health officer	−.31	.20	.22	.31	.12
Earnings, noneducated employees	.13	−.01	.04	.17	.11
General personnel department	.00	.11	−.24	.09	−.14
Percent employees under general personnel department	−.01	.19	−.05	.07	.06
Washington lobby office	.14	.20	.05	.05	−.02
Presidential Influence					
Republican governor, 1972	.08	−.11	.22	.25	.22
Over twenty electoral votes	.22	.23	.15	.26	−.06
Size of victory margin, 1968[b]	.17	.15	.04	.13	.10
States carried by Nixon, 1968	.13	−.28	−.07	−.18	.03

Note: The dependent variable in each case is the difference between shares of funds awarded and allocated to each state. N = 50 except as noted.

[a]N = 48 for correlations with this variable.

[b]Positive correlations indicate a tendency for those states in which the victory margin was narrowest to receive larger shares.

3

Politics in the Distribution of Federal Grants: The Case of the Economic Development Administration

J. Theodore Anagnoson

Introduction

The distributional characteristics of federal expenditures have been extensively analyzed in recent years. Total federal expenditures, individual programs, even individual projects have been scrutinized in an effort to determine how federal funds have been allocated among the ten federal regions, the states, congressional districts, and counties.[1] For the most part these studies have suggested that federal spending is distributed in broad accordance with population, with a tendency in some programs to redistribute some money to rural or poorer areas.

The subject of this study is the factor which often determines these broad economic tendencies: politics. Although they are not always analyzed, political factors are important in federal spending because it is the political process that determines the extent to which factors like population, income, or need will be important in the distribution of funds. Political considerations are also important because of the extent to which federal agencies, unlike private businesses or corporations, are dependent on the external environment—a basically political environment—for their funding and the rules under which they operate.

Sources of outside political influence include congressional committees, the political leadership of the agency or department, the Office of Management and Budget (OMB), and the White House. Each of these can affect the distribution of spending in the programs under its jurisdiction. Congress as a whole, usually operating at the behest of its committees, specifies the rules under which the executive branch operates programs, widening or narrowing applicant eligibility, suggesting (or mandating) criteria for discretionary spending, or setting a formula to distribute funds.

An earlier version of this paper was presented at the Fifth Seminar on National Policy Issues, California Institute of Technology, Pasadena, California, November 12, 1977. I would like to thank John Ferejohn, Morris Fiorina, Will Price and Helene Smockler for their comments. In addition, Daryl M. Bladen, Richard F. Fenno, Jr., Bruce Jacobs, and Richard Thaler commented on the dissertation on which this chapter is based (Anagnoson, 1977).

In addition, individual congressmen may attempt to influence executive branch decisions when federal administrators have the authority to grant, terminate, or shape the flow of funds. The White House or OMB can also influence individual executive branch decisions, or even, as during the Nixon administration, refuse to spend congressionally appropriated funds.

It is usually acknowledged that special treatment on the part of executive branch administrators influences the approval of at least some individual decisions. One crucial question in this study, then, is whether special treatment results in an entire distribution of spending biased toward those who are presumed to be influential with an agency. It is generally assumed that those who are influential with an agency are those in Congress who hold institutional positions overseeing the agency, the members of its authorizing and appropriating committees. Influence with the agency is also assumed to lie with those in the executive branch who have some authority over the agency; that is, its own leadership, departmental leadership, and so on, through OMB, and the White House.

This paper is a report on the politics of the distribution of federal grants-in-aid in one program, a program whose structural characteristics make it an excellent vehicle for the measurement of the potential political benefits that flow to the members of congressional committees overseeing agencies. The program is the public works program of the U.S. Department of Commerce's Economic Development Administration (EDA).

Politics and Grants: Structure and Influence

The structural configurations of federal programs reflect the different kinds of political influence operating in them. The major distinction is between programs for which Congress makes the distributional decisions directly (for example, most formula grant programs), and programs for which that authority is delegated to the executive branch (most project grant programs).

Studies of programs for which distributional decision making is centered in Congress have generally found considerable congressional influence in the distribution of spending. Gerald S. Strom, for example, found that the House Public Works Committee had arranged the formula distributing the Environmental Protection Agency's sewage treatment program so that states represented on the committee received more money from the formula than states not on the committee. States represented by more than one member received more funds than states represented by only one member, and so on (Strom, 1973, 1976).

In a major study of a program for which Congress allocates individual projects in committee, John A. Ferejohn found that the 1969 new U.S. Army

Corps of Engineers rivers and harbors projects were distributed " . . . in rough conformity to formal authority over the legislative arena under consideration" (Ferejohn, 1972, 1973). That is, members of the overseeing committees tended to receive more projects for their states than did nonmembers; senior members more than junior members; and, in some cases, Republicans more than Democrats.[2]

Whatever the particular configuration of influence, the structure of congressional decision making is quite conducive to a policy outcome which reflects the internal congressional distribution of power. With subcommittees reporting to full committees, and full committees reporting to the floor, the way is open for committee members to follow one or both of two impulses. First, they can universalize the project distribution, including in it members who do not sit on the committees but whose votes will be needed on the floor of the house. And second, since the committee members are proposing each allocation, they are able to see to it, if they want to, that committee members are not neglected in each year's allocations. Neither Strom nor Ferejohn tested the universalization notion, but it is quite clear in both works that the internal distribution of power in Congress is reflected in the output of its committees.

When the authority to make these distributional decisions is transferred to the executive branch, however, several additional—and complicating—factors emerge. For one thing, congressmen are no longer the decision makers; bureaucrats are. And bureaucrats respond not only to congressmen, but to the other parts of their external political environments (the department, OMB, the White House), as well as to their own desires for rationality in their decision-making processes. Furthermore, it seems likely that federal executives desire both to insulate their decision making from the external environment and at the same time to ensure the future political stability of their programs. The result is a system which from the congressional standpoint is much less certain of yielding political benefits, and, from our analytical standpoint, more complex.

R. Douglas Arnold, for example, after analyzing the employment histories of military installations from 1952 to 1974, concludes that there is

> . . . no support for the hypothesis that members of military committees are able to affect employment at installations in their districts, either by promoting their expansion or by slowing their contraction. In fact, installations with committee representation suffered greater than average losses in employment (Arnold, 1977, p. 32).

Barry S. Rundquist, in a study of the distribution in 1960 of prime military contracts, similarly concludes that there is

> almost no support for the notion that the districts of members of the military committees benefit disproportionately from the distribution of

prime military contracts. . . . The preponderant conclusion from this
analysis is that contrary to the distributive theory and the argument about a
defense subgovernment, the districts of members of the military committees do not benefit disproportionately from the distribution of prime
military contracts (Rundquist, 1973, pp. 270-271).

And Carol F. Goss, in a cross-sectional analysis of defense plant employment, defense civilian employment, and private defense-related employment, found that " . . . members of the military committees obtain advantages for their constituencies in the form of high employment on military
bases, but not in the form of high employment in private plants" (Goss,
1972, p. 231).

Only one study of executive-centered decision making unequivocally
supports the notion that overseeing congressmen benefit from their committee membership. Charles R. Plott found, using a simple expected-value
analysis, that members of the House Banking and Currency Committee
received twice the amount of urban renewal expenditures as one would expect, based on average amounts of urban renewal nationwide (Plott, 1968).

Thus, executive-centered decision processes produce much less clear-cut
results than congressionally-centered processes; the overseeing congressmen
seem less likely to benefit when agencies in the executive branch make
distributional decisions.

The Distributive Theory

The hypotheses tested in these studies are ably summarized by Rundquist
and Ferejohn under the rubric of the "distributive theory." The theory
assumes

> that Congressmen are motivated to serve the economic interests of their
> constituencies. The theory states simply that congressmen are best able to
> benefit their constituencies if they are members of standing committees
> with jurisdiction over government activities that affect their constituencies
> (Rundquist and Ferejohn, 1974, p. 88).

I am interested in the third of the three hypotheses which follow from
this assumption:

> Hypothesis 3, the benefit hypothesis, is that, relative to those of other con-
> gressmen, the constituencies of committee members benefit dispropor-
> tionately from the distribution of expenditures under their jurisdiction
> (Rundquist and Ferejohn, 1974, p. 88).

The theory is clearly the embodiment of the "special treatment" notion
mentioned earlier and the "subgovernment" or "little triangle" notions.

The essence of these ideas is that policy is made by congressional committees, bureaucrats, and the relevant interest groups, neglecting the interests of the public at large.

The springboard for this study is the observation that the distributive theory is flawed, both theoretically and as previously tested. The theoretical problem is that, in emphasizing exclusively political factors to explain the distribution of federal expenditures, the distributive theory does not specify which of the numerous units in Congress sought to benefit from funds under their jurisdiction; similarly, the theory does not specify what accounts for funds expended in areas lacking any political clout. Thus, the theory does not specify whether it includes both authorizing and appropriating committees, whether it operates at both the full committee and the subcommittee level, whether party membership is important on either the committee or the subcommittee, whether the appropriate unit benefiting is the congressional district or the state, and a whole host of similar problems. Like many notions of policy making, it is simply vague.

Some of these problems can be partially ameliorated through empirical analysis. There is evidence, for example, that congressmen work on expenditures for their entire states in programs like the U.S. Army Corps of Engineers or formula grants which distribute money directly to the states. But for many project grants, particularly the smaller programs, there is no evidence to assume that congressmen work for benefits outside their districts, or senators, their states.

The methodological problem with the distributive theory is that, with few exceptions, the tests of the theory's benefit hypothesis have been flawed. In assessing the influence of politics on the distribution of projects, one must control for the relative eligibilities or needs of different spatial areas. In that way a measure can be obtained for the funds each area would receive from the program, regardless of political considerations. Testing the benefit hypothesis requires that the benefit (usually measured in money or projects) to some area, the dependent variable, be a function of two sets of independent variables: (1) need or eligibility considerations, and (2) political considerations. Neither can be omitted.

Yet precisely this circumstance of omission has occurred. Several tests of the benefit hypothesis have omitted the need variables entirely (Goss, 1972; Stafford, 1973). Others have aggregated programs and data so different that the few need and eligibility variables included (usually population and income) seem theoretically dubious (Ray, 1976a, 1976b). And others have omitted potentially important political variables in estimating the size of other political variables (Rundquist, 1973, 1971; Rundquist and Ferejohn, 1974).

In sum, the distributive theory is appealing, for it embodies many popular notions of the operation of power in Washington. But when it is examined closely, the theory has some theoretical problems. And several tests of the theory have not been convincing. There is, however, another explanation for the distribution of federal funds.

Universalization

David R. Mayhew has suggested that

> . . . in giving out particularized benefits where the costs are diffuse (falling on taxpayer or consumer) and where in the long run to reward one congressman is not obviously to deprive others, the members follow a policy of universalism (Mayhew, 1974, p. 88).

Universalism means that "every member . . . has a right to his share of the benefits" (Mayhew, 1974, p. 88). The distributive theory emphasizes the benefits that congressmen receive from the programs they oversee, but universalism emphasizes the shares of program benefits that all members receive. Moreover, the implication is that the shares are not dependent on party, seniority, or other political factors. Any inequality among different areas of the country is due to their different needs for the particular program. I call the tendency to distribute expenditures in this manner "universalization."

Mayhew asserts that universalized distributions of projects have been noted in studies of several congressional committees, although these have noted the phenomenon only indirectly (Mayhew, 1974, pp. 88-89). Charles L. Schultze calls the phenomenon "functional logrolling," a tendency, as he puts it, for programs with narrow geographical concentrations to be broadened in Congress to include "all areas, whether they need . . . (aid) or not" (Schultze, 1969, p. 134). Reinforcing Schultze's point are the geographical restrictions in many federal programs restricting any single state from receiving more than 10 or 15 percent of the funds. Sometimes congressional committee decision rules have the same effect: Murphy found in studying the House Public Works Committee's treatment of rivers and harbors legislation that the committee followed a general rule that no more than one new project per year per state could be approved (Murphy, 1974).

Yet universalization is also inadequate as a theoretical explanation for the distribution of federal expenditures in particularlized programs, for it too is vague as to the size of the share that each member of Congress should receive. The different-sized shares could result form differing needs among the various spatial areas, or from eligibility considerations built into programs by Congress. And it should further be noted that universalizing federal expenditures is not totally incompatible with the distributive theory. It could be that, within a basically universalized pattern of federal expenditure distribution, there are small benefits for some committee members. But the two notions do represent different emphases. The distributive theory emphasizes the *concentration* of funds in the districts of the overseeing members. (Naturally, funds could also be concentrated on the basis of efficiency or equity criteria.) On the other hand, a tendency toward universalization represents the opposite emphasis, the *dispersal* of funds among different areas.

Why EDA's Public Works Program?

The larger study from which this report is drawn is an analysis of the project distributions of two federal project grant programs, EDA's public works program and HUD's water and sewer program (Anagnoson, 1977). (For general analyses of EDA, see Levitan and Zickler, 1976; Cameron, 1970; Cumberland, 1971; Martin and Leone, 1977; and Hansen, 1970, 1972.) EDA was selected for several reasons.

1. EDA's public works program is a project grant with moderate-sized projects. Moderate-sized projects are those which include from about $100,000 in federal funds to approximately $5 million. The project restriction focuses us on programs which, on the one hand, are significant enough to interest congressmen, and on the other, are not so large that each project approval involves a prolonged redistributional conflict, like NASA's decision on the location of its manned flight center (Murphy, 1974, pp. 271-277).

2. The effects of EDA public works projects are particularized; that is, they do not affect more than a single congressional district. This requirement tends to eliminate urban-oriented programs, where project benefits can easily spill over to adjacent congressional districts; or where projects, such as Model Cities, urban renewal, or Title I of the Elementary and Secondary Education Act, typically affect several congressional districts. Should the projects affect more than a single congressional district, it would not be possible to assume the project benefits accrue to a single congressman, and the measurement problems would become quite difficult.

3. EDA administrators claim that they have controlled political pressures for the special treatment of individual applications through the use of a preapplication process, which shifts basic project selection decisions out of Washington. Under the preapplication process, EDA local representatives and regional directors make the basic project selection decisions within one to two weeks after the applicant's first substantial contact with the agency. Once there is an initial decision that the application is fundable, the time that the applicant spends on the paperwork and that EDA spends on processing the full application is basically designed to ensure that the application fits the legislative/bureaucratic criteria. While

there are no actual data, EDA administrators involved in the process indicate that upwards of 90 to 95 percent of the completed applications that have survived this initial decision point are eventually funded. Thus, any congressional or White House pressure to accelerate the processing of a favored application is received *after* the agency has made its project decisions in relative quiet.

Thus, considering the extent of political benefits present in EDA's project distribution in a sense enables us to evaluate whether the preapplication procedures can achieve what EDA officials claim they achieve, as well as whether, in any distributive program, it is possible to minimize political conflicts over redistributional goals.

4. The most important reason for selecting EDA is that the structural characteristics of the program make measuring what each spatial area would receive in the absence of political considerations relatively easy. There are two ways to measure political influence in the distribution of governmental expenditures. One way is a longitudinal design, in which spatial areas are examined over periods of time, including times when they have been represented on the relevant overseeing committees and times when they have not. The disadvantage of this method is that congressional redistrictings and internal changes within the geographic areas (fortunately, these occur over very long time periods) make it difficult in practice to use this method (although see Arnold, 1977). The other design is cross-sectional, in which the characteristics of the spatial area which would otherwise result in its receiving funds are controlled, while the political characteristics are varied. The disadvantage of this method is that it is difficult to devise good quality need and eligibility variables for most programs.

EDA, however, is an exception, for Congress has legislated criteria which markedly vary the eligibility of different congressional districts for EDA's programs. Each county in the nation is either eligible or ineligible to apply for EDA funds, depending on whether it qualifies on one of eight criteria: substantial and persistent unemployment, a median family income less than 40 percent of the national median, the presence of one of the nation's poorer Indian reservations, an area likely to experience a sudden rise in unemployment, and the like. The criteria, specified in the agency's legislation, remove almost all of EDA's discretion in determining which areas should be eligible for the program. Areas are designated for periods of three years, although since 1971 Congress has legislated a moratorium on the dedesignation of areas from the program. The moratorium resulted from frequent complaints from areas that their statistics justified their inclusion in the program one year and their exclusion the next. At any rate, the existence of the designation criteria provides marked variations in the number of eligible counties per congressional district, their populations, and their median family incomes. Thus, by controlling for these variables (among others; see below), the extent to which the agency is favoring overseeing congressmen can be ascertained. Since EDA has existed only since 1965, a period of relatively low turnover in Congress until the last two to four years, it would not be possible to use the longitudinal method.

Data

The principal data source in this paper is EDA project data, organized by congressional district, for the fiscal years 1968, 1969, and 1970. These three years were chosen to vary the political control of the executive branch by providing a year of Democratic administration (1968), a year of Republican administration (1970), and a divided year, containing an election campaign, in between. Thus I can ascertain whether the distribution of projects varies with a change of administration or during the congressional election campaign of 1968.

In addition to varying the control of the administration, the selection of these years minimizes the problem of redistricting. Since the assumption is that the benefits of a project accrue to the political representatives of the area in which the project is located, it is necessary to assign each EDA project, the location of which was obtained from an EDA project directory, to a state and congressional district. States which have realigned their congressional districts during these years make this attribution tenuous in the areas changing from one congressional district to another.

Fortunately, most congressional redistrictings took place immediately after the Supreme Court's decision in 1964 and then again after the 1970 census. During the three fiscal years from 1968 to 1970, sixteen states redistricted their congressional districts, but four of these were within one month of the beginning of FY 1968 and were ignored.[3] For the others, I wished to assign a project to its congressional district during the period when the agency was processing it, since any political influence would have been exercised during that time. Thus, as a working rule, projects announced within two months after a redistricting were assigned to the previous congressional district.

The second problem arose in counties split between congressional districts. Since split counties occur most often in large urban areas and the program has a decidedly rural emphasis, this was not a major problem. In some cases, data at the subcounty level was used to apportion the population or income variables. In other cases the portion of the county split off was very small (both in size and population), and was ignored.

Projects crossing county or congressional district borders presented a third problem. EDA, however, indicated the specific geographic location of projects at the subcounty level, and this information helped in placing the projects in the correct congressional district. Projects which still crossed borders were assigned to both districts, but the money was split between them.[4]

There were four additional sources for the quantitative data: (1) EDA documents on the eligibility of each county for the program (U.S., EDA, 1970); (2) census background data on each county (U.S., Department of Commerce, 1973, 1971); (3) Congressional Quarterly *Almanacs* for congressional committee and other political information (Congressional Quarterly, 1968-1971); and, (4) the *Congressional District Atlas* for reference maps of each congressional district. Much of the information concerning EDA already discussed came from a series of almost fifty interviews conducted in Washington during 1975.

Methodological Considerations

The basic model to be tested in this paper posits that the distribution of funds to different spatial areas is a function of two sets of independent variables: the need or eligibility of each area and the political representation of that area. The dependent variable is the number of projects or amount of money obligated in that district during the given time period.

The analysis that follows generally focuses on the number of projects dependent variable because EDA controls the decision to give a grant in the first place, to a much greater extent than it controls the amount of money the applicant receives. An example may help to clarify this point. A typical EDA project might be the provision of water and sewer lines for an industrial park. Once the decision to offer a grant is made, the project must meet certain standards. If any assistance is to provide sewers or sewage treatment, the Environmental Protection Agency must certify that the waste will be adequately treated. Simply running water and sewer lines to an industrial park may not be adequate; the community may need its sewage treatment plant upgraded. Similarly, land for an industrial park may be available only outside the city limits, where services will be more expensive. Or, if water service is to be provided to a part of town serviced by wells, other parts of the town serviced by wells may not be equitably excluded from the project.

For all of these reasons, the amount of money provided an applicant is less controllable, from the agency's point of view, than the initial decision to make the award.[5] And while there is a substantial correlation between the amount of money and the number of grants provided each area, that correlation (.62, .75, and .67 for the three fiscal years respectively) is not a perfect one. Consequently, the emphasis here is placed on the number of grants per congressional district dependent variable, although results with the amount of money as the dependent variable are presented also.

The method used to determine the relative strength of each independent variable is linear multiple regression, in which the number of projects received by each congressional district is regressed on the need, eligibility, and political variables.[6] The procedure used is weighted least squares to counteract the heteroscedasticity typically found in aggregate data where a wider range on the dependent variable is available to the larger aggregate units (Lemiux, 1976). Additional heteroscedasticity results from restrictions on the dependent variable, which, while still interval level, is essentially restricted from varying below zero in all the time periods, and above three in the shortest time period, the four-month election period at the beginning of FY 1969. That time period is sufficiently restrictive that I have not used a multivariate method for the small group of projects funded during that period. (See the discussion in Tufte, 1974, pp. 108-134, and Acton, 1959, pp. 219-233. In previous analyses I have also used a log-log model to avoid this problem, with very similar results. See Anagnoson, 1977.)

Initially I combined the three fiscal years to remove the influence of single-year idiosyncracies (for a similar procedure see Tufte, 1974, chapter 1). Then each fiscal year is analyzed independently, since the provision of public works projects in any single year does not commit the agency to further funding. In fact, quite the reverse may be true, as federal officials await the results of the first project before committing further funds. In addition, the first four months of FY 1969 are analyzed to detect any differences between the congressional election period of July to November 1968 and the rest of the year.

Each congressional district contains areas (usually counties, as mentioned above) which are eligible for EDA's public works program on the basis of criteria stated in the legislation, the Public Works and Economic Development Act of 1965. Districts with no eligible areas during any of the three fiscal years are excluded from the analysis, resulting in 211 congressional districts eligible during at least one of the three fiscal years, and 182 eligible during all three fiscal years.[7] Between fifteen and twenty are ineligible during any single fiscal year.

Three characteristics of the eligible portions of these 211 districts measure their relative need and eligibility for EDA's public works program:

1. A count of the number of eligible areas in each congressional district.
2. The 1970 population of these eligible areas.
3. The 1970 per capita income of these eligible areas.

Three characteristics of the 211 districts take account of particular idiosyncracies in the EDA program:

Whether the Eligible Areas Are Part of an Operating Economic Development District (EDD). EDA's planning grant program funds the staff of these multicounty development districts, which are composed of at least two (one after 1974) designated eligible areas and a growing community (called an Economic Development Center) that receives funds to channel some of its growth to the depressed redevelopment areas. Among the functions of the district staff, normally consisting of three to four professionals, is assisting applicants within the geographic confines of the EDD in applying for federal funds (U.S., EDA, 1970a).

Since EDA's domain is the worst-off economically of the nation's three thousand counties, the assumption of the district program is that these counties are unlikely to have the expertise and experience to apply for federal and state programs. Congressional districts whose counties are part of an operating EDD might be expected to receive more projects from the largest program of their parent agency. To test this possibility, a dummy variable is included for congressional districts whose counties are part of an EDD.

Whether the Eligible Areas Are Part of EDA's Selected Indian Reservation Program (SIRP). In early 1969, EDA and the Office of Economic Opportunity selected fifteen reservations, the "action group," on which to concentrate their available economic development assistance (U.S., EDA, 1969). The assumption behind the list was that a limited amount of aid might not be sufficient to provide enough help to any single reservation if all reservations were to receive projects. EDA has special personnel in both Washington and the regions to oversee its Indian program. Both these factors indicate that these fifteen Indian reservations should receive special attention from EDA. The congressional districts in which the reservations on the action list were located are included in a dummy variable.

Whether the Congressional District Is Located in a Large Urban Area. As with Indian projects, EDA gives urban projects special treatment, too.[8] Special project officers handle urban projects at both the Washington and regional levels. But after Eugene C. Foley, EDA's first assistant secetary, funded $23.3 million of EDA's first public works appropriation in Oakland, California, and the implementation of the projects proved difficult (see Pressman and Wildavsky, 1973), the agency funded few urban public works projects, particularly large ones. It seems reasonable to test the hypothesis that larger urban areas are treated differently in EDA public works funding through a dummy variable.

The political variables outline the distributive theory. The assumption here is that members of the committees and subcommittees overseeing the agency receive more projects than those not on those bodies. The four committees and subcommittees relevant here are:

House and Senate Public Works

(Subcommittees on Economic Development);

House and Senate Appropriations

(Subcommittees on the Departments of State, Justice and Commerce and the Judiciary).

Congressional districts represented on the committees and subcommittees are coded "1" on the particular dummy variable.[9] Table 3-1 describes each independent variable for reference purposes.

Findings

Table 3-2 reports four equations. The first three present the results with the dependent variable of the number of projects received by each congressional district over the three-year period from July 1, 1967, through June 30, 1970. Equation 1 contains the need variables alone; equation 2 contains the political variables alone; equation 3 contains both need and political variables. Equation 4 contains both need and poltical variables with the dependent variable of the total amount of money received by each congressional district. The political variables included are those for FY 1969; there is so little change in Congress during these three years that the substitution of FY 1968 or FY 1970 political variables yields almost identical results. Coefficients with T statistics less than 1.0 are omitted in the interest of clarity. The findings are divided into the following five areas.

The Consequence of a Misspecified Model

The first finding concerns the consequences of misspecified models. A misspecified model is one which omits important variables. It was noted previously that several analyses of political influence in federal programs had omitted altogether measures to account for the differing need of parts of the nation for the program. Other analyses had included poor quality measures of need. Here the consequences of this omission can be seen. When the need and eligibility variables are omitted from the model (equation 2 of table 3-2), it appears that there is more politics involved in the grant distributions than when the need and eligibility variables are included (equation 3). Some of the political coefficients change from significant and positive in the misspecified model to insignificant and close to zero in the

Table 3-1
Definition of Variables

N of Areas	The number of eligible redevelopment areas (usually counties) per congressional district.
Population	The 1970 population, in thousands, of the eligible areas in each congressional district.
Income	The 1970 per capita income of the eligible areas in each congressional district.
EDD membership	A dichotomous variable equalling 1 for congressional districts with more than 50 percent of the eligible counties belonging to a funded Economic Development District; zero otherwise.
Urban	A dichotomous variable equalling 1 for the thirteen urban areas that are part of EDA's urban entity program (see text); zero otherwise.
SIRP	A dichotomous variable equalling 1 for the congressional districts containing at least one of the fifteen reservations on the SIRP (see text) action list; zero otherwise.
HPWC seniority	A variable taking the form of the actual number of terms of membership (one term = two years) for members of the House Public Works Committee; zero otherwise.
HPWC sub	A dichotomous variable taking the form of 1 for members of the House Public Works Committee Subcommittee on Economic Development; zero otherwise.
HAC party	A dichotomous variable taking the form of 1 for Democrats on the House Appropriations Committee; zero otherwise.
HAC sub party	A dichotomous variable taking the form of 1 for Democrats on the House Appropriations Subcommittee on the Departments of State, Justice, and Commerce, and the Judiciary; zero otherwise.
Chairman HR	A dichotomous variable taking the form of 1 for the chairman and ranking minority member of the authorizing and appropriating committees and subcommittees, and the House leadership; zero otherwise.
HR party	A dichotomous variable taking the form of 1 for congressional districts represented by Democrats in the House of Representatives; zero otherwise.
HR seniority	The actual rank in House seniority for each member.
SPWC member	A dichotomous variable taking the form of 1 for members of the Senate Public Works Committee; zero otherwise.
SPWC sub seniority	A variable taking the form of the actual number of terms of membership on the full Senate Public Works Committee for the members of the Subcommittee on Economic Development; zero otherwise.
SPWC chairman	A dichotomous variable taking the form of 1 for the chairman and ranking minority member of the Senate Public Works Committee and its Subcommittee on Economic Development; zero otherwise.

Table 3-1 *(cont.)*

SAC sub seniority	A variable taking the form of the actual number of terms of membership for members of the Senate Appropriations Committee Subcommittee on the Departments of State, Justice and Commerce and the Judiciary; zero otherwise.
SAC chairman	A dichotomous variable taking the form of 1 for the states of the chairman and ranking minority member of the Senate Appropriations Committee and its Subcommittee on the Departments of State, Justice, Commerce and the Judiciary; zero otherwise.

correct model; others change in the opposite direction. These differences show that the extent to which politics governs the distribution of federal expenditures cannot be inferred from political considerations alone. The naturally differing needs of different parts of the nation, that is, what they would receive in the absence of political help, must also be examined.

Considerations of Need and Eligibility

The basic hypothesis is that considerations of need and eligibility will be far more important in determining EDA's distribution of public works projects than political considerations will be. This does not mean that if the hypothesis is supported there is no politics in the project distribution. The particular configuration of need and eligibility variables may itself be a political decision.

Two ways of comparing the strength of sets of variables are by comparing the proportion of the variance which is explained by each set, and by comparing the individual coefficients. The first three equations in table 3-2 indicate the proportion of the variance explained by need and eligibility characteristics alone (61 percent), politics alone (26 percent), and both need and politics (73 percent). It is clear from these figures that the major portion—indeed, almost the overwhelming portion—of the variance is explained by the need and eligibility of each congressional district.

The same picture emerges when individual coefficients are compared. The number of eligible areas coefficient is worth almost one project per eligible area during the three year-period (.92 in equation 3), with the districts varying from one to twenty plus eligible areas, and thus from one to twenty plus projects. Population is worth .004 projects per one thousand people, or .4 project per one hundred thousand people. Since the districts vary from one thousand or so people to as many as three hundred thousand in some areas, the maximum difference would be a little over one project between the largest areas and the smallest. The income variable at —1.2 indicates that each $1,000 decrease in per capita income results in about 1.2 projects more over the three-year period. Thus, the Indian reservations,

Table 3-2
The Effects of Need, Eligibility, and Politics on the Distribution of EDA Public Works Projects, Selected Equations, 1968-1970

Political Variable	Equation 1 Needs Only Projects $R^2 = .61$	Equation 2 Political Only Projects $R^2 = .26$	Equation 3 All Projects $R^2 = .73$	Equation 4 All Money $R^2 = .73$
Constant	1.41* (2.19)	4.39* (4.06)	1.92* (3.08)	206.9 (0.37)
N of areas	.96* (6.64)		.92* (6.91)	244.2* (2.02)
Population	.004* (2.91)		.004* (3.08)	1.4 (1.17)
Income	−.73* (2.79)		−1.20* (4.98)	
EDD membership	.83* 2.18		1.43* (3.87)	726.9* (2.18)
Urban				1086.4) (2.91)
SIRP	15.85* (15.67)		13.45* (12.14)	9819.5* (9.81)
HPWC seniority		.48 (1.30)	.21* (1.89)	927.6* (9.43)
HPWC sub		3.12 (1.39)		
HAC party		3.90* (1.95)	1.02* (1.80)	625.4 (1.22)
HAC sub-party		−9.24* (2.46)	−1.36 (1.25)	
HR chairman		9.30* (2.69)		−1078.7 (1.0)
HR party				389.0 (1.38)
HR seniority			.02* (2.56)	
SPWC member		−1.87 (1.57)	−1.11* (3.47)	−576.1* (2.0)
SPWC sub-seniority		1.16* (2.16)	1.22* (5.66)	985.3* (5.06)
SPWC chairman		6.69* (3.47)		
SAC sub-seniority			−.13* (2.29)	−76.4 (1.49)
SAC chairman		3.46* (1.96)	−5.50* (5.14)	−4849.8* (5.02)
F statistic[b] (d.f.)	46.08 (6,175)	4.87 (12,169)	25.00 (18,163)	24.96 (18,163)

Note: The dependent variable in all cases is the number of projects or amounts of money over all three fiscal years combined. Figures in parentheses are t statistics. Coefficients with t statistics less than 1.0 are excluded. All variables listed at the left are included in equations 3 and 4. An asterisk (*) indicates significance at .10.

*Approximate f statistics required for significance (.05): with 6 and 175 degrees of freedom, 2.14; with 12 and 169, 1.77; with 18 and 163, 1.68. For .01, the levels are 2.90, 2.22 and 1.98 respectively.

with per capita incomes less than $1,000, receive an average of about 2.5 projects more than the richest areas, which have per capita incomes of just over $3,000. Therefore, the most important variable is the number of eligible areas, a variable which tends to disperse the project distribution across the nation. Moreover, these three need and eligibility variables affect every single congressional district eligible for the program; the significant political variables affect, at the most, one-fourth of the districts.

(The same exercise, with similar results, can be performed with the money variable in equation 4. I have omitted it to save space.)

The substantive meaning of these findings is support for the universalization notion; for the strength of the population, eligible areas, and income variables indicate that the project distribution is spread across the nation, with every congressional district receiving projects in proporiton to its eligibility. It is not the case, for example, that the population variable alone is strong, which would indicate that the projects are concentrated in the more populous areas.

All of these variables have signs in the expected direction; income and population were expected a priori to be more important than the number of eligible areas.

Three variables attempt to tap particular EDA need and eligibility characteristics:

1. The *Economic Development District* (EDD) variable indicates that congressional districts where there is a functioning EDD received 1.43 more projects and almost $727,000 more money over the three-year period.
2. The *SIRP* variable indicates that the reservations included in the Selected Indian Reservation program (SIRP) benefit greatly from that designation. The designation is worth an average of thirteen extra projects per congressional district over the three year-period, and substantially more money also.
3. The *Urban* variable is negative but not statistically significant in the projects equation, but positive in the money equation, reflecting the larger project size of the urban projects. Only the population variable among all the needs variables favors large urban areas, since each constitutes only one eligible area and their incomes tend to be relatively high. Clearly they receive no special treatment.

Thus, of the six need and eligibility variables, five are relatively precise and significant; only the urban variable has such a large standard error as to render difficult any predictions. Of the six, the strongest are population, income, and the number of eligible areas per congressional district. Collectively they account for the major proportion of the variance in the dependent variable. Their coefficients are also relatively stable under different specifications of the equations. It is interesting that the number of eligible areas variable is strongest, for during EDA's first five years, through the early 1970s, the EDA project distribution tended to favor the South. In the South, projects tended to locate the largest number of jobs, and the criterion for project success was the number of jobs located by the project. Southern states tend to have larger numbers of counties; these counties are poorer, and have smaller average populations. The makeup of EDA's overseeing committees also reflected a stronger Southern representation than in the period since 1972.

The Political Variables

The political variables as a group are quite different. Many are insignificant, and the coefficients of those with low T statistics are quite unstable under different specifications of the models. Four, however, are both significant and relatively stable, and these shed some light on the distributive theory.

The House Public Works Committee. If the distributive theory is to receive any support at all, House Public Works ought to be the committee to provide it. It is EDA's most important committee in terms of the influence Congress has over EDA project selections. It contains the subcommittee that has held the major portion of EDA's hearings, a subcommittee whose jurisdiction includes only EDA and the Appalachia Regional Commission's programs. It is a subcommittee that is involved with the program, although not to the extent that it includes only heavily eligible members. Two variables are included to represent the committee: one for the seniority of the full committee, the other for the Economic Development Subcommittee. The seniority variable models the "public works club," the group of senior members who are reputed to dominate the committee (Ferejohn, 1972, pp. 258-261; Murphy, 1974). The subcommittee includes a number of junior members and is not particularly prestigious, as reflected in its relatively high turnover.

The results indicate that the senior members of the full committee benefit from EDA public works projects over and above what they receive on the basis of need and eligibility. While the senior members seem to average about one-fifth of a project more (.21) for each two years that they sit on the committee (a figure which is barely statistically significant), they definitely received almost $1 million extra for each two years ($927.6 million), which is highly statistically significant. Membership on the subcommittee is statistically insignificant.

The seniority variable thus indicates that the committee's senior members, the so-called public works club, profit from membership on the committee. These are mostly Democrats, since there were almost no senior Republicans on the committee during these years.

The House Appropriations Committee. On the full House Appropriations Committee sit several Democrats whose pursuit of federal public works infrastructure is legendary. These include Representatives Joe Evins, Robert Sikes, George Andrews, Jamie Whitten, Otto Passman, and William Natcher. The senior members of the House Appropriations Committee are usually considered among the more influential members of the House.

A dummy variable is included for the House Appropriations Committee Democrats. The coefficient is positive and barely significant, in terms of projects but not money, indicating that the Democratic majority on the committee gained about one extra project each during this period. Democrats on the committee do seem to benefit from the program, although there are no particular advantages to membership on the subcommittee. This seems to be a refleciton of the Cannon/Tabor rule (Fenno, 1966).

Party and Seniority. The party variable in the House is not significant, but the seniority variable (.02) indicates that the most senior members of the House received about 2.5 projects more than the most junior (since there are approximately 125-150 seniority ranks).

Senate Public Works Committee. Three variables for the Senate Public Works Committee are included in each equation. The first of these is a dichotomous variable for membership on the committee. It is negative and significant, indicating that general membership on the committee does not lead automatically to increased benefits. The second variable is the number of terms of committee seniority for the members of the Economic Development Subcommittee; it is positive and significant. A variable for the committee leadership is positive and statistically significant for projects but not for money. Thus, the benefits of membership on the Senate Public Works Committee are received by the states of the chairman, the minority leader, and the senior members of the Economic Development Subcommittee.

Senate Appropriations Committee. On the Senate Appropriations Committee only two variables could be incorporated into the analysis, because most of the members of the full committee sit on all the subcommittees. A variable for the seniority of the members of the State-Justice-Commerce subcommittee was included, and it is negative and significant with the project dependent variable, and approaching significance with the money dependent variable. This indicates that the senior members of the subcommittee receive fewer projects than otherwise. The states of the chairman and minority leaders of the Senate Appropriations Committee receive less money and fewer projects than otherwise.

Thus far, the overall distribution of EDA projects seems to be in broad accordance with need and eligibility, governed primarily by the number of eligible areas in each congressional district, population, and income. To this basic distribution there are six adjustments: (1) more projects for the Indian reservations in the SIRP program; (2) more projects and money for functioning EDD's; (3) more money for the senior members of the House Public Works Committee; (4) more projects for the Democrats on the full House Appropriations Committee; (5) more projects for the senior members of the Senate Economic Development Subcommittee; and (6) fewer projects for the senior members of the Senate Appropriations Subcommittee on the Departments of State, Justice and Commerce. Almost all of the benefiting groups of politicians share two things in common: they are both senior members on the committees and subcommittees overseeing EDA, and, at the same time, they are very public-works oriented. This factor raises some interesting questions about the distributive theory. Before discussing these questions, however, we examine the three fiscal years to see if control of the administration makes any difference.

Party Control

Only the equations with the project dependent variables for each of the three fiscal years are contained in table 3-3, because of space considerations. The most immediate result is, with some notable exceptions, considerable consistency with the previous results. The exceptions, however, are interesting.

Among the need and eligibility variables, population and the number of eligible areas per congressional district are again statistically significant, and with the same signs as previously. Again they account for the major portion of the variance explained in each fiscal year.

The political variables show much less consistency across the three-year period. Even those which were positive and significant when the three years were combined above are now more idiosyncratic. For example, the senior members on the House Public Works Committee benefited greatly from EDA projects when the three fiscal years were combined, but here they benefit in 1968 only.

The party variable is insignificant in all three fiscal years. Thus, there is no systematic trend in favor of Democratic house districts in 1968, under the Democratic administration, and Republican districts in 1970, under the

Table 3-3
The Effects of Need, Eligibility, and Politics on the Distribution of EDA Public Works Projects, Fiscal Years 1968, 1969, and 1970[a]

Political Variable	Equation 1 1968 $R^2 = .44$	Equation 2 1969 N of Projects $R^2 = .51$	Equation 3 1970 $R^2 = .65$
Constant	.14 (0.50)	1.13* (3.42)	− .22 (0.98)
N of areas	.40* (5.61)	.28* (4.07)	.34* (5.17)
Population		.001* (1.72)	.002* (2.88)
Income	− .13 (1.30)	− .50* (4.41)	
EDD membership		.34* (1.87)	.39* (2.28)
Urban	− .44* (2.10)	.52* (2.57)	− .43* (2.43)
SIRP	3.71* (6.06)	4.42* (7.79)	5.64* (10.11)
HPWC seniority	.20* (3.33)	.07 (1.18)	
HPWC sub		− .54 (1.52)	.77* (1.88)
HAC party		.34 (1.28)	
HAC sub-party	− .55 (1.0)		.58 (1.08)
HR chairman			− .64 (1.08)
Party	.19 (1.24)	− .18 (1.09)	
HR seniority		.006 (1.47)	.01* (2.83)
SPWC member	.37* (1.99)	− .43* (2.89)	− .56* (3.70)
SPWC sub-seniority	.40* (3.36)	.28* (2.78)	.25* (2.32)
SPWC chairman	− 1.63* (1.23)		
SAC sub-seniority		− .09* (3.16)	− .04 (1.40)
SAC chairman		− .87* (2.33)	− 1.36* (2.74)
F statistic (d.f.)	7.61 (18,174)	10.05 (18,177)	17.47 (18,173)

[a]See notes in Table 3-2.

Republican administration. According to agency officials, there was an effort to do this by the Republicans when they first took office under President Nixon in 1969, but the EDA project selection process is so decentralized that the crucial decisions are clearly difficult to manipulate in this manner.

Thus, the three fiscal years are chiefly important for what they tell us about the political benefits. Political benefits from EDA's distribution of projects do not automatically accrue to any group in a position overseeing EDA's program. Instead the benefits are idiosyncratic, occurring in some years and not in others. They are, moreover, not very large; not very many projects are involved when they are totalled individually. And the benefits which are present accrue mostly to the senior members, not to entire committees or subcommittees.

The 1968 Congressional Election Campaign

The most overtly political event, at least according to EDA officials, in the entire project selection process is the project announcement. Many actions connected with the project awards are politically manipulable, in contrast to the other parts of the project selection process. Thus an announcement can be accelerated or delayed, or different politicians can be allowed to make the announcements at different times. During each election period in EDA there are many projects whose processing is accelerated so that the announcement can be made before the election; others are left to sit until after the election. Announcements, moreover, are almost always made from Washington, not from the field, and the person making the announcement of the project's approval is usually the congressman representing the district or the senator(s) representing the state.

According to agency officials interviewed for this study, there are few (some even said no) special projects approved under political duress during the election period. The fact that FY 1969 is not systematically different from FYs 1968 and 1970 tends to confirm this. Instead, the basic rule is that the processing of a regular project application will be accelerated or deferred so that the announcement will be made during the campaign to help the relevant congressman.

An examination (not shown) of the project approvals announced during the 1968 election campaign (defined to include the period from July 1 to October 30) indicates that the projects do not go systematically to those comprising EDA's congressional power structure. But one might not necessarily expect announcements to benefit only the committee members overseeing EDA. A look at the twenty-three congressional districts receiving two or more projects during the campaign period tends to confirm this. The twenty-three received 74 percent of the ninety-six projects announced during this four-month period.

Eighteen, or 78 percent, of the twenty-three districts are represented in Congress by Democrats, a percentage much higher than the 57 percent Democratic among the 211 districts eligible for EDA. Moreover, of the five Republican districts, three received only Indian projects, a program which EDA has administered impartially, and the fourth was that of Rep. John Paul Hammerschmidt (R., Ark.), who at the time was a member of the House Public Works Committee's Subcommittee on Economic Development and later became its ranking minority member. (The fifth Republican district is that of Tennessee's William Brock.)

Among the eighteen Democratic districts, senior Democrats are quite overrepresented. Five are House committee chairmen (Staggers, Patman, McMillan, Colmer and Perkins); two are House Appropriations subcommittee chairmen (Evins and Natcher); and the eighth is Representative Ed Edmundson, the chairman of the House Public Works Committee's Subcommittee on Economic Development.

Political considerations clearly dominate project announcements during the election period, with the districts of Democrats being assisted disproportionately. Many of those receiving projects during this period are House committee chairmen; but, with the exception of Edmundson and Hammerschmidt, they are not in a position to oversee the agency. Both Edmundson and Hammerschmidt, however, are extremely eligible for the EDA program, with twelve and seventeen eligible counties in their districts respectively.

Summary

The primary question here has been the extent and nature of political influence in EDA's project distribution. It seems that universalization explains the overwhelming portion of the project distribution. It was found that EDA projects are spread out over the entire nation, with the most significant determinants of that distribution being the number of eligible areas per congressional district, population, and income.

At the same time, the distributive theory should not be abandoned, for there are significant benefits to some of those overseeing the agency. These include the senior members of the full House Public Works Committee (a group known as the "public works club"), the Democrats on the House Appropriations Committee, and the senior members of the Senate Public Works Committee Subcommittee on Economic Development. All of these groups have in common a strong public works orientation. Their members are congressmen and senators interested in federal public works projects, and, in the case of EDA, they are positioned well to transform their interest into benefits for their districts.

But when we look at the project distributions for the individual fiscal years, it is clear that the same groups are not benefiting each year. In fact, in some years certain groups of congressmen do significantly worse than would be expected solely on the basis of their need and eligibility. What this indicates is that benefits do not flow automatically to those in these high positions; they must take advantage of the potential, urge local communities to apply for the grants, follow up the applications with correspondence with the agency. There are times when this process does not take place, when either local communities do not apply or their applications are not very good ones. Thus it is not simply a position overseeing the agency which produces benefits for influential congressmen, but the combination of position, choice on the part of the congressman that these are the kinds of benefits that he wishes to emphasize, and local initiative in producing good quality applications. It does not appear that the agency is favoring politically well-situated congressmen with easier standards of approval, and the decentralized EDA project selection process argues against this. Neither does it appear that the agency is reacting to actual political pressures, a contention agency officials deny and the routine nature of congressional casework procedures weighs against (see Anagnoson, 1979a). Rather it appears to me after studying EDA procedures for some years that the reason EDA project distributions favor some politically well-situated congressmen but not others, as the data indicate, is that local officials in their districts know which committees the congressman is on; the committees tend to oversee programs the district is eligible for; and ultimately, local officials simply apply more often to these programs. This contention is supported by interviews with agency officials, who routinely deny poor quality projects in important congressmen's districts, and by the data, which indicate that the benefits from EDA's public works program do not seem to flow automatically to those overseeing the program.

While there is some evidence of politics in the distribution of EDA projects, some rather obvious political phenomena do not occur in the way one might imagine. There is little systematic difference, for example, between the distribution of projects in FY 1968, under President Lyndon B. Johnson's Democratic administration, and the distribution in 1970 under Richard M. Nixon's Republican administration. And the people who benefit from the distribution of projects during the election campaign were not those overseeing the agency but senior Democrats in general. At the same time the distribution for FY 1969 seems to indicate that the election approvals are those applications already received by the agency whose processing it is deemed politically expedient to accelerate.

Why is EDA's project distribution universalized? There are three reasons. First, within the agency, EDA officials have chosen to use a basically incremental strategy for approving project applications, a rolling review of project proposals at the preapplication level. The reason why project decisions are made both quickly and outside Washington is so that political pressure from either Congress or the executive branch will be minimized. This procedure seems to be quite successful in accomplishing its chief goal, giving the agency the freedom of action to choose projects without letters and phone calls from congressmen pressuring the agency for favorable decisions. Accompanying the preapplication project criteria (the number of jobs, quality of the economic development process, services to the poor and unemployed) which are sufficiently vague as to permit the regional directors and EDR's to choose almost any projects they wish. The second reason concerns the restraints. The restraints serve the purpose of ensuring to Washington that the ultimate project distribution will be spread out, with no area of the nation receiving too few or too many projects. The restraints are four: (1) the agency allocates its funds by regional office mainly on the basis of the eligible population; (2) it looks askance at very large, especially large urban, projects; (3) the legislation gives one state each eligible area regardless of the state's economic distress; and (4) the legislation limits each state to no more than 15 percent of the annual public works appropriation.

The third reason why EDA has a basically universalized project distribution is that Congress has not permitted the agency to alter these flexible and ambiguous project selection methods in the direction of making them more precise and, most important, producing a more concentrated project distribution. EDA has twice attempted to do this on its own. In 1966-1967 the agency attempted to favor the poorest eligible areas with the worst-first policy. From the agency's point of view the policy had a sound justification, including the fact that a full third of the areas receiving EDA projects during the first fiscal year were dedesignated at the end of that year because their unemployment statistics no longer qualified them as depressed areas. (The dedesignation occurred before EDA had constructed the projects.) But congressional and internal opposition, operating within the context of a decentralized agency where it is difficult for Washington to know what its regional and local officials are doing anyway, was sufficiently strong to prevent the policy from being implemented in some regions at all, and in no region for longer than one year. The same was true in 1974-1975 when the agency attempted to rank areas by the quality of their development efforts so as to favor those likely to yield the largest payoff for EDA's money. In both of these cases members of the House Public Works Committee led the congressional opposition.

So EDA's project distribution is unversalized for three reasons: (1) because of the agency's goal of making its project selections without outside pressure, which results in a very decentralized project selection process; (2) because of the Washington-imposed restraints which operate to spread the money out regardless of the distribution of good quality projects; and (3) because of congressional pressure to maintain the equal eligibility of all parts of the nation for the program.

Let me conclude by discussing the implications of universalization on the performance of federal programs. It has been said in another context that "the most difficult problems of political economy are those where goals of efficiency, freedom of choice and equality conflict" (Tobin, 1970). This statement is certainly true of federal community development programs in general and EDA specifically. In EDA's public works program, the tradeoffs among these three qualities overwhelmingly emphasize equality of area and freedom of choice for the recipient to determine his own priorities. EDA emphasizes neither efficiency nor equity criteria, for these tend to single out particular categories of areas, breaking political coalitions laboriously worked out in Congress.

Universalization is important in federal programs because of its implications: ultimately, the use of criteria which treat every area on an equal basis means that agencies are reacting to local demand, not imposing federal priorities in their funding decisions. And if the federal government limits its role to reacting to local demand, that role will be a minimal one. At the same time, a universalized project distribution also implies that the funds available to any one particular place will be too small to produce much change, since the limited pot is spread widely to give as many applicants as possible their fair share. Indeed, the most telling criticism of EDA's program is that the funds are scattered thinly around the nation (see U.S., Office of Management and Budget, 1974, for an example).

These twin phenomena—a universalized project distribution and a minimal federal role—are not unusual among federal programs. The central criticism of the Nixon administration, reflected in such works as David Stockman's "The Social Pork Barrel" (1975) and OMB's Bellmon report on EDA (U.S., O.M.B., 1974), is that many Great Society programs scattered funds too thinly to accomplish any good. Frequently mentioned in this connection are programs like Title I of the Elementary and Secondary Education Act, Model Cities, or the educational impact program.

This phenomenon is quite general among federal programs. Consider two basic kinds of federal grant programs. First, there are programs where the objective is "simply to provide financial help for lower level governments in pursuing their own purposes," programs where the federal role is appropriately minimal and the project distribution appropriately universalized. Programs like general revenue sharing and the highway trust fund fit within this category. The other kind of federal program is one where the purpose is truly national, where the goal of the federal government is either to change the way some function is being performed at the state and local level or to emphasize one way a function is being performed at the expense of others. Programs with national objectives are ones like EDA or the poverty programs formerly administered by the Office of Economic Opportunity.

The problem with universalization and the forces reinforcing universalizing tendencies is that they tend to change national purpose programs into ones with a minimal federal role. If all areas are to be treated equally, what is the sense of having strong federal involvement in some policy area? EDA has resolved the difficulty by emphasizing essentially a "political rationality," by structuring the program so that acceptable economic development projects are funded within the constraint that all areas of the nation receive projects. But some programs are not able to resolve the difficulty: one of the main arguments over Title I of the Elementary and Secondary Education Act is whether the program is one with a national purpose or one where the purpose is to aid local school systems in accomplishing their own objectives (Murphy, 1971; McLaughlin, 1975).

The myth about federal programs is that politics reigns supreme, with the bureaucrats and senior congressmen on the overseeing committees cooperating through the concentration of grants in the congressmen's districts in return for increased appropriations. If there is any program where this should be the case, it is EDA, a seemingly pork barrel program. We have seen that the myth is largely untrue, but, at the same time, universalization is in a sense more constraining than having to pay off one's senior overseers. Instead of a few congressional districts or states obligated to receive projects, most of the nation is obligated—a far more difficult situation to change.

Notes

1. Some representative examples, in addition to those cited in this paper, include Weidenbaum and Larkins (1972); Ray (1976a, 1976b); Lave and Lave (1974); Murphy (1974); Russett (1970); Bahl and Warford (1972); Fried (1975); and Brunn and Hoffmann (1969). See Kaufman and Jones (1974), on the distribution of urban services.

2. It should be noted that the Corps is not a grant program, for the Army constructs and manages the projects itself. Its decision making, however, is congressionally centered, like that of formula grants.

3. In FY 1968 it was still the case that well over half of each year's projects were approved during the last half of the fiscal year. Moreover, very few (much less than one-quarter) were approved during the first quarter of the year. The other twelve states and the months of their redistrictings are: Arizona (1/1/70); California (3/8/68); Hawaii (7/14/69); Indiana (2/15/68); Louisiana (6/30/69); Missouri (10/13/69); Nebraska (1/1/68); New Jersey (2/8/68); New Mexico (5/15/68); New York (1/23/70); Ohio (1/29/68); West Virginia (1/6/68).

4. In EDA there are very few projects (less than 10 of some 1,000 over the three-year FY 1968-1970 period) affecting two or more congressional districts.

5. This is probably less true for grants providing salaries and general organizational support like community action than grants for physical facilities and infrastructure like EDA.

6. An alternative model is path analytic, where need and eligibility stand prior to the political factors. I have not done this for several reasons. First, using either ordinary least squares or discriminant analysis there is virtually no relationship between need/eligibility and committee membership when the latter is regressed on the former. Second, the estimating procedure for that path should take account of the 0,1 dependent variable. It is difficult to use such estimating procedures in path analysis. Third, the sheer complexity of the task, given the number of political variables, argues against it.

7. If municipalities within the district are legally prohibited from applying, they will of course receive no grants. Were these 200 districts included, in addition to increasing the R2 substantially, they would serve no purpose other than to constrain the regression planes through the origin, producing more heteroscedasticity.

8. The cities included within the urban program are Oakland, Los Angeles (Watts/Compton only), and San Diego, California; Chicago (Stockyards area only), Illinois; East St. Louis, Illinois; South St. Paul, Minnesota; St. Louis, Missouri; Omaha, Nebraska; Camden and Newark, New Jersey; Brooklyn (Navy yard area only), New York; Cleveland, Ohio; Providence, Rhode Island.

9. There is some multicollinearity among the political variables, which are extremely intercorrelated at the committee and subcommittee level. On each committee and subcommittee, party and seniority correlate in the .60 to .90 range, in part because of the small number of committee and subcommittee members whose districts are eligible for EDA. Also there are few or no senior Republicans on several bodies concerned, resulting in a senior membership almost exclusively Democratic; and sometimes almost all of a committee will sit on a given subcommittee, particularly in the Senate. Fortunately, this does not affect the need and eligibility variables, for they do not correlate highly with the political variables or with each other. In dealing with this problem, I used a general decision rule that the variables least correlated with each other and most correlated with the dependent variable would be included in the equations. The actual choices were based on both the bivariate correlations and the behavior of the different variables in the actual regressions.

References

Acton, Forman, S. *Analysis of Straight Line Data*. New York: Wiley, 1959.
Anagnoson, J. Theodore. "Political Influence in the Distribution of Federal Grants: A Study of the Implementation of Federal Policy." Ph.D. Dissertation, University of Rochester, 1977.

———— . "Bureaucratic Reactions to Political Pressures." Paper presented at the annual meeting of the American Political Science Association, 1979.

———— . "Targeting the Federal Grant System: An Impossible Dream?" In *The Success and Failure of Public Policies*, edited by H. Ingram and D. Mann. Beverly Hills: Sage, 1979.

Arnold, R. Douglas. "Congressmen, Bureaucrats, and Constituency Benefits: The Case of Military Employment, 1952-1974." Paper presented at the 1977 Annual Meeting of the Northeastern Political Science Association.

Bahl, Roy W., and Jeremy J. Warford. "Real and Monetary Dimensions of Federal Aid to States." In *Redistribution to the Rich and the Poor, the Grants Economics of Income Distribution*, edited by Kenneth E. Boulding and Martin Pfaff. Belmont: Wadsworth, 1972.

Brunn, S.D., and W.L. Hoffmann. "The Geography of Federal Grants-in-aid to States." *Economic Geography* 45(1969):226-238.

Cameron, Gordon C. *Regional Economic Development, the Federal Role*. Baltimore: Johns Hopkins, 1970.

Congressional Quarterly, 1968-1971. *Congressional Quarterly Almanac*. Washington: Congressional Quarterly, 1968-1971.

Cumberland, John H. *Regional Development Experiences and Prospects in the United States of America*. Paris: Mouton, 1971.

Fenno, Richard F. *The Power of the Purse*. Boston, Little Brown, 1966.

Ferejohn, John F. "Congressional Influences on Water Politics." Ph.D. Dissertation, Stanford University, 1972.

———— . *Pork Barrel Politics*. Stanford: Stanford University Press, 1973.

Fried, R.C. "Comparative Urban Policy and Performance." In *Policies and Policy-Making*, edited by F.I. Greenstein and N.W. Polsby. Reading: Addison-Wesley, 1975.

Goss, Carol F. "Congress and Defense Policy: Strategies and Patterns of Committee Influence." Ph.D. Dissertation, University of Arizona, 1971.

———— . "Military Committee Membership and Defense Related Benefits in the House of Representatives." *Western Political Quarterly* 25(1972):215-233.

Hansen, Niles M. *Rural Poverty and the Urban Crisis: A Strategy for Regional Development*. Bloomington: Indiana, 1970.

———— . *Growth Centers in Regional Economic Development*. New York: Free Press, 1972.

Kaufman, Clifford, and Bryan D. Jones. "Political Demography and the Distribution of Urban Public Services." In *Political Issues in U.S. Population Policy*, edited by V. Gray and E. Bergman. Lexington: Lexington Books, D.C. Heath and Company, 1974.

Lave, Judith R., and Lester B. Lave. *The Hospital Construction Act, An Evaluation of the Hill-Burton Program, 1948-1973*. Washington: American Enterprise Institute, 1974.

Lemieux, Peter. "Heteroscedasticy and Causal Inference in Political Research." *Political Methodology* 3(1976):287-316.

Levitan, Sar A. *Federal Aid to Depressed Areas, An Evaluation of the Area Redevelopment Administration*. Baltimore: Johns Hopkins, 1964.

Levitan, Sar A., and Joyce K. Zickler. *Too Little but not Too Late, Federal Aid to Lagging Areas*. Lexington: Lexington Books, D.C. Heath and Company, 1976.

Martin, Curtis, H., and Robert A. Leone. *Local Economic Development, The Federal Connection*. Lexington: Lexington Books, D.C. Heath and Company, 1977.

Mayhew, David. *Congress: The Electoral Connection*. New Haven: Yale, 1974.

McLaughlin, Milbrey W. *Evaluation and Reform: The Elementary Education Act of 1965/Title I*. Cambridge: Ballinger, 1975.

Murphy, James T. "Political Parties and the Porkbarrel: Party Conflict and Cooperation in House Public Works Committee Decision-making." *American Political Science Review* 65(1974):169-186.

Murphy, Jerome T. "Title I of ESEA: The Politics of Implementing Federal Education Reform." *Harvard Educational Review* 41(February 1971):35-63.

Murphy, Thomas P. *the New Politics Congress*. Lexington: Lexington Books, D.C. Heath and Company, 1974.

Plott, Charles R. "Some Organizational Influences on Urban Renewal Decisions." *American Economic Review, Papers and Proceedings* 58(1968):306-333.

Pressman, Jeffrey R., and Aaron Wildavsky. *Implementation*. Berkeley: University of California, 1973.

Ray, Bruce A. "Congressional Committees and the Geographic Distribution of Federal Spending." Paper presented at the Annual Meeting of the Midwest Political Science Association, 1976a.

_____ . "Investigating the Myth of Congressional Influence: The Geographic Distribution of Federal Spending." Paper presented at the Annual Meeting of the American Political Science Association, 1976b.

Rundquist, Barry S. "Congressional Influences on the Distribution of Prime Military Contracts." Ph.D. Dissertation, Stanford University, 1973.

_____ . "The House Seniority System and the Distribution of Prime Military Contracts." Paper presented at the annual meeting of the American Political Science Association, 1971.

Rundquist, Barry S., and John A. Ferejohn. "Observations on a Distributive Theory of Policy Making: Two American Expenditure Programs Compared." In Craig Liske, et al, eds., *Comparative Public Policy: Theories, Methods, and Issues*. Beverly Hills: Sage, 1974.

Rundquist, Barry S., and David Griffith. "The States, Congressional
    Committees, and Military Spending: Longitudinal Observations on the
    Distributive Theory of Policy Making." Paper presented at the Con-
    ference on Mathematical Models of Congress, 1974.

Russett, Bruce A. *What Price Vigilance?* New Haven: Yale, 1970.

Schultze, Charles L. *The Politics and Economics of Public Spending.*
    Washington: Brookings Institute, 1969.

Stafford, Walter W. "An Analysis of Grants and Public Housing Units Ap-
    proved for Municipalities by the Department of Housing and Urban
    Development 1965-1970 and Their Relationships to the Black Popula-
    tion." Ph.D. Dissertation, University of Pittsburgh, 1973.

Stockman, David A. "The Social Pork Barrel." *The Public Interest*
    39(1975):3-30.

Strom, Gerald S. "Congressional Policy Making and the Federal Waste
    Treatment Construction Grant Program." Ph.D. Dissertation, Univer-
    sity of Illinois, 1973.

_____ . "Congressional Policy Making: A Test of a Theory." *Journal of
    Politics* 37(1975):711-735.

Tobin, J. "On Limiting the Domain of Inequality." *Journal of Law and
    Economics* 13(1970).

Tufte, Edward R. *Data Analysis for Politics and Policy.* Englewood Cliffs:
    Prentice-Hall, 1974.

U.S., Department of Commerce. *Congressional District Atlas. (Districts of
    the 92nd Congress).* 1970.

_____ . *Congressional District Data, Districts of the 92nd Congress.* Series
    DD-92. 1971.

_____ . *City-County Data Book, A Statistical Abstract Supplement.* 1973.

U.S., Department of Commerce, Economic Development Administration.
    *Qualified Areas . . . Criteria and Data under the Public Works and
    Economic Development Act of 1965.* February 2, 1970.

_____ . *Evaluation of Economic Development Administration Planning
    Grants.* 1970a.

_____ . *Selected Indian Reservation Program.* 1969.

U.S., Office of Management and Budget and Department of Commerce,
    1974. *Report to the Congress on the Proposal for an Economic Adjust-
    ment Program.* February 1, 1974.

Weidenbaum, Murray, and Dan Larkins. *The Federal Budget for 1973,
    A Review and Analysis.* Washington: American Enterprise Institute,
    1972.

4

Distributive Benefits, Congressional Support, and Agency Growth: The Cases of the National Endowments for the Arts and Humanities

Ralph Carlton, Timothy Russell, and *Richard Winters*

Introduction

In 1965, the Congress of the United States began supporting a segment of our society that had long remained outside its consideration. The arts and humanities in America had traditionally been the domain of the private sector, and government support to this broad field had been rare up until this point.[1] Even in the few instances where the government did lend substantial support, such as during the Great Depression, aid to the arts was generally the means to another, noncultural end.[2] In 1965, Congress for the first time recognized the arts as worthwhile and needy ends in themselves.

After considerable debate, the National Arts and Humanities Foundations Act was passed, authorizing the establishment of a National Foundation on the Arts and Humanities. With the formation of this new agency, Congress had taken a decisive and bold step in the area of arts support. Though the initial appropriation was a modest $5 million, the establishment of this agency was a clear indication of Congress's commitment to this field. The National Foundation on the Arts and the Humanities (NFAH) was set up as a broad administrative unit so that all the arts and humanities could fall under the aegis of one single agency. The act called for the establishment of the National Endowment for the Arts (NEA) and the National Endowment for the Humanities (NEH). These two organizations were to function as the operating subunits of the NFAH. All decisions would be made within either endowment. The NEA or HEH would not have to answer to the chief administrator of the Foundation, would decide its own fate, and would defend itself in the face of congressional scrutiny. The NFAH was to deal only with administrative matters, such as the personnel needs of the two endowments.

The dividing line between the endowments was the clientele they were to serve. The NEA would serve the arts, which were broadly defined to include music, drama, dance, and virtually all the so-called performing arts, along with architecture, photography, graphic arts, and a host of related areas.

The NEH encompassed the more academic areas: study of language, literature, history, philosophy, law, religion, and just about anything else that could claim a humanistic base.

Politics of the Arts and Humanities Appropriations

The endowments are only two of hundreds of federal agencies, each with its own distinctive appropriations politics. Why, therefore, focus on these two agencies? First of all, unlike many federal agencies, the endowments are new agencies begun in 1965. Thus, we can study not only forces shaping the origins of the agency but also forces maintaining or changing the agency and its programs. Political forces creating an agency may be distinct from those shaping its ongoing program.

Second, prior to 1965, the private market and charity funded the arts; yet the producers of the arts and humanities (artists and scholars), and consumers of the arts and the humanities (patrons and scholars or students) tend to be the well-educated, the affluent, and the politically active.[3] Thus, these constituencies probably overlap the politically attentive and conscious constituency. If this is true, then unusually active and persistent political pressures may have surrounded the origin of the endowments and may continue to shape their maintenance. Third, the growth rate of these two agencies has consistently outstripped the growth rate of the federal budget in every year of their existence. While the federal budget increased 72 percent from 1965 to 1978, the arts and humanities endowments grew 800 percent for that period. Factors accounting for this extraordinary growth rate will concern us here.

Also, there can be little agreement within the endowments over the specific objects of their support. Competitors and claimants for support are diverse as well as numerous, and there exists no decision rule to distinguish among them. Complicating the lack of agreement on the deserving is the geographical basis of representation in Congress. While a compelling economic and cultural argument can be made for geographical specialization and concentration of funds in such arts centers as New York, Washington, Chicago, Minneapolis, and elsewhere, such arguments are difficult to sustain in Congress, as the following exchange between Senator Stevens (Dem., Alaska), Chairman of the Appropriations Subcommittee on Interior and Related Agencies, and Nancy Hanks, head of NEA, demonstrates:

Senator Stevens: Eighteen percent of your 1976 total of grants went to New York. Is that grant concentration necessary? Is it wise?

Miss Hanks: I believe it to be. I believe that we have to consider that so many of the institutions exist in New York and, anticipating that you might ask this question, there was an article in *The New York Times* this morning of a report that has been published by the city of New York, so you can imagine it will not be totally objective advising us all of how important they are. . . .

But they do talk about how their groups are performing all over the country. Of course, they do happen to mention even going to Anchorage.

Senator Stevens: On their way to where? [laughter]

There is little doubt about the source of pressures for equity as their exchange continues.

S. If we get down to per capita, I think they sent one fiddle up to our place. Is there a per capita concept in this in your grant distribution?

H: No; but we run per capita figures, because we have been asked to do so by the committee.

S: The other committee?

H: In the House, that is correct. Our figures per capita are basically very high in small states. When you get down to New York, for example, New York receives less per capita than New Hampshire, Rhode Island, Wyoming, Vermont, an unnamed state, beginning with the first letter of the alphabet, Guam, Washington, and American Somoa.[4]

Any of the annual reports from the arts or humanities endowments list many hundreds of grants by state. These grants, by and large, are perfectly selective, particularistic, or distributive goods and services.[5] As Lowi notes, distributive policies "are characterized by the ease with which they can be disaggregated and dispensed unit by small unit, each unit more or less in isolation from other units and from any general rule."[6] In distributive policy making, "the indulged and the deprived, the loser and the recipient, need never come into direct confrontation. Indeed, in many instances of distributive policy, the deprived cannot as a class be identified, because the most influential among them can be accommodated by further disaggregation of the stakes."[7]

Thus, five attributes single out the endowments as interesting objects of analysis: their relatively recent founding date, which allows analysis of origin as well as maintenance of the agency; rapid growth; their politically vocal and active constituency; their lack of any obvious decision rule to distinguish among the many competitors for funding; and finally, the fact that their output—grants in support of the arts and humanities—are classic distributive goods, discrete and segmented benefits to constituents.

The notion of distributive benefits has interested congressional analysts for several years. Of particular interest to these specialists has been the consequence of institutional position on the distribution of benefits. Do senior, powerful, and prestigious members gain more of these benefits for their constituencies? Do members on the appropriations or oversight committees gain more benefits from the agencies they oversee? Do members who support the agency's request on the floor of the House or Senate gain favors from the agency in the distribution of agency grants? It is this last question and the House of Representatives which will ultimately concern us in this essay.

Existing studies indicate that the nature of the relationships between congressional variables and the allocation of distributive benefits by government agencies ranges from very weak to nonexistent. To cite an example, Russett discovers that the correlation between the distribution of military contracts, personnel, bases, and so on, and support of the defense budget in the Senate is weak at best. Most correlations are simply not reported, as they are less than $\pm.10$.[8] Likewise, Rundquist reports that, despite the prominent example of the late Mendel Rivers, chairman of House Armed Services Committee, assignment to that committee or its parallel appropriations subcommittees does not lead to greater than expected defense contracts. In fact, party and seniority on the committees are also unrelated to defense contracts.[9] Again, though Ferejohn reports positive relationships between committee assignment to the House Public Work Committee, party affiliation, and seniority on that committee and new starts of the Corps of Engineers, yet that relationship is weaker than we would expect and does not hold in the Senate.[10] Ray, in this volume, examines a broader number of committees and programs and discovers little if any correlation between assignment, position, and constituency benefits.[11]

But while these studies indicate that the relationship between Congressional variables and the allocation of distributive benefits by government agencies is weak at best, this may be due to the institutionalization of recipients within the nation in general and in districts in particular. That is, existing capabilities within the array of specific districts determine in large part the allocation of distributive benefits by an agency. While this may be true, the existing capability of a district might well have been shaped by the allocation of benefits by the agency in the early years of the agency's existence in return for initial political support by the constituency's or state's representatives. If this is so, then cutting into the analysis at any one point in time will yield an imperfect specification of the relationship for most agencies. This distinction might best be seen as that of a genetic explanation of agency development versus a maintaining explanation. We will test the hypothesis that the early years—the origin of an agency—might be shaped by a sophisticated strategy of benefit allocation promoting an agency's congressional friends. With time, the agency's support becomes established as the recipients of its services become established. If this is so, then we suggest that the explanatory variables involved in the budget of a new agency will change over time. Political support variables will explain the initial distribution of benefits. Over time, incremental variables will gradually increase in power, supplanting the political variables.

The Rapid Growth of the Endowments

The most striking phenomenon about the two endowments in their brief history has been the extraordinary increase in the level of funding of both organizations. In a decade, the NEA (and NEH) budget has grown from $2.5 million in its initial year to $116 million in 1978. That represents a growth of over 800 percent. The average annual growth rate for the NEA over this period has been 37 percent per annum, compared to a growth of 9.3 percent for the federal budget outlays and 4.5 percent rise in prices.[12] The NEA growth rate from 1971 to 1975 was an astonishing 58.1 percent per year. Even calculated in constant dollars, the growth rate over the whole period averages 27.7 percent a year. Or as Senator Stevens once put it in a hearing on the NEH appropriations: "You know, it is an interesting thing. I don't know of any area of the budget that has gone like this, $2 million, then $3.8, then $4.9, then $8, then $13, $28, $51, $73, $87 million. That is a continual increase in a period of declining budgets, and it is getting tougher and tougher to defend them."[13]

Some Possible Factors in Endowment Growth

The hypotheses covered in this chapter fall into three broad categories. The first set is based on aggregate, longitudinal data. Given the limited amount of data—an eleven-year span from 1965 to 1976—it is most difficult to reach concrete conclusions on the relevant factors. This is aggravated by the problem of multicollinearity of the variables. Despite these shortcomings the analysis has its value, though it is clearly the weakest of the methods employed in the chapter. The first two hypotheses explore the growth in the government budget and inflation as explanations for the high growth rate of the endowments. The third hypothesis states that the high growth rates are a function of societal demand for the arts; that is, the growth in the NEA is simply a function of the growth in demand for the arts.

The second set of hypotheses shifts attention to the distributive quality of the endowments' grants. We hypothesize that equality in funding across the states comes about slowly as the agency endeavors to reward its friends in its initial years. Given the limited amount of benefits available for distribution, this must imply a less equal allocation in per capita terms across the fifty states in the early years of an agency's development. We initially examine the hypothesis by testing a corollary: that the variability (technically, the coefficient of variation) in per capita allocations across the fifty states will begin at a high and unequal level, and consistently decline across time as the agency's funds increase and its political support consolidates.

The final set of hypotheses tests the distributive benefits hypothesis more directly. We first establish the limits of state population and personal income in explaining the state-by-state distribution of endowment funds. Noting that both factors are poor predictors of allocations—population is weakly and negatively related, and wealth is weakly and positively related—we then turn to evidence of congressional voting support for the agency as a possible explanation of the endowment's growth. We cannot test directly for the proposition, only corollaries, that the relationship between state-by-state allocation of endowment funds and state delegation vote support in the House will be positive. Second, the relationship is likely to be greater in the early, formative years of the agency's existence and decays over time. Finally, the shape of this decaying relationship will remain despite the imposition of plausible controls.

The Effects of Aggregate Economic Variables

The simple regression between aggregate federal spending and endowment spending indicates the existence of a strong positive relation. But this finding can easily be explained by the high degree of collinearity in both the variables. This problem, which will crop up often, is a result of the fact that aggregate indicators, such as the budget, agency spending, or the Consumer Price Index, all tend to grow in a highly linear fashion, somewhere between 8 percent and 10 percent per year. A more interesting test, and one which controls for some of the collinearity among the variables, is to shift to the first differences of the variables and pose the question: Are changes in arts and humanities spending largely due to changes in government spending? That is, when the government budget grows by large amounts, do arts and humanities budgets also surge in growth? If that and its converse are true, then the endowments budgets can largely be thought of as some large multiple, certainly greater than 1.00, of the government budget. If the first differences or changes are unrelated, then different forces are probably driving the two spending processes.

The simple correlations among the first difference variables are all greater than .70, and the simple bivariate regression indicates a strong and significant relationship for both endowments. After controlling for changes in inflation, however, the effects of changes in government spending on endowment spending levels are negligible. The combined variables of changes in government spending and changes in inflation account for about 72 percent of the variance in changes for NEA spending and 57 percent for NEH spending. Thus, while substantial portions of the variance in endowment spending can be accounted for by these simple variables, large unexplained portions remain.

The Effects of the Demand for the Arts

On an aggregate level, the best estimate of national demand for the arts comes from the yearly accounting of personal consumption expenditures (PCEs) by the U.S. Department of Commerce.[14] This category, a numerical estimate of the total dollars spent, serves as an indicator of the demand for the arts, or at least for the performing arts on a national level.

We tried three models, each expressing demand in a different manner. The first viewed demand as the percentage of total personal consumption expenditures that the performing arts category comprised. A second calculated the arts demand variable as a percentage of total personal disposable income, a figure that approximated in some ways the notion of income elasticity for the arts. Only the third model, using the theater PCE category all by itself, was a success. This variable was successful in even the most stringent, dynamic tests. The simple correlation between arts demand and NEA appropriations indicated an R^2 at a .90 level. Controlled for a time-series variable, the theater variable remained significant, with a 4.12 *t*-ratio. Controlled for the GNP deflator, a similar result appeared, with the theater PCE the more important factor by a ratio of 2:1. Even using both the deflator and time together, the theater demand variable remained highly significant. A final control against disposable personal income yielded similar results. Thus, theater PCE remained highly significant in all the status-controlled models.

Still, any variable with this high a degree of linearity must be subjected to more stringent tests. In a simple dynamic model employing first differences, the theater PCE was the only time variable studied that remained clearly significant. The *t*-ratio was 2.75, significant even with limited degree of freedom. The R^2 was a strong .52. Even controlled for other variables, the dynamic model of the theater PCE retained most of its significance. Controlling for the GNP deflator, the theater PCE was significant, with a *t*-ratio of 2.57. The R^2 remained high, and the borderline *t*-ratio could be chalked up to the very low degrees of freedom. In addition, the beta weight ratio was 5:1 in favor of the demand variable. We encountered virtually the same results when theater PCE was controlled for by the change in the government budget.

Since it survived this multitude of tough tests, the theater PCE variable is apparently related to NEA growth in a significant way. The national demand for the arts, as represented by this theater consumption variable, appears to be a clearly operative factor in the level of funding of the NEA and HEH. While this finding is quite important, it can only be stated as a broad positive relation, that as demand for the arts rises in this country, the level of NEA and NEH funding will rise with it. Unfortunately, the data here are too limited to even consider tackling the complicated question of causality, that is, a specific definition of the interaction between these two factors.[15] The most direct explanation for the relationship between government spending on the arts and personal consumption for the arts is that the former stimulates the latter, and that the latter draws forth the former. The relationship is complicated by the two-way causation, an example of a nonrecursive relationship.

The Evenness of Allocations

NEA or NEH growth may be related to each endowment's ability to allocate its grants evenly to the several states. Ideal equality would be identical NEA or NEH per capita contribution to each state. This hypothesis assumes that as the ideal is reached, as each constituency receives its fair share, more and more congressmen support the NFAH and its substantial growth.

To quantify this notion of evenness, we developed a very simple statistical model. First, we calculated the grant levels for each state for each endowment computed on a per capita basis, and then the "coefficient of variation,"[19] allowing for simple comparison. The coefficient of variation is a proportional function, and a negative one; that is, the lower the coefficient, the greater the evenness. That the function is proportional implies that a year with a coefficient of 1.0 would be twice as even as a year with a coefficient of 2.0; and so on.

The results of this test for both the NEA and NEH are shown in figure 4-1. Note that in the discussion of evenness, the differences between the NEA and NEH will almost always be relevant. A simple view of the figures indicates that the theorized downward drift of the coefficients of variation is actually there, albeit with substantial deviations during some of the years. The pattern especially for the last years of both Endowments is most striking. Indeed, an equilibrium seems to have been reached by both endowments within a few years of their birth.

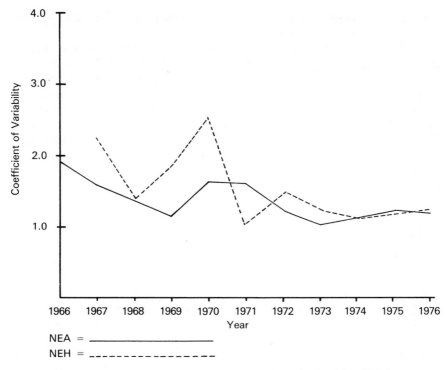

Figure 4-1. The Evenness of NEA and NEH Per Capita Grants

The Effects of Population and Wealth
on State Grants

While an examination of population and wealth will do little to explain endowment growth, it serves as an excellent introduction to the patterns of
allocation employed by both the NEA and the NEH.[17] Simple correlation
between population and absolute state grant levels year by year reveals a
high correlation between these two factors, ranging from .69 to .86 for the
NEA in 1972. While it is not surprising that the larger states receive more
money, they actually receive less money on a per capita basis. For the NEA,
the simple r's are low and negative, ranging from $-.28$ to $-.47$. Thus,
while the large states do receive more money than the small states, they are
clearly and consistently discriminated against by the NEA, which favors the
small states with its grant allocation.

The pattern for the NEH is harder to isolate. None of the simple correlations for per capita grants are larger, but the coefficients are negative in
six out of eight cases. While the NEH is clearly not as sensitive as the NEA

to population, this finding suggests that the relationship between endowment funding and state population is negative.

Per capita personal income is not as strong a factor in the determination of absolute grant levels. $\overline{R}^2$s are between .09 and .27. Like population, the relation was positive, and it carried over equally to both endowments. Wealth is a weak indicator of state grant levels. This same pattern carries over to a consideration of wealth and per capita state grant levels, though the relation is even weaker. For the NEA, only four (including the last three years) of eight years were significant, the coefficient positive in all cases. The pattern for the NEH is somewhat stronger, with six out of eight years at significant levels. Again, the relation was positive, and all the simple *r*s were very low.

Congressional Vote Support

The final factor to be studied in this paper is the relation between congressional vote support and state levels of funding by the NEA and the NEH. We explore several hypotheses in depth. The simplest asks whether vote support in one year has any relation to the amount of money a state receives the next year. The data employed in this section were from six roll-call votes in the House of Representatives on the NFAH budget level. The votes covered nine years (1965, 1968, 1970, 1973, 1974), spanning the history of both endowments fairly evenly.[18]

An original measure considered vote support to be the ratio of the number of yes votes in a delegation to the total number of votes. A second form of the variable took the ratio of yes votes to the total number of yes and no votes. Both possess qualities that make them poor indicators of vote support. Briefly, both are highly susceptible to variation stemming from the number of abstentions.[19] They also tend to exaggerate changes in vote support among the smaller states. For these reasons, and others, both were discarded in favor of a much simpler model—the simple number of votes in support of spending for the endowments. Of course, the model is biased, since the large states have a larger vote pool. To correct for this, a population variable is always used as a control, alongside the number of yes votes. These two variables combined give an unbiased view of the level of vote support in a state delegation.

Before examining the specific hypotheses, we shall outline a few facts about the series of roll-call votes. The vote support for the NFAH varied from a low of about 54 percent in the conference report extending authorization in 1968 (H.R. 11308), to a high of about 77 percent in favor of extending authorization in 1970 (S. 3215). These years also just about span the highs and lows of absolute votes in support as well—194 in favor in 1968, with 166 votes in opposition, to a high of 294 votes in support of authorization in 1973 (with 106 in opposition on S. 795). By and large, we suspect that the last three votes indicate a gradual acceptance and routinization of the vote for NFAH: the margins of victory were within a few percentage points of one another, and absolute vote support was well above one-half of the House. Not surprisingly, the vote support variables of NFAH are highly intercorrelated.

Our first hypothesis relates arts and humanities grants to statewide vote support, in its simplest form relating the number of support votes in a state delegation in t_1 to statewide grant levels in t_2, controlling for statewide population. Tables 4-1 and 4-2 relate the series of votes for NEA and NEH for the 1965-1974 series of roll-call votes. Of the eleven regressions, the partial regression coefficients for the state vote support variable are, as expected, positive; and ten of the eleven are twice their standard error, a convenient measure of statistical robustness. The multiple correlation coefficients for the combined effects of population and vote support all exceed .53, with eight of the eleven exceeding .65.

A pattern asserts itself in the regressions of vote support and NEA allocations. The vote support variables begins with a very powerful relationship with grant allocations and then systematically decays over time. The regression coefficient for the vote support variable in 1965 is 5.9 times the size of its standard error, and decays to 1.7 times its standard error by 1973. It regains some strength in 1974. Although this pattern of decaying strength does not appear in the explanation of NEH allocations, it does raise the question of whether or not congressional vote support explains early allocations—in fact, whether or not agency officials might use such support as a decision rule, with other more incremental decision rules asserting themselves later, as the agency establishes or institutionalizes itself.

Table 4-1
Vote Support and Population Predicting NEA Appropriations

Variable	Appropriations at $t+1$					
	1966	1969	1969	1971	1974	1975
1970 population	−.0023	−.003	.002	−.02	.05	.036
	(.002)	(.006)	(.008)	(.02)	(.12)	(.12)
Vote support at time t	7.9[a]	17.7[a]	12.3[a]	48[a]	126	206[a]
	(1.3)	(4.3)	(5.3)	(13)	(73)	(75)
R − Bar^2	.75	.62	.53	.68	.65	.70

Note: Standard errors of regression coefficient in parentheses.
[a]Regression coefficient greater than ±1.96 times its standard error.

Table 4-2
Vote Support and Population Predicting NEH Appropriations

Variable	Appropriations at $t+1$				
	1969	1969	1971	1974	1975
1970 population	.01	.009	− .02	− .13	.10
	(.005)	(.006)	(.02)	(.20)	(.10)
Vote support at time t	9[a]	9[a]	50[a]	296[a]	159[a]
	(3.5)	(4)	(16)	(122)	(65)
$R - \mathrm{Bar}^2$	.70	.69	.65	.55	.75

Note: Standard errors of regression coefficient in parentheses.
[a]Regression coefficient greater than ± 1.96 times its standard error.

Such an explanation of a decaying relationship over time between vote support and allocations might be worth greater investigation if the pattern of decay remained after controls are imposed on the hypothesis. We selected as an initial control an indicator of "arts demand," a measure closely akin to personal consumption on arts expenditures. According to our earlier analysis, the personal consumption figure at the aggregate national level was the single most important factor in accounting for changes in arts expenditures. For our purposes, the 1963, 1967, and 1972 Census of Selected Services records the state-by-state number of establishments and the gross receipts of "Producers, orchestras and entertainers," the inclusive 792 Standard Industrial Code. These two variables are our indicators of the state-by-state public demand for spending in the arts and humanities. Not surprisingly, the two variables of number of establishments and their receipts for the three census years are closely related, with each other and across the half-decade time span. Each of the variables is closely related to appropriations for the endowments as well, ranging from a low of .80 to a high of .97.

We shall retain the population variable of the state and use the appropriate census figures for places and receipts in explaining NEA allocations. Table 4-3 reports the results for the six roll-call votes for the NEA. Only one variable, census reports of arts establishment receipts, consistently relates to NEA allocations. All other variables, except for the 1965 roll-call vote regressed on 1966 NEA appropriations (which retains a robust regression coefficient 3.8 times its standard error), pale into insignificance.

Figure 4.2, part A, displays the changing powers, as indicated by the beta weights, of the two main variables of interest—vote support and the Census Bureau record of state-by-state arts receipts. Vote support starts off with an initial high power in explaining allocation and rapidly trails off. On the other hand, the state-by-state figures on the dollar receipts of arts establishment, our indicator of statewide demand of arts support, begins

Table 4-3
Vote Support, Population, and Arts Demand Predicting NEA Appropriations

Variable	Appropriations at $t+1$					
	1966	1969	1969	1971	1974	1975
Population	-.001 (.002)	.00005 (.005)	.0005 (.005)	.003 (.01)	.04 (.09)	-.007 (.09)
1967 census of arts establishments	-.007 (.03)	-.008 (.07)	-.002 (.06)	.04 (.15)		
1972 census of arts establishments					.18 (.37)	-.27 (.42)
1967 census of arts receipts in dollars	.0005[a] (.0002)	.003[a] (.0005)	.003[a] (.0005)	.004[a] (.001)		
1972 census of arts receipts in dollars					.01[a] (.003)	.02[a] (.0042)
Vote support at time t	5.5[a] (1.4)	2.2 (3.1)	1.1 (3.1)	7.4 (10.4)	-6.5 (54.7)	36 (54)
R - Bar^2	.81	.80	.88	.88	.85	.88

Note: Standard error of regression coefficients in parentheses.
[a]Regression coefficient greater than ± 1.96 times its standard error.

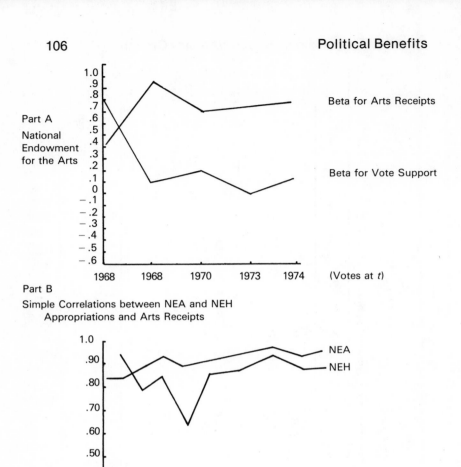

Figure 4-2. Explanatory Power of Vote Support and Census Arts Receipts on NEA Appropriations

with a very modest beta of + .42 and rapidly increases over time. This is as expected if the decision rule employed by the endowment is initially political and is transformed into the institutional. The early years of an agency's life are concerned with survival through establishing the political worth of the agency's program. One natural constituency for such a calculation are those supporters among Congress. As the agency becomes better and better established and as the controversy which surrounded its origin fades, it can then respond to the needs of existing institutional demand.

We searched for a testable corollary of this hypothesis and discovered it almost by accident. If the NEA transforms itself over time from political to institutional allocation, then the correlation between statewide arts receipts and NEA state grants would increase. As the agency reflected the arts institutions more and more, it would probably reflect more and more the established base of the arts across the nation. And that should be reflected in the increasing correlation between grants and receipts. The predicted correlations exist regardless of whether the 1967 or 1972 figures are used separately or in combination. But these relationships are entangled in problems of causality. NEA grants contribute to and shape the arts demand, defined in terms of arts receipts. We discovered, however, that the relationship also exists with the 1963 census figures on arts receipts—statewide figures calculated well before the founding of the endowment. Figure 4-2, part B, indicates the changing simple correlation between NEA grants and the 1963 Census Bureau figure for arts receipts by year. The correlations for the first two years, and those most proximate in time, are in the low 80s; and the correlations increase, though not at a consistent rate, over time. Thus the correlation between what a state receives in NEA grants in 1974 and its arts establishments' receipts eleven years before, in 1963, is substantially higher than the correlation between grants in 1965 and receipts in 1963. The likely cause, we suggest, is that, over time, the NEA gradually began to reflect objective arts demand in the nation. But in its formative years, political considerations weighed more heavily.

An Alternative Political Model

We would be more comfortable with our interpretation of the decaying relationship between vote support and grant allocations if the relationship held up despite the imposition of a series of plausible political control variables. We considered three as rival variables in explaining grant allocations for the NEA. First of all, the well-institutionalized homes of the arts have always been the cities of America. New York, Washington, Minneapolis, Chicago, and Detroit are associated with large and expensive arts installations. Second, the North, with its cities, is more likely to receive benefits than the South. Finally, the endowments were created in the last years of the Democratic administration of Lyndon Johnson; the Arts Endowment was first headed by a longtime Johnson associate, Nancy Hanks; and both endowments have been controlled by a Democratic Congress. Thus, we expect the endowments to be strongly supported by House delegations dominated by members of the Democratic party.

We were particularly interested in whether the initial relationship between vote support and allocations is seriously vitiated controlling for urbanization, region, and party. For if that is true, then the observed decaying relationship might well be a simple artifact of the effects of one or more of these rival variables. Table 4-4 presents the multiple regression analysis of the rival variables. The 1970 population of the states and their respective arts receipts are included as controls. Urbanization is included simply as the percentage of the state's population considered urban in the 1970 Census. The regional variable is coded as a dummy variable with 1 = North and 0 = South. The Democratic members of Congress are indicated by the number of Democrats in the state delegations.

Not one of the control variables in any of the fiscal years examined approaches statistical significance—that is, that the regression coefficient be at least twice the standard error. The vote support variable for the initial year retains its power. The power of the equation is substantial, as the R-Bar^2 coefficients at the bottom of the table indicate. The equation accounts for about 80 percent of the variance initially, and that mounts into the upper 80s by the end of the time period.

Because the proportion of a state's delegation who are members of the Democratic Party struck us as such a plausible rival variable to simple vote support, we decided to extend the test one step further. We retained as a control variable the Census Bureau measure for arts receipts in dollars.[20] We also included the number of Democrats in the state delegation and the vote support variable in a reduced equation predicting NEA appropriations. We used these variables, however, to predict not just the $t + 7$ appropriations, but all 1966-1975 appropriations. For example, we used the 1965 vote support figure, the 1963 Census Bureau arts receipts, and the 1966 number of Democrats in the state delegations to predict 1966 NEA appropriations. We used the 1965 vote support, the 1967 Census Bureau arts receipt figure, and the 1967 number of Democrats to predict the 1967 NEA appropriations, and so on.

If the major hypothesis of this essay is sustained, then the relative power of the arts receipt variable, as measured by its beta weight, ought initially to be low to moderate and over time rise in power and become dominant as the NEA slowly comes to reflect the power of the institutionalized arts. The vote support variable, conversely, ought to begin at a relatively moderate-to-high positive beta and slowly trail off in power. Finally, the beta weight of the Democratic party variable should be lower than the vote support variable. All beta weights should be positive.

Figure 4-3 displays the results of this final test. All of our expectations were fulfilled. The top line measures the cumulative power of the three variables at each of the ten time periods from 1966 to 1975. The R-Bar^2 initially is at the .70-.80 range over the first three years of the agency's life,

Table 4-4
Vote Support, Population, and Arts Demand Predicting NEH Appropriations

Variable	Appropriations at $t+1$					
	1966	1969	1969	1971	1974	1975
Population	-.002 (.003)	-.002 (.006)	-.0015 (.007)	-.003 (.02)	.01 (10)	.065 (.11)
Census of arts receipts	.0005[a] (.00015)	.002[a] (.0002)	.002[a] (.0002)	.004[a] (.0004)	.014[a] (.002)	.019[a] (.002)
Urbanization (% urban, 1970)	-.05 (.16)	.08 (.31)	.10 (.31)	1 (.70)	4.6 (3.8)	4 (4)
North (North = 1, South = 0)	-11 (12)	-10 (23)	-4 (22)	72 (43)	331 (230)	342 (252)
Democrats (no. in delegation)	-.82 (1.99)	-1.4 (3.8)	-1.2 (3.8)	7.7 (8.8)	73 (43)	13 (54)
Vote support	6.4[a] (1.8)	3.5 (3.9)	2 (3.8)	5 (10)	-31 (58)	-7 (57)
R – Bar^2	.79	.87	.87	.88	.85	.88

Note: Standard error of regression coefficients in parentheses.
[a]Regression coefficient greater than ± 1.96 times its standard error.

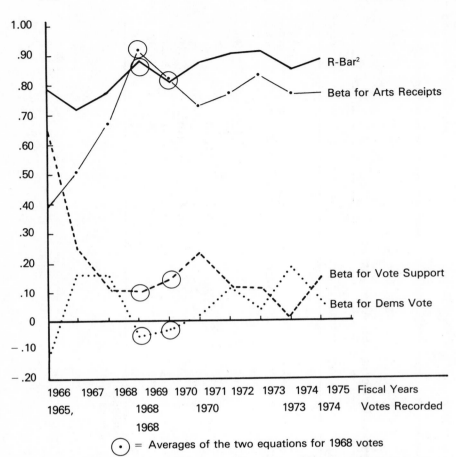

= Averages of the two equations for 1968 votes

Figure 4-3. Cumulative and Relative Power of Arts Receipts, Vote Support, and Democratic Vote in Explaining NEA Appropriations

and then gradually rises to the .85-.90 range, where it has stabilized over the last five years of the agency's life. The second line is the beta weight for the arts receipt variable—our measure of the institutionalized arts in the state. As predicted, it begins with a modest beta of .38, rises to .50 and .67, and then stabilizes in the range between .70 and .85.

The next line is our measure of vote support; as predicted, the beta is initially at a high point of .66, trails off to .25, and then falls to .11. Except for 1974, it seems to reach an equilibrium point somewhere between .10 and .20. The Democratic Party variable, on the other hand, initially has a negative beta weight, but gradually assumes a positive level and has seemed to stabilize at the range between .0 and .10. All of the betas for vote support and arts receipts are positive, as expected.

We are persuaded that the determinants of the distribution of allocations and benefits of the National Endowments of the Arts changed over its history. We suggest that during the first several years of the agency's life, several standards competed in shaping the endowment's pattern of allocations. Naturally, the existing distribution of arts institutions, the state-by-state array of existing arts investments across the nation, determined in part where the agency funneled its funds. But the existing distribution of arts institutions was an imperfect decision rule for the agency in these early years. Political controversy and debate are usually greatest during the early years of an agency's life, when its fate is not as yet determined. The agency must seek to satisfy not only what we term its objective clientele—in this case, the arts establishments in America—but must also solidify its relationships with congressional supporters and advocates. One method of stabilizing such relationships is to generate a flow of benefits into the states and districts represented by these supporters—and thus, the observed relationship between early vote support and initial grant allocations. But as the agency achieves stability, as the political controversy which surrounded its origins fades, and as its appropriations are folded into the ongoing operations of the budgetary process, the need for such a tactic fades. At that point the agency can begin to reflect in its grant allocations the national, objective demand for the arts. And that is observed in the increasing relationship between the Census Bureau record of arts establishment receipts and grant allocations.

So far, we have focused on the endowment's distribution of political benefits as an internal decision rule applied in its formative years to consolidate political support. There is, however, a rival, plausible hypothesis which focuses on the changing activity of recipient organizations.

As Baumol and Bowen point out, leadership of the arts was not wholeheartedly in favor of the National Endowments. They report, for example, that a 1953 nationwide survey of the governing boards of American symphony orchestras indicated that 99 percent of the directors "strongly opposed . . . federal aid."[21] That typical position had changed by 1962, when the majority took a somewhat middle position; and by 1965, "in a dramatic reversal of position . . . presidents and managers of nearly forty symphony orchestras endorsed federal support."[22] This support could hardly be unanimous, however. Some orchestra boards were probably less quick to favor federal support. And other arts may well have lagged behind the symphonies of America in their desire for support. Thus, in its early years, the endowment faced an unrepresentative set of claimants for grants and support, with many states overrepresented among claimants and many other states underrepresented or not represented at all. And it is likely that vote support will be greatest among those overrepresented states precisely because of the location of the vocal and active set of beneficiaries. It may be the activity of beneficiaries that motivates both the early allocation and vote support.

Second, the technical and political skills necessary to present a proposal to the endowment in 1966 were probably unequally distributed across the national arts institutions, and were probably centered in those institutions most publicly committed to the endowment. And these personal and institutional commitments probably were transmitted to the respective member of the House and resulted in early voting support for the endowment. Thus, the relationship between agency benefits and voting support is likely to be the result of a similar determinant: atypical patterns of political activity on behalf of likely beneficiaries.

Both of these factors are likely to decline in importance over time and result in the observed benefit-vote decay. Board members opposed to federal support will change their minds as they see that none of the gloomy forecasts about the effects of federal control occur, or they are replaced by members convinced that financial problems plaguing their institutions can be solved by federal aid. For whatever reason, over a short period of time, opposition to arts funding is likely to decline, and the array of claimants for such monies is likely to better reflect existing distribution of arts institutions. Today, opposition to federal money is likely in only a few widely scattered outposts.

And while a larger number and wider array of institutions are seeking endowment support over the middle years of the agency's life, more and more money is being appropriated. Thus the early claimants for agency grants can remain sated with continuing appropriations, while new money is being used for more recent claimants. And the observed relationship between vote support and NEA allocations declines largely because increasing agency appropriations allow a wider and more equitable distribution. This equity increases over time across House districts. We conclude that the declining correlation between vote support and allocation may simply reflect the *unchanging* vote of incumbent congressmen and the *changing* NEA allocations. A wider and more equitable distribution of grants occurs, as the declining coefficient of variation in figure 4-1 indicates. But the vote totals, pro and con, changed very little over the history of the endowments. We suspect that the initial positive correlation between vote support and allocations comes about because of the atypical nature of requests in the early period. Early requesters were proably concentrated in the very constituencies of early congressional supporters. Eventually a national pattern of requests developed, but the vote divisions in the House remained relatively unchanged, possibly because of such enduring cleavages as ideology or other budgetary cleavages.

Finally, we cannot ignore the anomalous role of the Humanities Endowment. Simply put, the analysis of the NEH does not confirm our most important hypotheses. The critical test regressing arts expenditure, vote support, and Democratic delegation support, analogous to the NEA test in figure 4-3, resulted in wildly varying estimates for the three variables. The $R\text{-}Bar^2$ varied from .52 to .88, with a sharp decline from the initial figure of .85 to the low figure, and then a rise toward the end of the time series to the high point. The beta weights for vote support and arts receipts averaged about the same, yet they vary wildly from one time period to the next and generally in opposite directions. For example, the initial betas for votes and receipts are .85 and .10, and two years later have become .05 and .55. Yet, three years later, they are .85 and .02. The only constant series is the low, almost nonexistent series of beta weights for Democratic Party support. Thus, of the two agencies examined in this essay, the vote support-distributive benefit hyphothesis holds only for the Arts Endowment. We had early indications of some of the differences between these two agencies. The variability of the state grant allocations, as indicated in figure 4-1, was generally higher and more volatile in the NEH than in the NEA. Similarly, the correlations between the Census Bureau record of statewide arts receipts and statewide NEH allocations were also lower and more volatile. The lesser size of the correlations may be due simply to the less appropriate nature of arts receipts as an indicator of the presence and size of humanities institutions. But the volatility probably measures lower year-to-year cor-relations of humanities allocations to the states. And that is the case. The average intercorrelation of the NEH annual state allocations (a total of 45 coeffecients across 1966-1976) is .87, compared to .90 for the NEA. The range of the coefficients is greater as well, from .70 to .95 for the NEH, and .77 to .99 for the NEA.[23].

Summary

For the early years of the National Endowments for the Arts, the distribu-tion of state grants seems to have been related to support for that agency on the House floor by state delegations. Put simply, the more support, the more grants. That relationship declined over the first years of the agency's life. As the relationship between voting and grants declined for the NEA, the relationship between the objective demand for NEA grants, our measure of arts institutionalization, or between the Census Bureau record of state-by-state arts receipts and NEA allocations, increased. Our inter-pretation is that as the agency's appropriations became established and its need for political support lessened, it could then more accurately reflect the demand for the arts in the nation. We could not, however, test an alter-native explanation that the early vote support from House members and the large numbers of grants received by some states flowed from the activities, both political and grant-seeking, of large arts institutions in those states. Our analysis did not hold for the National Endowment for the Humanities.

Notes

1. The most helpful review of the status of the "performing arts" was William J. Baumol and William G. Bowen, *Performing Arts—The Economic Dilemma* (New York: Twentieth Century Fund, 1966). Chapters 15 and 16 are especially good reviews of the history of government support for the arts and its rationale. They note that prior to the passage of the bill organizing the National Foundation for the Arts, government assistance was generally limited to "forty chamber music concerts at the Library of Congress and some concerts at the National Gallery of Art and the State Department program that sends American performing groups abroad as a cultural exchange with other countries" (p. 356). They go on to note ironically that "to more than one dance company and chamber group, the cultural exchange program has literally proved a lifesaver, but several observers have commented on the irony of an arrangement which provides American funds to American groups only when they perform in other countries. Particularly curious are cases (reported to us by performing groups we interviewed) in which groups had been forced to disband, at least temporarily, because of economic pressures, and reconstituted with the aid of State Department funds so that they could be sent abroad to represent typical American cultural activity" (p. 357).

2. We refer of course to the Works Projects Administration. The size of their arts support is impressive even by contemporary standards of federal support for the arts. Baumol and Bowen report that from 1936 to 1939 thirty-four symphony orchestras were supported, employing 2500 musicians, and the Federal Theater Project produced sixty thousand performances at a cost of over $45 million (pp. 356-357).

3. We have no evidence on the political activity rates of either patron or artist. However, Baumol and Bowen report on the general socioeconomic characteristics of arts audiences. The survey was based on a Twentieth Century Fund audience study of over twenty-four thousand respondents attending six types of events. The audience, compared to the urban population in 1960, was slightly more male (53 percent versus 48 percent), older (median age of 38 versus 30), professional (63 percent versus 13 percent), well-educated (55 percent had attended graduate school versus 5 percent), and had twice the median income ($12,804 versus $6,166). That profile strikes us as very similar to that of the active and attentive political public.

4. Testimony recorded in Senate Hearings before the Committee on Appropriations on the Department of Interior and Related Agencies, Fiscal Year 1978, Ninety-fifth Congress, First Session on H.R. 7636, Part 3, pp. 175-176.

5. The analysis of distributive or selective benefits is ably developed in David Mayhew, *Congress: The Electoral Connection* (New Haven: Yale University Press, 1974), pp. 53-54. The concept first received prominent

treatment in Theodore Lowi, "American Business, Public Policy, Case Studies, and Political Theory," *World Politics* (1964).

6. Lowi, "American Business, Public Policy, Case Studies, and Political Theory," p. 690.

7. Lowi, "American Business, Public Policy, Case Studies, and Political Theory," p. 690.

8. See, for examples, tables 3.4 and 3.5 in Bruce Russett, *What Price Vigilance* (New Haven: Yale University Press, 1970), pp. 73, 76.

9. Barry Rundquist, "On Testing a Military Industrial Complex Theory," *American Politics Quarterly* (January 1978).

10. John Ferejohn, *Pork Barrel Politics* (Palo Alto: Stanford University Press, 1974).

11. See chapter 1 in this volume.

12. The figures are for total NEA appropriations, excluding the "Treasury Fund." These are the figures referred to throughout this essay. The budget figures and the implicit price deflator are drawn from the Council of Economic Advisors, *The Economic Report of the President* (Washington, D.C., 1976), pp. 245, 174.

13. Testimony recorded in Senate Hearings before the Committee on Appropriations on the Department of Interior and Related Agencies, Fiscal Year 1977, Ninety-forth Congress, Second Session on H.R. 14231, Part 3, p. 651.

14. This variable was used by William J. Baumol and William C. Bowen as an indicator of arts demand in their study, *Performing Arts—The Economic Dilemma*, pp. 41-50 and Appendix III. The source for this variable is the *Survey of Current Business* (Washington, D.C.: Department of Commerce), in their annual July issues, which include accounting of individual personal consumption expenditures for the previous year.

15. A further limitation should also be noted. There is an interaction between the independent and dependent variable. This stems from the fact that as NEA grows, the money it doles out will probably be reflected in the theatre demand figure, to some extent. And it is the level of involvement that is really important. If the influx of endowment money has little direct bearing on the level of the theatre demand category, then the findings of this section still retain much of their import. But, if the NEA money makes up a substantial portion of the increase in the theatre demand category itself, then the findings of this section are not accurately testable by normal regression analysis.

16. The coefficient of variation is specifically the standard deviation divided by the mean.

17. The source is the *1970 United States Census* as reported in the *Statistical Abstract of the United States* (Washington, D.C., 1976).

18. The specific votes used in the analysis were:

For 1965, HR9460, on the original establishment of the NFAH—Griffen motion to kill the bill.

For 1968, HR11308, a House vote to authorize NFAH funding at $11.2 million for FY 1969 only.

For 1968, HR11308, a House vote on adoption of Conference Report to extend authorization of NFAH for FY 1969-1970.

For 1970, on S3215, a House adoption of Conference Report authorizing NFAH through FY 1973.

For 1973, on S795, a House adoption of Conference Report authorizing NFAH from FY 1974 to 1976.

For 1974, a vote on HR16027 on the Ichord substitute for Gross Amendment that supported a cut of $39.7 million for NFAH and proposed the cuts be divided equally among the two endowments.

19. The questioning of these models stemmed from a series of observations, two of which are noteworthy. First, the correlation among the yes votes was very high from one vote to the next, not a surprising result since voting patterns tend to remain the same from one equal vote to another. Second, in a state with only three congressional votes, a randomly induced abstention can cause as much as a 33 percent change in the vote support figure. The models might be reflecting the existence of state political dinners in Vermont as much as it is showing support for the NFAH. The same line of argument extends to the impact of vote shifts on large states and small states. Both models tend to exaggerate the shift in a small state while they probably undervalue the shift from a yes to a no vote in a large state.

20. In order to achieve the simplest and most parsimonious equation, the state population variable was dropped. However, it is closely correlated with the several measures of arts receipts (a correlation of +.81 with the 1972 arts receipt variable).

21. Baumol and Bowen, *Performing Arts,* p. 369.

22. Baumol and Bowen, *Performing Arts,* p. 369.

23. The data and a complete listing of data sources are available from Richard Winters.

5 Objective Need versus Political Interference: The Administration of the New York State Pure Waters Program

Richard T. Sylves

Introduction

Many political scientists are beginning to investigate the implementation of intergovernmental grant-in-aid programs.[1] However, few studies have acknowledged the importance of *state* grant administrators in the implementation of these intergovernmental programs.[2] In order to assess the influence of state grant administrators it is necessary to consider the intrastate distribution of grant money. Without considering the way in which state-level bureaucrats make decisions regarding the flow of funds to municipal governments, one cannot explain why some such governments are benefited and others are deprived in intergovernmental grant programs.

This study examines how political partisanship influenced the allocation of environmental construction grants in New York State. Grant decision making was investigated by analyzing the distribution of waste treatment construction grants among municipal governments during the final two years of the state's original Pure Waters program (1971-1972). It was assumed that party control affected the review and approval of municipal grant applications by officials of the NYS Pure Waters Division. We hypothesized that municipalities located in constituencies controlled by the majority party would enjoy a measurable advantage in securing approval of their grant applications.

Under the Pure Waters program, municipal officials of New York State made application for state and federal waste treatment construction grants in order to have the cost of building local wastewater treatment facilities subsidized. Competition for available state and federal construction grant money was keen among New York's municipal governments. This was because combined state and federal grant assistance could cover as much as 80 percent of a project's costs.[3]

The grant review process within the Pure Waters Division is highly complex, only partially visible to the public, and composed of numerous and

The author wishes to gratefully acknowledge the assistance of Barry S. Rundquist in the preparation of this chapter. However, errors or omissions are those of the author alone.

117

collective decision points. Studying the grant review process involves analysis of institutional decision making. Inferences about the division's decision making process are made on the basis of where grant money went during the implementation of the Pure Waters program.

In order to analyze the behavior of state grant administrators, a general simplifying assumption is put forward. This assumption is that individuals occupying decision making positions in a bureaucracy are attempting to be either administratively efficient, politically efficient, or, where possible, both. In the construction grant field, division officials are administratively efficient when they distribute grants in accord with existing environmental needs. Division officials are politically efficient when they distribute grants to areas represented by members in the party controlling the congress, the state senate,[4] and the governorship. Finally, division officials are both politically and administratively efficient when they approve grants to municipalities that exhibit high environmental need and potentially strong (majority) political party influence. Consequently, political and administrative factors are examiend together in this study.

Administrative Features of Pure Waters

As governor, Nelson A. Rockefeller advanced the concept of the Pure Waters program in an executive-sponsored bill submitted to the NYS State Legislature in early 1965. The bill was approved with few alterations in unanimous votes of both houses of the state legislature. State legislative approval insured that the measure would be brought before the state's voters as a bond referendum. In a 1965 voter referendum the Pure Waters Bond Act was passed by a four to one margin.[5]

The act establishing the Pure Waters program authorized a $1 billion bond issue which should ". . . enable the waters of the State to be cleansed within six years."[6] Bond money would cover 30 percent of eligible project cost for municipal treatment plant construction or improvements across the state. In other words, the state would subsidize a flat rate 30 percent of the cost of constructing wastewater treatment facilities for municipalities initiating such capital construction enterprises.

The NYS Pure Waters Division has been the exclusive administering unit of the Pure Waters program since the program's inception. For the first five years of the program, the Pure Waters Division was under the jurisdiction of the NYS Health Department. However, under a major administrative reorganization in 1970, the division was transferred from the Health Department to the new Department of Environment Conservation (EnCon or NYSDEC).

The Pure Waters Division itself contained the Bureau of Construction

Grants, the Bureau of Municipal Wastes, the Bureau of Water Quality Management, and the Bureau of Industrial Wastes. The decision to approve state construction grant applications of various project sponsoring municipalities was the responsibility of the Bureau of Construction Grants in conjunction with the Bureau of Municipal Wastes.

As an administrative entity, the Pure Waters Division was relatively "self-contained" in the sense that March and Simon apply the term. March and Simon maintain that, "A unit is self-contained to the extent and degree that the conditions for carrying out its activities are independent of what is done in other organizational units."[7] The division has been insulated from penetration and interference by other divisions or bureaus of its host department. Most division personnel are state-certified civil engineers with a sanitary engineering specialization.

From an intergovernmental perspective, the Pure Waters program paralleled the federal water pollution construction grant program. However, there were a few major differences between the state and federal programs which served to underscore the importance of the state grant administrator. For example, while conferral of the state Pure Waters grant required only Pure Waters Division approval, the conferral of a federal construction grant needed both federal and state agency approval. No federal grant could be approved unless a project was first aproved by the state agency. The way in which the federal grant application process was staged gave state agencies considerable power in determining which municipalities would receive federal grant assistance.[8] Robert D. Thomas explains that, throughout the statutory life of the federal pollution control program, the federal administering agency emphasized that the states were the key actors through whom national pollution control programs should be implemented.[9]

Even though a project may have been approved by a state environmental agency, the federal agency was not obligated to approve a federal grant for the project. However, Pure Waters officials claimed that, during the period investigated here, federal agency officials of the Environmental Protection Agency's Water Quality Office (EPA-WQO) seldom rejected projects once they were approved by the Pure Waters Division. Because few projects were rejected after state agency approval, it seems that federal construction grant officials deferred program responsibility to, and expressed confidence in, the grant decision making process of the NYS Pure Waters Division. Two major factors which could account for weak federal agency involvement in the state program are given below. First, the frequent administrative reorganizations of the federal water pollution control agency could have had a detrimental effect upon the productivity and performance of federal grant administrators.[10] Second, the failure of federal appropriations to match agency contract authorizations almost certainly undermined federal agency operations at the state level.[11]

Thus, administrators of the state's $1 billion construction grant program faced little internal administrative interference within the department, and they encountered little opposition or domination by the federal water-pollution control construction grant agency.

Party Hypotheses and the Political Environment

Having briefly discussed some administrative features of the Pure Waters program, it is now necessary to address some political factors which may have affected program implementation. In addition, the hypotheses which follow restate the assertions made in the introduction in the form of testable propositions.

> Hypothesis 1. Projects located in Democratic congressional districts (following the 1970 election) will receive a significantly larger amount of Pure Waters grant funds relative to Republican congressional district projects, with control for population served by the completed project.

This hypothesis, as well as several which follow, were based on the supposition that a majority party advantage existed in the intercity competition to secure Pure Waters grants. Because the Democrats held a majority of seats in the NYS congressional delegation after the 1970 general election, municipal projects located in Democratic congressional districts were thought to have a better chance of favorable Pure Waters Division review than those projects initiated by municipalities represented by Republican congressmen. Furthermore, since the Democratic party occupied a majority of seats in the total House of Representatives, and because the majority party of the House traditionally controls committee chairmanships as well as other important political resources, Democrats in the delegation were expected be in an advantageous position to influence state grant administrators.[12]

Admittedly, this study concerns a state, rather than a federal, program. Nevertheless, state Pure Waters officials were acutely aware of the importance of the state's congressmen. New York State's forty-one representatives (1970) frequently considered federal environmental legislation which either directly or indirectly affected the state environmental program. If members of the state delegation contributed to expansion of the federal waste treatment construction grant program, or if they were instrumental in increasing the amount of federal money available to NYS municipalities, the Pure Waters Division and the state program would benefit.

This was because, if more federal grant money were made available, or if a larger percentage of municipal project cost became eligible for federal grant assistance, local governments would want to build more projects. The effect of this increased project demand is to encourage Pure Waters Division expansion in order to facilitate review and approval of more grant applications. This increased federal grant share would have the indirect effect of raising the level of municipal demand for state grant money.[13] As more municipalities apply for federal grant assistance, the demand for the 30 percent state grant (which, as mentioned, must be approved before the federal grant request can be made) correspondingly increases. Therefore, the linkage of state and federal agency grant approval procedures made consideration of federal- (congressional-) level political forces a necessity for Pure Waters administrators.

The partisan composition of the New York State delegation during the final two years of the original Pure Waters program is depicted in table 5-1. Democrats held twenty-four districts and this was 58.5 percent of all delegation seats. Table 5-1 also reveals that Republicans controlled seventeen districts, 41.5 percent of all delegation seats.

Besides expressing concern about what the congressional delegation could do for the state program, it seems reasonable to expect that Pure Waters officials would also be concerned about their relations with the NYS State Legislature. In this study, the state senate (upper chamber) of the legislature was given special attention. The state assembly (lower chamber) was not considered.[14]

Pure Waters officials were obviously aware that the state senate acts on confirmations of the governor's appointments to state agency positions. EnCon's commissioner and numerous deputy commissioners must have their appointments confirmed by the state senate. Both the senate and assembly considered appropriations legislation for a number of division programs and functions. Since Pure Waters was a bond-supported program, it was not subject to an annual appropriation approved by the legislature. However, senate and assembly passage of environmental bond issues was required before the issues could be placed on the ballot for approval in a statewide referendum. In other words, division officials were cognizant of the fact that state senate approval of construction grant bond issues was absolutely necessary if the state program were to be maintained.

Table 5-1
NYS Party Seats Controlled by Level of Government, 1970

Political Party	Congressional Delegation Seats	Percent of Total	State Senate Seats	Percent of Total
Democrat	24	58.5	25	43.9
Republican	17	41.5	32	56.1
Total	41	100.0	57	100.0

For these reasons, it would seem to be in the division's interest for grant administrators to maximize support among legislators of the majority party in the state senate. Division officials could conceivably use their substantial discretion in project review to insure that sufficient votes will carry beneficial legislation to passage on the senate floor. Division officials might reason that supporting the interests of majority party legislators will help to protect the division from reductions in state support for the Pure Waters mission.

Therefore, the second hypothesis posits that a majority party advantage will be detected in the allocation of Pure Waters grants over state senate districts.

Hypothesis 2. Projects located in Republican state senate districts (following the 1970 election) will receive a significantly larger amount of Pure Waters grant funds relative to Democratic state senate district projects, with control for population served by the completed project.

Table 5-1 reveals that Republicans held a majority of seats in the state senate following the 1970 general election. Consequently, a majority party bias in grant distribution will be evident if Republican state senate district projects secure a disproportionately large share of Pure Waters grant funds obligated in the period investigated. After the 1970 election, Republicans controlled thirty-two districts and occupied 56 percent of all senate seats. Democrats controlled twenty-five districts, which was 44 percent of all senate seats.

The third hypothesis is executive-oriented.

Hypothesis 3. Projects located in counties which voted for the Republican incumbent governor (in 1970) will receive a significantly larger amount of Pure Waters grant funds than projects located in counties which voted in the majority for the Democratic gubernatorial candidate, with control for population served by the completed project.

In other words, Pure Waters grant administrators were constrained to favor projects proposed by municipalities of Republican-governor-voting counties in 1970. This assumed constraint would be apparent if there was evidence that project-sponsoring municipalities of Republican-governor-voting counties received a disproportionately large amount of Pure Waters funds. The reasoning behind this assertion is that EnCon and division political appointees owe their appointment to the incumbent Republican governor, and so they might be expected to repay their benefactor by expeditiously approving projects proposed by municipalities of counties which vote majorities for him.

Table 5-2 indicates that the incumbent Republican governor (Rockefeller) carried fifty-seven of the state's sixty-two counties.[15]

Table 5-2
NYS Counties Carried by Each Party's Gubernatorial Candidate and Major Party Vote, 1970

Political Party	Counties Carried	Percent of Total	Major Party Vote	Major Vote Percentage
Democrat	5	8.1	2,421,426	43.5
Republican[a]	57	91.9	3,151,432	56.5
Total	62	100.0	5,572,858	100.0

[a]Incumbent

This study includes a scale of need for project grant funding conceived in terms of environmental damage produced by preconstruction project treatment facilities. The variable used to represent need was BOD removal. BOD stands for *biochemical oxygen demand*, and is the amount of water-borne oxygen consumed by wastes.[16] The question was whether approved grants were highly correlated with the degree of need reflected in BOD removals of existing facilities. In other words, how well were the existing facilities functioning in the removal of pollutants before grant approval for a project at the site was secured?

Use of BOD removal as the sole indicator of project need may be disputable; however, few other need-related variables could be operationalized and tested in this study.[17] J. Clarence Davies explains, "While there is no single measure of the degree of water pollution, the standard most often used is 'biochemical oxygen demand.' "[18] Therefore, BOD removal was selected as the variable most indicative of project need.

BOD removal is a percentagized variable (0-100 percent). The closer a facility gets to 100 percent BOD removal, the higher the level of treatment, and thus, the less the need for projects and, correspondingly, grant money at the facility site. It follows that the lower the BOD removal value, especially for primary-level treatment or for sites with no treatment facility whatsoever (BOD removal = 0 in the latter instance), the less adequate and sanitary the treatment and the more a municipality manifests need for a waste treatment construction project of some kind.

Consideration of project need made it possible to determine whether the program was "pork-barreled" during implementation. J. Roland Pennock defines a pork barrel program as one which ". . . authorizes appropriations for public works in many districts . . . in excess of what a rational apportionment of resources to needs would justify."[19] In this case, the Pure Waters program will be considered a pork barrel program if objective need based upon BOD removals of preproject facilities was not shown to be a statistically and substantively significant factor in receipt of Pure Waters grant funding.

The fourth hypothesis is stated in the affirmative and it assumes that division administrators will take project need into account in their project review decision making.

Hypothesis 4. Projects built at sites with previously low mean annual BOD removals will receive a significantly large share of Pure Waters grant funds, with control for population served by the completed project.

Confirmation of this hypothesis will constitute modest evidence that the Pure Waters program was not pork-barreled during its implementation by division administrators. A high and significantly large negative correlation between preproject treatment plant BOD removal and Pure Waters grant funding will mean that division grant administrators apportioned grant resources in accord with project need.

Partisan pork-barreling in program implementation is addressed in the set of hypotheses presented below. Here tests will concern the correlation of project need with Pure Waters grants conferred, by party of the district (or county) in which the project is located. For each level of government investigated (congressional delegation, state senate, and governor), projects will be grouped by party, and the correlation of need with grants conferred will be calculated.

Hypothesis 5. Projects in districts of Democratic congressmen will exhibit a weaker association of need with Pure Waters grants received than will projects of Republican congressional districts, with control for population served by the completed project.

Hypothesis 6. Projects in districts of Republican state senators will exhibit a weaker association of need with Pure Waters grants received than will projects of Democratic state senate districts, with control for population served by the completed project.

Hypothesis 7. Projects in counties voting for the Republican incumbent governor will exhibit a weaker association of need with Pure Waters grants received than will projects of counties which voted in majority for the Democratic gubernatorial candidate, with control for population served by the completed project.

The experiments used to test hypotheses 5-7 select out projects by party and then address the question of need. It is assumed in each of these hypotheses that if a project is located in a majority party district (or county), need will be a less salient factor in the decision to confer a Pure Waters grant to the project, than it will be in the case of a project located in a minority party district or county. A simpler way to express this relationship is, the Division administrator has a great incentive to discount or deemphasize the need variable in grant decision making when a project is located in a majority party district or county. On the other hand, the minority party district or county status of other projects affords no advantage to those projects, and may in fact be disadvantageous in project review. As a result, project need must be very great in order for minority party district or county projects to receive Pure Waters grant funding.

Tests of Hypotheses

Tests which follow were performed through use of multiple regression in order to measure both the degree and direction of influence which partisan political forces and need considerations had upon the distribution of Pure Waters construction grants for the period 1971-1972. Table 5-3 is a regression analysis test for hypotheses 1-4. NYS Pure Waters construction grant money was the dependent variable (Y). Three political independent variables utilized were: congressional district party of project location (X_2), state senate district party of project location (X_3), and party of governor

Table 5-3
The Influence of Political Party and Project Need on Distribution of NYS Pure Waters Grants, 1971-1972[a]

Variable	Beta Weight	F	Significance Level
X_1 Population served	.74054	77.546	.001
X_2 Congressional district party of project[c]	− .08659	1.862	not significant
X_3 State Senate district party of project[c]	.19545	6.314	.05
X_4 Governor county party of project[c]	.10750	1.838	not significant
X_5 Mean annual BOD removal (1971) for preproject facilities	− .21069	13.420	.001

Multiple $R = .65729$; $N = 190$; variance explained (R^2) = .43203; significance of the model (F) = 27.99202 (Significant at .001 level); $Y^b = -3569.535 + .09908X_1 - 1930.889X_2 + 5137.822X_3 + 3320.789X_4 - 65.075X_5$

[a]Table is based on regression analysis with NYS Pure Waters construction grants to completed or approved municipal projects for the period 1/1/71 to 3/31/72 as the dependent variable.

[b]Numeric values in the equation are unstandardized regression coefficients, with the exception of the first number in the equation.

[c]Political party is based upon majority party vote in the 1970 general election; minor parties do not apply in the study.

vote by county of project location (X_4). Each of these variables is dichotomous, with Democratic districts or counties assigned the value "0", and Republican districts or counties assigned the value "1". Mean annual BOD removal of preproject facilities is an interval scale variable and is independent variable (X_5). In addition, population served by the completed project is introduced as control variable (X_1). Population served is also an interval scale variable.

The test investigated a set of 190 projects approved for Pure Waters grant funding between January 1, 1971, and March 31, 1972. Some projects were actually completed before March 31, 1972; however, most projects were in some stage of construction on that program expiration date. The cost of these 190 projects amounted to $820 million, or about 91 percent of all Pure Waters bond funds committed during the seven-year life of the program.[20]

Review of the findings in table 5-3 indicates that population served by the completed project (X_1) was strongly associated with Pure Waters grants conferred. Population served was employed as a control variable in measuring the influence of the independent variables upon the dependent variable. Therefore, its strong association with the dependent variable is of no theoretical importance. The population-served variable helped to eliminate distortions in grant distribution attributable to large-scale projects. The key point is that once population served (X_1) has explained its portion of the variance in the model, is there any variance then explained by incorporation of the independent variables?[21]

A check of the beta weight column in table 5-3 reveals that two of the four independent variables in the model have explained a portion of the variance in the dependent variable and are statistically signficant. Variables (X_5), mean annual BOD removal of preproject facilities, has a moderately large and negative beta weight ($-.21069$). The negative sign for BOD removal was predicted in so much as BOD removals of preproject facilities should be inversely related to Pure Waters grants obligated, even with control for population served by the completed project.[22]

This finding serves to confirm hypothesis 4. That is, the magnitude and statistical significance of the project need variable signifies that projects built at sites with previously low mean annual BOD removals have received a significantly large share of the period's Pure Waters grant funds, even with control for population served by the completed project.

In statistical terms, the hypothesis was confirmed by the magnitude and significance of the beta weight for variable (X_5). The F value in table 5-3 is a measure of statistical significance for the beta weights of the independent variables. In a sense, the F value is an indicator of the reliability of the beta weights for the independent variables. The F value for (X_5) is 13.42, and this value is significant at the .001 level. The standard significance level used by most social scientists is .05, and it is the significance level used here.[23] Therefore, (X_5) falls well within the predicted critical region, and this affirms that the need variable is statistically significant and reliable in explaining the variance of the dependent variable.

Hence, there was a moderately strong association between project need and grants conferred in the model. This can be taken as evidence that Pure Waters grants distribution by state administrators was partially in accord with need, based upon BOD removals of existing treatment facilities before project construction. If BOD removals of preproject facilities are ranked highest to lowest, as one moves down the list to lower levels of BOD removal more project grant money is likely to go to low-ranked projects, even when controlling for the size of the project based upon population served by the completed project. This suggests that Pure Waters administrators were not simply responding to partisan or majoritarian pressures exclusive of project need.

However, one political independent variable does turn up as important in table 5-3. The beta weight for state senate district party is sufficiently large enough (.19545) to be asociated with the variance in the dependent variable. Because the beta weight is positive in sign, a Republican state senate district advantage is indicated. The F value for the state senate party variable (X_3) is (6.314), and this value falls within the .05 critical region employed for these tests. Therefore, the state senate party variable is associated with Pure Waters grant distribution, and the beta weight for this variable is moderately large and statistically significant.

This serves to conform hypothesis 2. Projects located in Republican state senate districts have received a significantly larger amount of Pure Waters grant money relative to Democratic state senate district projects, even with control for population served by the completed project. This holds true even with inclusion of the congressional and gubernatorial party variables in the model. This demonstrates that Pure Waters grant administrators tended to approve more project money for Republican state senate district projects than for Democratic state senate district projects.

A logical question which could be raised at this point is, was there actually a greater need for project grants in Republican state senate districts relative to need for project grants in Democratic state senate districts? If this is the case, Republican state senate district advantages in project grant acquisition may only be a legitimate division response to environmental need unrelated to state senate district partisanship. This issue can be resolved by reviewing test results for hypothesis 6. However, before pursuing this matter, a few final points regarding the findings of table 5-3 must be discussed.

There seems to be no evidence to confirm hypothesis 1 and hypothesis 3. Projects located in Democratic congressional districts have not received a significantly larger amount of Pure Waters grant funds relative to

Republican congressional district projects. This is revealed by the relatively small beta weight for (X_2) and its statistical insignificance. Thus, the congressional district party of project location does not appear to be an important factor in explaining how Pure Waters grants are distributed to NYS municipalities.

Likewise, executive-oriented hyphothesis 3 stands unconfirmed. Projects located in counties which voted for the incumbent Republican governor in 1970 have not received a significantly larger amount of Pure Waters funds than projects located in counties voting in majority for the 1970 Democratic gubernatorial contender. The small and statistically insignificant beta weight for (X_4) produced in the test was the reason for drawing this conclusion.

Table 5-4 contains a series of regression equations which test hypotheses 5-7. As before, NYS Pure Waters construction grant money is the dependent

Table 5-4
The Influence of Project Need on Distribution of NYS Pure Waters Grants by Political Party, 1971-1972

Variable		Beta Weight	F	Significance Level	N
X_2^a	BOD removal for Democratic state senate district projects	− .53397	16.844	.001	39
X_2^b	BOD removal for Republican state senate district projects	− .14938	5.825	.05	151
X_2^c	BOD removal for Democratic congressional district projects	− .45453	27.149	.001	66
X_2^d	BOD removal for Republican congressional district projects	− .09903	1.684	not significant	124
X_2^e	BOD removal for Democratic governor county projects	− .63129	30.745	.001	26
X_2^f	BOD removal for Republican governor county projects	− .15804	5.720	.05	164

Notes: Levels of analysis are by party of State Senate district, Congressional district, and Governor County.

Equations, (Rs), and (R²s) are simply furnished to show source from which beta weights for the need variables were derived.

[a]$Y = 18357.203 + .05034X_1 − 297.10363X_2$ R $= .70694$ R$^2 = .49976$
[b]$Y = 1964.368 + .10588X_1 − 36.98799X_2$ R $= .66238$ R$^2 = .43875$
[c]$Y = 11639.187 + .08494X_1 − 226.43537X_2$ R $= .72664$ R$^2 = .52800$
[d]$Y = 1583.700 + .05397X_1 − 15.90132X_2$ R $= .54611$ R$^2 = .29823$
[e]$Y = 16506.072 + .10004X_1 − 442.69522X_2$ R $= .86600$ R$^2 = .74995$
[f]$Y = 2381.215 + .07115X_1 − 33.58676X_2$ R $= .54530$ R$^2 = .54530$

Y = Pure Waters construction grant to each project
X_1 = Population to be served by each completed grant project

variable; this is grant money committed to building the same 190 projects as before. Yet, these tests select our projects by party, and then project need is correlated with grants conferred, controlling again for population served by the completed project. Independent variable (X_2) and control variable (X_1) are the only variables used in the correlation with Pure Waters grant money committed (Y).

In table 5-4, beta weights for variable (X_2) are depicted for each equation with a corresponding letter subscript. For example, variable (X^a_2) represents preproject BOD removals for the thirty-nine projects built in Democratic state senate districts during the period. Similarly, (X^b_2) is a variable denoting preproject removals for the 151 projects built in Republican state senate districts during the same period. Table 5-4 discloses that the beta weight for (X^a_2) and the beta weight for (X^b_2) are large enough to be statistically significant. In so much as beta weights are standardized regression coefficients, the fact that there are only thirty-nine cases for the first equation (a) and 151 cases for the second equation (b) should make no significant difference in comparing beta weights on variable (X_2). The beta weight for (X^a_2) is considerably larger than the beta weight for (X^b_2). Moreover, the beta weight for (X^a_2) is significant at the .001 level, while the beta weight for (X^b_2) is only significant at the .05 level.

What this means is that the thirty-nine projects approved for Democratic state senate district municipalities exhibit a very strong association of need, based upon preproject BOD removals, with Pure Waters grant money obligated. While an association of need with grants conferred also exists for the 151 projects located in Republican state senate districts, the relative strength of that association is much less than that for the Democratic state senate district set of projects. This confirms hypothesis 6. That is, projects in districts of Republican state senators do exhibit a weaker association of need with Pure Waters grants received than do projects of Democratic state senate districts, with control for population served by the completed project.

Returning to the question posed above regarding why Republican state senate district projects have an advantage over Democratic state senate district projects in grant acquisition, it can now be shown that a comparatively higher level of project need does not exist in the case of Republican state senate district projects. The advantage enjoyed in grant acquisition by Republican state senate district projects is not attributable to greater project need, and may well be explained by efforts of division grant administrators to satisfy the constituency service interests of majority party legislators in the state senate.

Using the same set of 190 projects, what can be said regarding the congressional delegation level of analysis? Table 5-4 indicates that for the sixty-six projects built in Democratic congressional districts, the beta weight (X^c_2)

reveals a strong association of need with grant money conferred, with control for population served by the completed project. What is remarkable is that the beta weight for (X^d_2) is not statistically significant. This signifies that there is no meaningful association of need with grant money received in the case of 124 Republican congressional district projects. Within the narrow confines of this study, the data disclose that partisan pork-barreling may have occurred for Republican congressional district projects for the period under review.

This finding is most interesting when one considers that the Republicans were the minority party in the delegation. It should be stressed that this finding does not mean that Republican congressional district projects acquired a larger share of grant money than their numbers would warrant. What it does suggest is that Republican congressional district projects received a modest share of Pure Waters money even though the money went to low need, rather than high need, projects. Need is in relative terms, not absolute terms. Further research may explain this finding in committe terms. That is, during the period investigated here, there were more NYS Republican congressmen on the House Public Works Committee than there were NYS Democrats on the committee.

Hypothesis 5 is not confirmed by the data. Projects in districts of Democratic congressmen do not exhibit a weaker association of need with Pure Waters grants received than do projects in districts of Republican congressmen.

For the same set of 190 projects, are there any discernible relationships for the governor-county-level of analysis? Table 5-4 points out that the twenty-six projects built in counties voting a majority for the Democratic gubernatorial contender in 1970 show a very strong association of need with grants conferred, with control for population served by the completed project. This is because the beta weight for variable (X^e_2) is quite large and statistically significant.

Only a moderate association of need with grants conferred exists for the 164 projects approved in counties which voted in majority for the incumbent Republican governor. Therefore, hypothesis 7 is confirmed. Projects in counties voting for the Republican incumbent governor do exhibit a weaker association of need with Pure Waters grants received than do projects of counties which voted in majority for the Democratic gubernatorial candidate. This applies even with control for population served by the completed projects. Confirmation of hypothesis 7 suggests that division grant administrators consider project need a slightly less important factor in grand decision making if it is a Republican-governor-county project they are reviewing. Similarly, need is a very important factor in their review of Democratic-governor-county projects.

A careful check of the beta weight column for table 5-4 reveals that the

Republican project variable at each level of analysis (X^b_2, X^d_2, and X^f_2) has a smaller beta weight than their Democratic project variable counterparts (X^a_2, X^c_2, and X^e_2). Moreover, Democratic project need variables all have beta weights which are significant at the .001 level. In no case does a Republican project need variable display a significance level better than .05. This means that need is a critical variable in the decision to approve grants to projects in Democratic state senate districts, Democratic congressional districts, and Democratic governor counties. Need obviously is a less important variable in the decision to approve grants to projects in Republican state senate districts, Republican congressional districts, and Republican governor counties.

This study is not implying that municipalities of Republican congressional districts are spending local funds to secure grants for projects they do not need. Instead, the argument is that the pre-existing treatment facilities, based upon the indicator of BOD removal alone, have levels of need not strongly correlated with the magnitude of grants conferred, even when controlling for population to be served by the completed project. It may be that projects of Republican districts or counties were being built to specifications which incorporate excess sewage treatment capacities, relative to the extant population served. However, this observation is purely speculation and it does not address the question as to why projects of Democratic districts or counties are not being built to incorporate larger future wastewater flows as well.

The argument that most of the money going to municipalities of Republican districts was to fund projects which include more sewerage construction than sewage treatment plant construction does not hold water. A very considerable portion of project cost for facilities serving Democratic district municipalities covered sewerage construction as well as treatment plant construction. Besides, the huge volume of wastewater conveyed and the expensive complications of in-city construction for urban (Democratic district) sewer systems were likely to inflate the cost of project construction in those areas. It was beyond the scope of this study to distinguish sewer construction cost data from wastewater treatment plant construction costs.

Summary

This study has examined how political partisanship influenced the allocation of environmental construction grants in New York State during 1971 and 1972. Grant decision making was investigated by analyzing the distribution of Pure Waters grants among municipal governments. It was assumed that party control would affect the Pure Waters Division review and approval of municipal grant applications. Hence we hypothesized that municipalities located in constituencies controlled by the majority party would enjoy an advantage in securing approval of their grant applications.

It was also assumed that Pure Waters officials occupying decision making positions attempted to be either administratively efficient, politically efficient, or, where possible, both. Division officials were considered administratively efficient when they distributed grants in accord with existing environmental needs. They were thought to be politically efficient when they distributed grants to areas represented by members in the party controlling congress, the state senate, and the governorship.

A most important conclusion revealed by regression analysis of tables 5-3 and 5-4 was that project need is a substantively and statistically significant variable in the correlation with Pure Waters grants conferred. Allegations that the Pure Waters program was a pork barrel enterprise in which resources were not apportioned in accord with what a rational assessment of need would justify are not valid. However, despite the positive response of Pure Waters officials to project need, a more focused analysis did reveal some evidence of partisan bias in grant distribution. When the need variable and three political party variables were incorporated in a multiple regression analysis, a strong association was found to exist between Republican state senate district projects and Pure Waters grants conferred. Municipalities located in Republican state senate districts received a disproportionately larger share of Pure Waters grant funds than did municipalities of Democratic state senate districts. Thus, grant decisions appear to have been influenced by project need *and* a political consideration.

In the second battery of tests (table 5-4), projects were selected out by party for each level of government and the need-grant correlation was again computed. Results showed that need was an important factor in the decision to approve grants to projects located in Democratic state senate districts, in Democratic congressional districts, and in counties voting Democrat for governor. Need was a less important concern in the decision to approve grants to projects in Republican state senate districts, Republican congressional districts, and in counties voting Republican for governor. Actually, need proved to be inconsequential in the case of projects in Republican congressional districts. We concluded that this represents evidence that grant administrators furnished grants to projects in Republican congressional districts on grounds that either discounted or ignored project need.

This analysis of the Pure Waters program revealed that municipalities in areas represented by the majority party in the state senate had an increased probability of success in grant acquisition. Nevertheless, the study also discloses that Pure Waters officials did frequently consider need as an important factor in grant decision making. While high-need projects could be identified in districts and counties of each party across the state, moderate- and high-need projects of Republican state senate districts were especially likely to receive Pure Waters grants. Less grant money went to a smaller pool of very high-need projects in Democratic state senate districts. In a sense, Pure Waters officials were both politically and administratively efficient in grant decision making. The program's grant administrators apparently balanced their responsiveness to constituency service interests of majority party state senators with their professional concern for meeting New York State's water pollution control priorities.

It seems that future research of distributive programs should take into account the behavior of grant administrators and their political as well as administrative and professional constraints.

Notes

1. One of the best-known works on the subject is by Jeffrey L. Pressman and Aaron B. Wildavsky, *Implementation* (Berkeley: University of California Press, 1973). Examples of other works on the subject are: Eugene Bardach, *The Implementation Game: What Happens After a Bill Becomes a Law* (Cambridge, Mass: The MIT Press, 1977); Edwin C. Hargrove, *The Missing Link: The Study of Implementation of Social Policy* (Washington, D.C.: The Urban Institute, 1975); Martha Derthick, *Uncontrollable Spending for Social Service Grants* (Washington, D.C.: Brookings Institution, 1975); Rufus P. Browning and Dale Rogers Marshall, "Implementation of Model Cities and Revenue Sharing in Ten Bay Area Cities: Design and First Findings," in ed. Charles O. Jones and Robert D. Thomas, *Public Policy Making in a Federal System* (Beverly Hills, Calif.: Sage, 1976), 191-216; Jerome Murphy, "Title I of ESEA: The Politics of Implementing Education Reform," *Harvard Educational Review* 41(February 1971):35-63.

Examples of implementation-related studies of intergovernmental environmental programs are, Robert D. Thomas, "Intergovernmental Coordination in the Implementation of National Air and Water Pollution Policies," in *Public Policy Making in a Federal System*, ed. Charles O. Jones and Robert D. Thomas (Beverly Hills, Calif.: Sage, 1976), 129-148; Robert D. Thomas and Ralph A. Luken, "Balancing Incentives and Conditions in the Evolution of a Federal Program: A Perspective on Construction Grants for Waste Water Treatment Plants," *Publius* 3(Summer 1974):43-63; Harvey Lieber, *Federalism and Clean Waters: The 1972 Water Pollution Control Act* (Lexington, Mass.: Lexington Books, D.C. Heath and Company, 1975).

2. Several notable exceptions are: Martha Derthick, *The Influence of Federal Grants: Public Assistance in Massachusetts* (Cambridge, Mass.: Harvard University Press, 1970); Elizabeth A. Haskell and Victoria S.

Price, *State Environmental Management Case Studies of Nine States* (New York: Praeger, 1973); and Lieber, *Federalism and Clean Waters.*

3. Under the terms of the federal Clean Waters Restoration Act of 1966, as much as 55 percent of a project's total eligible cost could be subsidized by a federal construction grant. State construction grant support was at a flat 30 percent of total eligible project cost under the NYS Environmental Conservation Law of 1965. See Office of the State Comptroller (New York State), Division of Audits and Accounts, *Audit Report of the Pure Waters Program,* Report Al-St-15-73, pp. 4-9 (hereafter cited as State Comptroller).

4. This study investigates the influence of the state legislature's upper chamber on the state program. The study does not include an analysis of grant distribution over assembly districts of the state, nor does it address the issue of political interference exercised by state assemblymen in the area of grant administration. Disaggregation of grants to assembly districts was beyond the scope of the study. However, in New York State each state senate district is composed of three assembly districts, and the partisan composition of the state senate district is often indicative of the partisan character of the assembly districts within it. This is particularly true during the years of the Pure Waters program.

5. NYS Health Department, *Pure Waters Progress 1969* (Albany, N.Y.: NYS Health Department, 1969), p. 1.

6. State Comptroller, p. 6.

7. James G. March and Herbert A. Simon, *Organizations* (New York: John Wiley & Sons, 1958), p. 28.

8. State Comptroller, Exhibit C, pp. 1-2.

9. Thomas, "Intergovernmental Coordination," p. 130.

10. J. Clarence Davies, III, and Barbara S. Davies, *The Politics of Pollution,* 2nd ed. (Indianapolis: Pegasus, 1975), pp. 109-110.

11. Robert D. Thomas argues, "The uncertainty of federal allocations not only works as a bargaining tool for state administrators to negotiate with their legislators, it also works for them as a bargaining tool in their negotiations with federal administrators. See Thomas, "Intergovernmental Coordination," p. 135.

12. This assertion is based upon Elazar's concept of "legislative interference" in administrative affairs on behalf of constituents. Elazar claims that legislative interference

... is a most useful device for gaining administrative consideration for state and local needs after legislation has been enacted and at the point where administrative discretion in statutory interpretation comes into play.

See Daniel J. Elazar, *American Federalism: A View From the States,* 2nd ed. (New York: Thomas Y. Crowell, 1972), p. 159. Here it is assumed that majority party legislators have an advantage in exercising legislative interference during the Pure Waters Division project review process.

13. It also holds out the prospect that the state 30 percent grant can be reduced to a lower percentage level, thus allowing extension of the Pure Waters program over a longer time period, in as much as state grant money could be stretched to support more projects. It is important to note that the term *municipality* in this study refers to counties, cities, towns, villages, or any designated agency thereof which could sponsor a grant-supportable project.

14. See footnote 4.

15. From Richard M. Scammon, *America Votes,* (Washington, D.C.: Governmental Affairs Institute, Congressional Quarterly, 1972), 9:229.

16. Davies and Davies, p. 10.

17. Considerable effort was applied to creating a need index based upon a combination of variables. Among them were preproject BOD and suspended-solids removals along with plant overload data. BOD removal was found to be very highly correlated with suspended-solids removal, and, therefore, use of suspended-solids data would be redundant if BOD removals were to be used. Flow data regarding overloads were incomplete and questionable. Besides, seasonal variations in combined sewer flow systems made use of an annual flow average somewhat dubious. Therefore, BOD removal (mean annual five-day BOD removal in correct technical terms) was employed as the most superior need variable. BOD removal data were obtained from an NYS Department of Environmental Conservation, Bureau of Municipal Wastes, "Municipal S.T.W. Inventory" (unpublished computer printout, 1972).

18. Davies and Davies, p. 10.

19. J. Roland Pennock, "Pork Barrel and Majority Rule," *Journal of Politics* 32(August 1970):709-716.

20. Pure Waters grant data were found in NYS Department of Environmental Conservation, Division of Pure Waters, Bureau of Construction Grants, *Quarterly Report of Status of Inactive and Approved Federal and State Grants Projects for Construction of Municipal Treatment Works*, March 31, 1972.

All information concerning the congressional district location of municipal projects was researched through the *Congressional Directory*, (Washington, D.C.: U.S. Government Printing Office, Annual Volumes, 1964-1970). All information regarding state senate district location of municipal projects was researched through the *New York State Legislative Reference Service*, 1964-1972 (New York: NYS Legislative Reference Service, 1964-1972).

21. Population served by the completed project was obtained from project data contained in the "Inventory" and "Quarterly Report" cited above.

22. A negative sign for the beta weight was anticipated, in as much as need should be inversely related to grants received. Recall that, as BOD removals of ranked preproject facilities increase, the amount of Pure Waters grants conferred should decrease, again with control for population served by the completed projects.

Most of the statistical associations discussed in this study involve the size and significance of beta weights for various independent variables in the regression equations. Below is a brief definition of beta weights.

> If each variable is standardized by dividing by its standard deviation . . . we can obtain adjusted slopes which are comparable from one variable to the next. We thus measure changes in the dependent variable in terms of standard deviation units for each of the other variables, a fact which assures us of the same variability in each of these variables. These adjusted partial slopes are thus standardized *b*'s which are often called *beta weights*. . . . The beta weight can be obtained by multiplying the comparable *b* by the ratio of the standard deviation of the independent variable to that of the dependent variable. The beta weights . . . indicate how much change in the dependent variable is produced by a standardized change in one of the independent variables when the others are controlled.

See Hubert M. Blalock, Jr., *Social Statistics*, 2nd ed. (New York: McGraw-Hill 1972), pp. 452-453.

23. See James K. Skipper, Jr.; Anthony L. Guenther; and Gilbert Nass, ''The Sacredness of .05: A Note Concerning the Uses of Statistical Levels of Significance in Social Science,'' in (*The Significance Test Controversy—A Reader*) ed. Denton E. Morrison and Ramon E. Henkel, (Chicago: Aldine Publishing, 1970), 155-160. The .05 convention prescribes that the null hypothesis is automatically rejected whenever the probability of being wrong is 5 percent or less (Ibid., p. 156).

6 Paying for the "Bloody Shirt:" The Politics of Civil War Pensions

Heywood T. Sanders

Introduction

The year 1896 marked a turning point in American electoral history: a shift from a period of close party competition to an era of Republican hegemony. Yet, even as the "Gilded Age" grew to a close, the single dominant burden on the federal treasury remained a legacy of the Civil War—pensions for Union veterans and their survivors. Pensions accounted for 39.6 percent of all federal spending in 1896, a slight decrease from its highest point, 41.6 percent, in 1893. The Bureau of Pensions provided monthly benefits to roughly 750,000 veterans and 222,000 dependents in 1896, aiding over 63 percent of all surviving veterans. Pension payments averaged about $12 per month, a substantial payment at a time when average annual income for industiral workers came to $462.[1]

The pension system was not simply an early social welfare scheme. It evolved in a series of fits and starts, matching the increasing needs of the Republican party and the organization of the veterans themselves. While the system had begun as a means of assisting those injured during military service, its expansion ultimately included all veterans with some physical need, real or imagined. In its final form, in the years after 1890, it represented a central element in Republican party strategy for insuring the continuing loyalty and political participation of one of the party's traditional constituencies.

This article will examine the development and impact of this system of benefits, both to explain the conditions under which such a national machine developed and to determine its actual impact on partisan voting. The initial focus will be on the legislative arena and the course of pensions legislation through Congress. The executive branch, through the Bureau of Pensions, also affected the distribution of pension benefits. This will be the focus of the second major section. Finally, a case study of voting behavior in Ohio will be used to explore the relationship between pension benefits and group voting.

The use of veterans' pensions for partisan gain developed in a complex manner in a number of political arenas. Union veterans were a natural constituency for the Republicans, for "(t)he great majority of the soldiers who voted in the field in 1864 supported Lincoln, and in the next two decades the Republicans retained the affection of most of those.''[2] Their political influence was, however, greatly strengthened as they became organized in such groups as the Grand Army of the Republic. The G.A.R. grew from 31,000 members in 1878, to 295,000 in 1885, and finally to 409,000 in 1890. The increased organization of veterans both paced the rise of the pension issue and provided additional fuel for Republican activity. From the late 1870s through 1891, the Republican members of Congress consistently pressed for broader and more liberal pension benefits, while simultaneously sponsoring a flood of special legislation for individual ex-soldiers. When a Republican occupied the White House, the Bureau of Pensions could be assisted (or potentially manipulated) to further demonstrate the special relationship between Union veterans and the party.

The end product of this special relationship has been described by Wallace Davies.

> Through the pension system, the Republicans had devised for the benefit of the ex-soldiers a sort of early limited W.P.A. which, when combined with gifts of homesteads to Western pioneers, land grants to railroads, and tariff benefits to industrialists, was a striking demonstration of how lavish spending of Federal funds could long maintain a political party in power.[3]

In short, the Republican party had established, in the case of the ex-soldiers, a national political machine—a formal organization which provided specific material inducements to a mass of voters.

Congress and Pensions

The basic system of Civil War pensions was enacted into law in July of 1862. The system was designed to aid those who were disabled as a direct consequence of their military activities, and to provide for the widows and children of those killed during hostilities or due to war wounds. Payments were graded according to rank and level of disability, with a totally disabled private receiving $8 per month. Soldiers were required to formally apply for pension benefits, providing evidence of injury and military service. Where an application was filed within one year of discharge from the military, benefits started with the discharge date. In all other cases, the pension was paid as of the date of the application.[4]

A five-year extension of the filing period in 1868 was designed to insure that all eligible veterans were aided. It actually had the effect of creating substanial variations in individual benefits. For example, a claim filed before the end of the five-year grace period would generate a lump-sum payment of $480, while one filed immediately after the period would receive only the monthly stipend.

The existence of differences in pension benefits based on the delay or complexity involved in a single claim was disturbing, both to veterans and to government officials. The legislative response was the so-called arrears bill, which provided full back payments (based on the date of discharge) for all new and existing pension claims. The historical evidence suggests that a genuine concern for inequitable benefits was behind the early arrears legislation. Proposals for arrears were regularly introduced after 1873, but it was not until June 1878 that a bill was actually passed, in this case by the House. The vote was 164 to 61, with forty-eight Democrats joining 116 Republicans in the affirmative. All of the opposition came from the Democrats, largely those from the south and border areas. Senate action did not come until January 1879, when the arrears proposal passed by a vote of 44 to 4.[5]

Contemporary accounts suggest that the arrears legislation was seen as a question of fairness, rather than in partisan terms. There was little information or debate on the cost of the legislation, little pressure from veterans' groups (the G.A.R. counted only 45,000 members at the time). Indeed, the apolitical character of the legislation is suggested by congressional action in March of 1879, less than three months later, to reduce the scope and impact of arrears. Pensions were now to be dated as of the date of the disability (rather than discharge), with a one-year limit put on new claims. These actions substantially reduced the potential benefits for new claimants, and suggest that partisan gain was not the force behind passage of the arrears provisions.

Despite the retrenchment, passage of the arrears act in 1879 proved to be the flowering of pensions as a political issue. New claims flooded the Bureau of Pensions, jumping from 18,800 in 1878 to 36,900 in 1879 and 110,600 in 1880. Thus, the payment of arrears did not simply reduce the inequities of earlier pension benefits, but served to stimulate the financial interests of a sizable group of new claimants. These new applicants became vitally concerned with the efficiency and care with which the Pensions Bureau reviewed applications. The magnitude of that concern is suggested by the fact that first payments on new pension claims in the early 1880s averaged over $1,200. The increased concern of veterans for pension policy is also mirrored in the growth of the G.A.R. from 45,000 members in 1879 to 89,000 in 1882 and 215,000 in 1885. By the middle of the 1880s, the political impact of pensions policy and organized veterans was clear to both major parties.[6]

The emergence of pensions as a political issue was paralleled by a greater partisan divergence. The perception and response to veterans' concerns can be traced in the Democratic and Republican party platforms. In 1876, both parties acknowledged the soldier vote in general terms, with no commitment to pension benefits. The Democrats proclaimed that "the soldiers and sailors of the Republic . . . have a just claim upon the care, protection and gratitude of their fellow-citizens.'' The Republicans assured that "the pledges which our nation has given to our soldiers and sailors must be fulfilled.''[7]

By 1880, party differences had begun to emerge. The Democratic platform made no mention of either veterans or pensions. The Republicans indicated that "the pensions promised should be paid.'' Clearly, the pension issue was of only limited concern to the parties.[8]

In 1884, the clear appeal to the organized veterans is evident in both platforms. The Democrats endorsed the use of internal revenue taxes to "defray the expenses of the care and comfort of worthy soldiers disabled in the line of duty. . . .'' The Republican platform promised a far more substantial and beneficial pension system, "pledged to suitable pensions for all who were disabled . . . (and) repeal of the limitations contained in the arrears act of 1879.''[9]

The 1888 election platforms marked the high point of both party differences and concrete promises. The Democrats recalled their record in actually granting pensions "while carefully guarding the interests of the taxpayers and conforming strictly to the principles of justice and equity. . . .'' No mention was made of greater benefits or new legislation. In contrast, the Republican platform called for a system of payments ". . . so enlarged and extended as to provide against the possibility that any man who honorably wore the Federal uniform shall become the inmate of an almshouse or dependent on private charity.'' The party went on to denounce President Cleveland for his vetoes of pension legislation and the "action of the Democratic House of Representatives in refusing even a consideration of general pension legislation.''[10]

The platform statements of both parties show dramatic change from the 1870s to 1888. While pious symbolism and gratitude distinguished the earliest statements, they gradually grew to include clear promises and policy recommendations to benefit the veterans. Yet, the Republicans were able to press for specific new policies while the Democrats demurred on any true financial commitment.

The meshing of Republican support and G.A.R. pressures can be read in legislative action of the 1880s. The most optimistic proposals, universal-service pensions, were designed to provide a pension to all those who served in the military for a specific period. An alternative suggestion was for a dependent pension bill, with a grant to ex-soldiers who were disabled regardless of origin or date, and (in some proposals) who were "dependent" on their own daily labor for support. Such legislation would mean a complete revamping of the pension system, together with a new philosophy of the pension. Such service or disability legislation would merely single out all soldiers for special treatment, regardless of the fact that other, equally deserving, disabled, or dependent individuals could be found.

The Republican-controlled Senate proved most receptive to the demands of the ex-soldiers, passing a dependent pension bill in 1886. The House joined the Senate in supporting the pensions legislation the following year, only to see President Cleveland veto the final bill. The Democratic members of the House proved loyal to the president, and a veto override attempt failed by a vote of 175 to 125. Donald McMurray notes that all of the members who changed their yea votes were Democrats.[11]

While Cleveland's veto raised a material issue for the Grand Army and the Republicans, it also symbolized the distance between the Democratic party and the veterans. Cleveland's vetoes of private pension bills were unique for the time, and his order to return captured battle flags to the South raised a storm of disapproval. The Republicans were not about to pass up such desirable issues. The convention of 1888 endorsed a platform denouncing Cleveland's vetoes and calling for more substantial pension legislation. The delegates then nominated an ex-soldier, Benjamin Harrison, and moved to secure the veteran vote. While Harrison himself was somewhat close-mouthed on the pension issue, his partisan colleagues were not. James Tanner of the Grand Army (later appointed Commissioner of Pensions) boasted that he had "plastered Indiana with promises" of pensions under a Harrison administration.[12] Indeed, Indiana represented a major focus of Republican electioneering. One Republican veteran said the Grand Army in Indiana "became a machine in the hands of Republican politicians to awaken enthusiasm among the people on the one hand and to beat down the opposition to their candidates, both personal and political, on the other."[13]

The election proved a Republican triumph, with Republican control of the White House and Congress for the first time since 1875. The party was not long in attempting to repay its electoral debt to the old soldiers. Harrison advocated a dependent pension bill in his first annual message in December 1889. He argued that men who had served their country and were now in need should not be forced to rely on local charity.[14]

At this point, the only question that faced the Republicans was which pension scheme to take up. The Senate supported a Dependent Pension Bill providing $12 per month to soldiers who had served three months and were incapable of supporting themselves. The House supported somewhat more liberal legislation, including a provision for pensioning all veterans over 60 regardless of physical need. A conference committee resolved differences between the houses, and compromise legislation was passed by the House and Senate and signed by President Harrison on June 27, 1890.

The passage of pension legislation in 1890 was the product of many forces. Two clear influences stand out, however. The Republicans controlled both houses, with a seven-vote margin in the House of Representatives and a two-vote margin in the Senate. The Republicans were thus in a position to pass some new pension legislation and see it signed by the president. In the critical votes in the House and Senate, particularly on the adoption of the conference committee compromise, no Republicans voted against pensions. The issue posed a very difficult problem for the Democratic members of Congress from the east and midwest. The ex-soldier vote was a substantial and well-organized one, with only a single issue of concern. Any failure to support increased pensions would likely be punished at the polls. As a result, many Democrats supported the Republicans on the pension issue. In the Senate, the closest division came on the adoption of the compromise bill, with 34 yeas and 18 nays. Democratic Senators Call of Florida, Hearst of California, and Turpie of Indiana joined the Republicans in supporting new pensions. In the House, thirty-nine Democrats joined 140 Republicans in supporting legislation more generous than the final bill, including eleven from New York, seven from Indiana, five from Ohio, three from Illinois, and none from the South.[15]

The Pension Act of 1890 was quite a far-reaching measure. It provided a graded pension to the ex-soldier with ninety days' service who suffered from a disability and was incapable of performing manual labor. It significantly reduced the strictures on eligibility which had been in force since 1862. Even the Grand Army's pension committee was pleased, as it acknowledged that the new law opened the pension system "to all the survivors of the war whose conditions of health are not practically perfect."[16] The response by the veterans was immediate. In just one year, over 655,000 applications for new or increased pensions were received, and 116,000 were approved, bringing the pension rolls to some 676,000 veterans or dependents, and over $89 million in payments.[17]

The 1890 Act was the last major piece of Civil War pension legislation in the nineteenth century. Its passage provided a large strategic opening for the Republicans, which they capitalized on for the balance of the century. While the political question of pension benefits declined dramatically after 1890, the expenditure for the ex-soldiers did not. Civil War pensions remained a sizable portion of the federal budget into the twentieth century.

The full development of the pension system and the relationship between the veterans, the Grand Army, and the Republican party did not come about overnight. The historical evidence suggests that the issue of material benefits for the ex-soldiers did not emerge in partisan form until after the passage of the 1879 Arrears Act. That legislation simultaneously supported the organization of the Union veterans and their increased visibility to Republican politicians. For the Republicans, the pension issue provided three major political benefits. First, almost regardless of the legislative outcome, it provided a symbolic appeal to a central constituency of the party with a large membership of voters. Veterans were concentrated in the large eastern and midwestern states, and their votes could prove crucial in swinging the party balance. Second, the issue was one which

Table 6-1

Percentage of Total Federal Expenditures for Veteran Pensions and Number of Pension Recipients by Year

Fiscal Year Ending June	Percent of Expenditures for Pensions	Pension Recipients
1871	11.8	207,495
1872	10.3	232,189
1873	10.1	238,411
1874	9.6	236,241
1875	10.7	234,821
1876	10.7	232,137
1877	11.6	232,104
1878	11.5	223,998
1879	13.2	242,755
1880	21.2	250,802
1881	19.2	268,830
1882	23.8	285,697
1883	24.9	303,658
1884	22.7	322,756
1885	21.6	345,125
1886	26.1	365,783
1887	28.0	406,007
1888	30.0	452,557
1889	29.3	489,725
1890	33.6	537,944
1891	34.0	676,160
1892	39.0	876,068
1893	41.6	966,012
1894	38.4	969,544
1895	39.7	970,524
1896	39.6	970,678
1897	38.6	976,014
1898	33.3	993,714
1899	23.0	991,519

Source: U.S. Bureau of Pensions, *Report of the Commissioner of Pensions for the Year ending June 30, 1899,* p. 56.

severely divided the Democrats, particularly in the East and Midwest. Democrats, such as Congressman Matson of Indiana, often found it necessary to promise rewards to the veterans in order to gain (or at least not alienate) their votes. Such support aided the Republicans in enacting the 1890 legislation while it divided the Democratic party.

Finally, the Republican position on pensions aided the party in its position on what may have been the single most divisive issue of the era, the tariff. The Republican party consistently supported a high protective tariff to protect and develop American industries. One byproduct of this tariff wall was a huge governmental surplus in the federal treasury due to income from the customs houses. For example, in 1878 the government had surplus income of over $20 million, with the tariff providing over 50 percent of all revenue. Payments for arrears helped reduce the surplus to only $6.9 million in 1879, but, as Morton Keller notes, "(t)he most pressing fiscal problem of the 1880s was the large revenue surplus generated by rising tariff receipts."[18] An increasing surplus meant increasing Democratic pressure to reduce tariffs and provide for freer trade. Republican sponsorship of broader pension benefits promised to reduce or eliminate the nagging surplus at the same time it aided the veterans. The actual result was quite impressive, with the surplus reduced from $85 million in 1890 to about $27 million in 1891 and $9 million in 1892. Indeed, the national budget ran in the red from 1894 until 1900. The lack of any budgetary constraint, or the positive benefit of increasing government outlays, is a situation both critical to the pension program and unlikely to be repeated.[19]

The Executive Branch and Pensions

While Congress defined the general outline and scope of the pension system, responsibiity for the administration of the program, including the adjudication and payment of claims, fell on the Bureau of Pensions. The size of the Bureau grew with the increasing expenditures for pensions. By 1891, the Commissioner of Pensions could describe it as "the largest executive bureau in the world," including a clerical force of 2,000 in Washington, over 400 in the eighteen pensions agencies (responsible for actual payments), and 3,800 examining physicians spread across the country.[20]

The Bureau of Pensions was solely responsible for the fate of each individual pension claim, evaluating the evidence and information presented by each veteran. It was the bureau which defined the speed, order, and care with which claims were processed. This situation provided the potential for political manipulation of much of the pension system. As was the case with legislative action, it appears that little overt political manipulation took place until after the passage of the 1879 Arrears Act. The potential provided by the legislation was not lost on the new commissioner, W.W. Dudley, who took office in 1881 as President Garfield's appointee. While some contemporaries suggested that the appointment was a reward for Dudley's political services, his actions were calculated to aid the Republican cause. One historian has observed that "his one aim appears to have been that of building up a great political machine."[21]

Dudley pressed for increased personnel and more medical examiners in order to speed the processing of claims. He instructed the bureau to prepare a statement of the number of army enlistments from every state and the number of pension applications from both invalids and dependents. Of the total number of enlistees, only 26 percent had applied for pension benefits, leaving 1,000,469 ex-soldiers who had not yet filed a claim. Of the roughly three hundred thousand claims pending in 1882, over half came from the electorally critical states of Illinois, Indiana, Ohio, New York, and Pennsylvania. Obviously, the manner in which pending claims were handled had great promise for influencing elections.

Dudley moved to aid claimants by compiling a list of every surviving soldier of the Civil War, so that veterans could easily locate comrades and secure their testimony. The commissioner called on the Grand Army for aid, and after six months had acquired the names and addresses of over 189,000 veterans. This particular activity was cut short by Dudley's active participation in the presidential election of 1884.

Commissioner Dudley left Washington in September of 1884, and became a vital part of the Republican campaign organization in Ohio. It was charged that Dudley used his position in the bureau to foster Republican support in two ways. First, he instructed the clerks to reject no pension applications until after the election, so as to prevent any dissatisfaction among the veterans. Second, he ordered that the claims from Ohio and Indiana be taken before other outstanding claims. The Pension Bureau's records indicate that over five thousand pensions were allowed in Ohio and Indiana during the 1884 fiscal year, about 1,500 more than in the previous year.[22] Dudley's activities were not just confined to pension policy. He almost doubled the number of examiners in Ohio during September and October, and used them as organizers in the Republican campaign.

Dudley's activities proved fairly successful for the Republicans, and he moved into Indiana in an attempt to repeat them. Unfortunately for both the party and Dudley, Cleveland defeated Blaine. The commissioner resigned his post on November 10. The most interesting postscript to Dudley's peculiar version of public administration was provided by his Democratic successor, General John Black, in his annual report:

> At one time the Pension Bureau was all but avowedly a political machine, filled from border to border with the uncompromising adherents of a single organization, who had for the claimant other tests than those of the law, and who required, in addition to service in the field, submission to and support of a party before pensions were granted. . . . People of one faith filled every one of the great agencies. Examiners, trained in unscrupulous schools, traversed the land as recruiting sergeants for a party . . . leaves of absence were granted that the active men of the party might dominate over the elections . . . [23]

The actual impact of Commissioner Dudley's efforts on voting behavior in Indiana and Ohio is impossible to measure. His role as an innovator, in demonstrating the political potential of pensions administration, is quite clear. Dudley faced a situation which was characteristic of the Pension Bureau for the period from 1880 to the turn of the century. The monetary value of a pension to an individual veteran, particularly when arrears were included, was substantial. The performance and generosity of the Pension Bureau could cement the tie between the former soldier and the Republican party. The opportunity to build up that tie lay in the size of the claims backlog. The passage of the 1879 Arrears Act stimulated over 110,000 new pension claims in 1880 alone. Seven years later, roughly 42,000 of these claims were still pending, part of a backlog of unprocessed claims which totalled 374,354. By June of 1889, with increasing membership in the Grand Army of the Republic and a sympathetic Republican administration in office, new claims had brought the backlog to 479,008. The 1890 Act further stimulated new claims on pension funds, so that by 1892 the backlog stood at over 485,000.[24] The massive volume of pending pension claims throughout the period had two important effects. First, it provided wide discretion to the incumbent administration and the officers of the Pension Bureau. This discretion applied to the speed with which applications were processed, the states and communities from which they were drawn, and the rigor of the review (both medical and clerical). Second, the number of pending claims increased the pressures and benefits of faster processing. The Grand Army was continually demanding more funds and staff for the bureau, and these pressures supported Republican efforts to increase and spread pension benefits. A major effort to allow new claims and reduce the backlog also ensured the gratitude of those ex-soldiers whose applications had been held in abeyance for three or four or five years.

It is all but impossible to document the actual impact of the bureau's wide discretion on the processing of individual pension claims. It is possible to demonstrate the differences between Democratic and Republican administrations in their support of the Pension Bureau. Table 6-2 indicates the trends in the administrative expenditures of the bureau from 1879 to 1899, together with the party control of the executive branch. From 1879 to 1885, with a Republican in the White House, administrative spending increased rapidly—from $838,000 to over $3,393,000. During the first Cleveland administration, spending held steady at about $3.5 million. The Republican victory in 1888 and the 1890 Act brought a rapid increase, followed by a major drop in spending during Cleveland's second term. These trends parallel the changes in the number of employees authorized for the Pension Bureau. Changes in party control show a remarkable association with expenditure and staffing changes, with major increases in the bureau's resources under Republican administrations.

The record of Commissioner Dudley's administration stands out quite dramatically in the staffing figures. When Dudley assumed office in 1881, the Pension Bureau numbered 520 employees. By 1885, when control passed to the new Democratic administration, the bureau had grown to a total of 1,682.

Table 6-2
**Pension Bureau Administrative Expenditures, Employment, and
Presidential Party by Year**

Fiscal Year Ending June	Administrative Expenditures (in thousands)	Employees	Party
1879	$ 838	378	Rep.
1880	935	379	Rep.
1881	1,072	520	Rep.
1882	1,466	723	Rep.
1883	2,592	1,559	Rep.
1884	2,835	1,555	Rep.
1885	3,393	1,682	Rep./Dem.[a]
1886	3,245	1,682	Dem.
1887	3,753	1,554	Dem.
1888	3,515	1,554	Dem.
1889	3,467	1,554	Dem./Rep.
1890	3,526	1,554	Rep.
1891	4,700	2,009	Rep.
1892	4,899	2,009	Rep.
1893	4,868	2,009	Rep./Dem.
1894	3,964	2,009	Dem.
1895	4,338	2,005	Dem.
1896	3,991	1,836	Dem.
1897	3,988	1,836	Dem./Rep.
1898	4,114	1,836	Rep.
1899	4,147	1,741	Rep.

Source: U.S. Bureau of the Census, *Historical Statistics of the U.S., Part 2*, and U.S. Bureau of Pensions, *Report of the Commissioner of Pensions for the Year ending June 30, 1899*, p. 102.

[a]Slash indicates change in presidential party during fiscal year.

The administrative budget and staffing of the Bureau of Pensions provided only the inputs for its processing of claims. The Grand Army and the veterans were most concerned with the bureau's decisions on pending claims and pension awards. The record of invalid claims actually allowed by the bureau is shown in table 6-3. This table does not include pensions for widows or dependents because these were affected by legislation in the mid-1880s which did not affect the much larger number of veterans. The passage of the Arrears Act and the administration of Commissioner Dudley brought about a fourfold increase in allowed claims from 1878 to 1883. A slight decrease in 1884 and 1885 (which may be explained by the drop in the number of new applications filed in those years) was followed by a modest increase in the rate of new claims under Cleveland. The shift to Republican administrative control in March of 1889 brought about a rapid increase in new claims payments. It should be noted that the increase occured *prior* to the passage of broader pension legislation in June 1890. The new legislation

Table 6-3
Number of Army and Navy Invalid Claims Approved and Presidential
Party by Year

Fiscal Year Ending June	Claims Approved	Party
1878	7,414	Rep.
1879	7,242	Rep.
1880	10,176	Rep.
1881	21,394	Rep.
1882	22,946	Rep.
1883	32,014	Rep.
1884	27,414	Rep.
1885	27,580	Rep./Dem.[b]
1886	31,937	Dem.
1887	35,283	Dem.
1888	35,843	Dem.
1889	36,830	Dem./Rep.
1890	50,395	Rep.
1891	129,992[a]	Rep.
1892	180,772	Rep.
1893	72,523	Rep./Dem.
1894	14,939	Dem.
1895	22,855	Dem.
1896	22,853	Dem.
1897	27,574	Dem./Rep.
1898	32,517	Rep.
1899	20,500	Rep.

Source: U.S. Bureau of Pensions, *Report of the Commissioner of Pensions for the Year ending June 30, 1899,* p. 57.

Note: The term "invalid" refers to pensions for physical disabilities.

[a]Figures for claims approved in 1891 and after include claims under the Act of 1890.

[b]Slash indicates change in presidential party during fiscal year.

encouraged a flurry of new claims and a vast increase in approved claims, peaking in 1892. The shift back to the Democrats in early 1893 brought a dramatic decrease in allowed claims. The final partisan shift in the nineteenth century, in 1897, caused a final increase in the approval volume.

An indication of the relative treatment of pension claims can be provided by the ratio of approved claims to rejected claims. The rejection of a pension claim was not necessarily indicative of its ultimate fate, as rejected claims could be reinstated. The ratio does, however, suggest something of the Pension Bureau's willingness to accept the claims of the ex-soldiers. During the period of Republican control from 1881 to 1885, the approval rate averaged 74.9 percent annually. The high point of relative approvals came in 1881, with 88.9 percent, although the Republicans ended their tenure with a 75.1 percent rate. During the Democratic period under Cleveland, relative approvals dropped to 69.2 percent. Republican administration from 1889 until 1892 brought an annual average approval rate of 78.9 percent.[25]

The annual statistics on pension approvals suggest that partisan forces played a large role in the bureau's handling of claims. A more discriminating test of partisan influence can be made with the pension approval rate on a monthly basis, for those years in which control of the executive branch changed hands. Such a test can be illustrated with the figures for fiscal year 1889. That year began in July of 1888, with Democratic control until February 1889. In March 1889 the Republicans came into office. For the eight months' operation under Democratic control, 20,448 invalid pensions were approved—an average of 2,556 per month. Excluding the March figures (which were undoubtedly affected by the administrative change), the bureau approved 12,979 claims in April, May and June—an average of 4,326 per month.[26]

The failure of the Republicans to retain the White House after the 1892 election brought about another partisan shift and another change in the leadership of the Pension Bureau. During their tenure from July 1892 until February 1893, the Republicans approved an average of 6,574 pension claims per month. With Democratic occupancy from April through June of 1893, the approvals averaged only 734 per month. The enormous decrease in new pension allowances under Cleveland was not simply the result of a slow start on pension administration. Approvals averaged only about 700 per month during fiscal 1894.[27]

The final partisan shift of the century came following the 1896 elections. Democratic performance in the eight months prior to March 1897 yielded a monthly approval rate averaging 1,801 claims. Republican control in the last three months of the fiscal year brought the rate up to an average of 2,231, a level of activity which continued for the next twelve months.[28]

The impact of partisanship on administration of the pensions system is clear and consistent in each of the three test cases. A shift from Democratic to Republican control brought an immediate increase in pension approvals. A return of power to the Democrats resulted in a marked drop in the approval rate. The political parties could, and did, use administrative control to shape the outcomes of pension decisions.

By the decade of the 1890s, the partisan shape of pensions administration was clear. The Republicans pressed for a greater output and more resources for the bureau, to better reduce the claims backlog and distribute the benefits of pensions. They called for the most generous benefits and the most lenient review. The Democrats were left to protect the pension list as a "roll of honor," protesting improper decisions by previous administrations, and searching out and publicizing fraud and abuse. This difference in administrative styles is perhaps best illustrated by the implementation of the Act of 1890. The legislation provided pensions from $6 to $12 per month, graded on the "degree of inability to earn a support."[29] The Republican administration issued a directive (Order No. 164) basing the rates on the existing scheme for service-incurred disabilities. Pension applicants were also allowed to combine the benefits for several minor impairments so as to increase the total pension. The Republicans had provided for a more generous interpretation of the 1890 law.[30]

Such a generous mechanism for pension allowances did not sit well with the Democrats who assumed office in early 1893. The new Democratic Commissioner of Pensions stated in the Bureau's *Annual Report* for 1893,

> It is perfectly clear that under this order 164 in granting pensions under this act of June 27, 1890, the act itself was set aside and disregarded, with the result of granting pensions not authorized by any law. . . . The statement of the medical referee . . . made it appear probably that under order 164 many pensions were illegally granted.[31]

The bureau established a review committee to reconsider the pensions allowed under the now-defunct order. By 1894 the commissioner could report that 5,600 pensions were either reduced or completely eliminated. The following year saw the reduction of payments to 22,500 pension recipients and the dropping of over 4,100 from the rolls. Democratic vigilance and a desire to protect the sanctity of the federal treasury clearly prevailed over the electoral power of the ex-soldiers.[32]

During his tenure as Commissioner of Pensions, W.W. Dudley provided a model of the partisan use of pensions administration. His performance was not lost on the Republican party. The party used its occupancy of the White House as a vehicle for boosting the outputs and generosity of the Pension Bureau, fulfilling the demands of the organized veterans and its political needs. If the Republicans were able to create an enduring alliance with the ex-soldiers and build a national political machine, it was largely because they were willing and able to employ the pension bureaucracy in a partisan fashion. For the individual veteran, the choice was obvious. The Republicans promised increased support for the bureau and a more generous administration of pensions, and actually delivered more pensions than the partisan opposition. Electoral support for Republican candidates promised a better pension, delivered more quickly.

Pensions—A Statistical View

Commissioner Dudley's entrepreneurship, Cleveland's vetoes, and Harrison's promises all supported the position of the Republican party as the party of the veteran and the struggler for pensions. Yet, the comments of political contemporaries, particularly Democrats, suggest that the "party of the Union" was motivated by more than emotion and sentiment. Histories of pension legislation carry innumerable references to the political machine fostered and developed by pensions. The question of the actual electoral impact of pensions remains unanswered. This section will provide at least a partial answer.

From 1886 until 1890, the Bureau of Pensions reported the number of pensions and the dollar amount of pensions on a county-by-county basis for the United States. These data represent a unique resource for testing the performance of the Republican machine. For present purposes, the pensions data for the eighty-eight counties of Ohio were excerpted and keypunched. Ohio was chosen as a test case for a number of reasons. It was highly competitive on a regular basis throughout the 1880s and 1890s. For example, less than 1 percent of the vote divided the party in the 1888 presidential race, with a similar margin in 1884. Both parties finished almost even in 1892, with roughly 405,000 votes for each. The period was also marked by high participation and voter turnout in Ohio, with turnout rates of 91.9 percent in 1888, 86.2 percent in 1892, and 95.5 percent in 1896. It was seen by both parties as a critical state, and they lavished much attention on it. Finally, it had substantial populations of veterans and pension recipients. The state included 57,087 pensioners in 1890, more than any other state in the country.[33]

The measure of pensions at the county level is the number of pension recipients divided by the county population in 1890. The Pension Bureau reports combine invalid and dependent pensions of all types, so the recipient figures include widows as well as veterans. Figures for the number of veterans as of 1890, again adjusted for county population size, will also be examined. Finally, a number of variables from state and national census reports and election returns will also be discussed.[34]

The remainder of the discussion is concerned exclusively with Ohio, and is divided into two sections. The first examines the pattern of distribution of pensions within the state, while the second attempts to define the electoral impact of the pension system.

The balance of the analysis of pensions will focus on a single measure, the total number of pensioners per capita in 1890. The pension distribution varies from five recipients per thousand population in urban Cuyahoga County (which includes the immigrant population of Cleveland), t a high of thirty-three pensioners per thousand in Montgomery County (which includes Dayton). The average is eighteen pension recipients per thousand. This variable correlates with the number of pensioners per capita in 1886 at .889. Both variables appear very similar, and there are no substantial differences in their correlations with other measures discussed below. Of these other measures, 1890 pensions per capita has its highest correlation (.54) with the percent of the county population in 1890 that was native-born. There is a similar correlation with the percent of males over twenty-one, native-born. In addition, there is a negative relationship with population change from 1870 to 1880 (− .30), and with population change from 1880 to 1890 (− .35). There is another significant negative relationship with an index of urbanism, the percent of families in homes rather than on farms.

Generally, pensions were distributed to predominantly rural, Anglo-Saxon areas, with high population stability. These were areas of Republican strength, and 1890 pensions correlate positively with a variety of votes for Republican candidates, in both state and national elections.

A number of recent analyses of voting patterns in the Midwest during this period have emphasized the importance of religious differences. The major distinction employed is between "pietistic" and "liturgical" religions.[35] The pensions variable shows a significant negative correlation with one of the major pietistic groups, the Catholics ($-.47$). Similarly, there is a significant positive relationship with percent Baptist (.40), a major liturgical group. Pensions are also related negatively to per capita personal property, or wealth ($-.32$). It thus appears that pensions were highest in areas of Republican bias, and were distributed in a way that served to reflect the demographic correlates of Republicanism.

Pension increases follow the pattern noted for the 1890 variable. The increase correlates positively with 1886 pensions, indicating that the new pensions were going to areas already high in pensions per capita. The increase also correlates substantially with native-born population (.51), negatively with urbanism ($-.21$), negatively with Catholic population ($-.43$), positively with the proportion of Baptists (.45), negatively with wealth ($-.37$), and positively with measures of Republican voting. Thus, pension increases from 1886 to 1890 tended to reinforce a pre-existing bias toward Republican areas in Ohio. There is no question that the distribution of pensions favored the Republicans' electoral efforts.

One further element of pensions distribution remains. Distribution not only affected voting, but also probably exerted a pressure on voting turnout. The material incentives involved would give the voter a larger stake in the outcome of the election, and motivate him to vote. The intense partisan division of the times also created an incentive for both parties to maximize turnout. The 1890 pensions measure has a substantial correlation with turnout: .39 with the 1888 presidential election, .394 with the 1893 gubernatorial election. In addition, the 1886-1890 increase is significantly related to turnout, including a correlation of .43 with voting in the 1893 Ohio gubernatorial race.

The direct impact of the pension system on voting patterns is the most important question to be examined here. As before, the county-level data on voting and pensions for Ohio will be used. While the previous section indicated a positive relationship between pensions and Republican voting, some of this relationship may be due to their common relation to other independent variables. For example, the Republican vote is higher in native-born areas and lower in Catholic areas, and pensions are negatively associated with percent Catholic and positively related to percent native-born. An appropriate procedure for dealing with this problem is to examine the relationship between pensions and vote, controlling for other independent variables, with multiple regression analysis. Three sets of analyses were performed. First, pensions per capita in 1890 was related to a series of Republican votes (president in 1892, 1896; governor in 1893 and 1895), controlling for percent of males foreign-born; percent of males colored; percent foreign-born in Ireland; percent from England, Scotland, and Wales; percent from Germany; percent nonfarm families; value of personal property per capita; and percent Methodist. The results of these regressions are quite similar, and can be reported briefly. The regressions explain between 50 and 60 percent of the variance in Republican voting in each case. For example, in the 1892 presidential election, about 56 percent of the total variance is explained, with pensions the third most important variable (of 9), significant at the .001 level.

The initial regression results indicate that pensions had a positive relationship with Republican voting that cannot be explained by other measures or controlled away. However, given the modest proportion of variance explained by all of the independent variables, it seems entirely possible that an outside variable could be causing the pension results. Therefore a second series of regressions was run, using only pensions and the vote for Grant in 1868 as independent variables.

The strategy involved in this test was to use a general summary measure of party loyalty and vote which would be highly related to Republican voting in the 1880s, yet temporally prior to it, and isolated from the pension issues. The Grant vote was chosen for these reasons. It was correlated at over .90 with every later partisan vote.

The results of the analyses for 1892, 1893, and 1896 are presented in table 6-4. Both the Grant vote and pensions are able to explain a large percentage of the vote for Republican candidates. The impact of the pensions measure remains statistically significant in all cases. The actual impact of pensions on the partisan division can be estimated for 1892 using the regression coefficient for the pension measure, which excludes the influence of traditional Republican support. In a county (Cuyahoga) with the lowest level of pension recipients, the Republicans gained above 1.3 percent in the vote. At an average rate of pension participation, the Republicans received an additional 4.8 percent. Finally, at the highest values of pension distribution by county, 8.9 percent was added to the Republicans' share.

A final test of pension can be made by controlling one additional confounding influence: the county-by-county distribution of union veterans. A series of regressions, paralleling those discussed above but also including the number of veterans per capita, were run. These results are shown in table 6-5. With the exception of the 1893 Ohio gubernatorial contest, the impact of pensions continues to be statistically significant, even when controlling for the size of the veteran population.[36]

It now seems reasonable to reach some general conclusions about pensions

Table 6-4
Regression Analyses of Republican Voting

Variable	Coefficient	Standard Error	T
1892 presidential election—Harrison percentage			
Republican percentage 1868	0.69	0.03	23.61[a]
Pension per capita 1890	2.69	0.18	4.63[a]
$R^2 = 0.88$			
N = 88			
1896 presidential election—McKinley percentage			
Republican percentage 1868	0.71	0.04	19.60[a]
Pensions per capita 1890	1.46	0.73	2.02[c]
$R^2 = 0.83$			
N = 88			
1893 gubernatorial election—McKinley percentage			
Republican percentage 1868	0.75	0.03	25.60[c]
Pensions per capita 1890	1.46	0.58	2.51
$R^2 = 0.89$			
N = 88			

Significance level: [a] = .001, [b] = .01, [c] = .05

and voting in Ohio. It appears that pensions had an appreciable impact on voting, particularly in 1892. The impact took the form of raising the Republican vote beyond that which would be expected given the partisan division of 1868. In addition, pensions did not affect the level of turnout beyond what could be expected. Therefore, the distribution of these material incentives supported the Republican party without causing a general increase in turnout and possibly a Democratic backlash. Pension benefits were distributed unequally to Republican strongholds, particularly rural, nativist areas, with increases in pensions supporting this pattern.

Summary

Perhaps the most important conclusion supported by this paper about the pension system is its demonstrable impact on partisan voting in Ohio. The use of a single state in a limited time period must limit the strength of these conclusions. Still, it is apparent that the system of distributing material incentives like pensions contributed to Republican electoral success in a number of elections. The fact that material incentives influence voting will come as no surprise to the student of urban political machines. However, the evidence for the power of material incentives and political organization to affect voting comes at a very low level. The significance of the pensions system lies in its operation from a national level, highly removed from the

Table 6-5

Regression Analyses of Republican Voting, including Veterans, Per Capita

Variable	Coefficient	Standard Error	T
1892 presidential election—Harrison percentage			
Republican percentage 1868	0.68	0.03	22.76[a]
Pensions per capita 1890	1.82	0.75	2.42[c]
Veterans per capita	1.24	0.70	1.77
$R^2 = 0.88$			
N = 88			
1896 presidential election—McKinley percentage			
Republican percentage 1868	0.72	0.04	19.16[a]
Pensions per capita 1890	1.95	0.96	2.04[c]
Veterans per capita	−0.70	0.89	−0.79
$R^2 = 0.83$			
N = 88			
1893 gubernatorial election—McKinley percentage			
Republican percentage 1868	0.74	0.03	24.60[a]
Pensions per capita 1890	1.15	0.70	1.50
Veterans per capita	0.45	0.77	0.63
$R^2 = 0.89$			
N = 88			

Significance level: [a] = .001, [b] = .01, [c] = .05

individual voter, but with an effect on a large class of voters. While the national pensions policy may have supported a machine, it did not create one directly. That is, pensions probably had their greatest impact where they were supervised or controlled by an active political organization, or where social organization on a local level reinforced their impact. The Grand Army of the Republic was the epitome of such an organization. While data are not available to fully analyze this relationship, it is quite likely that pensions were most effective in areas with large, cohesive, and enduring GAR organizations, where veterans found their beliefs supported and reinforced.

The total impact of pensions was thus tied to a system of political and social organization. Some observers have attempted to explain the high levels of popular participation in the post-Civil War period on the basis of regular and bipartisan fraud which inflated vote tallies. A more plausible explanation is that the combination of widely distributed material incentives and local-level social and political organization tied individuals to the political system in a way never found since.

In contrast to the impact of pensions as material benefits, the pension as a political issue has been given a great deal of attention by historians. The issue did not develop until some years after the end of the Civil War. Its full impact did not come until after the passage of the 1879 Arrears Act. The 1890s saw an increasing divergence in party position and an increasing specificity of Republican promises. The 1880s also saw an explosive growth in organization of veterans, as shown in table 6-6. The increasing membership probably affected the development of the pension issue in two ways. First, it increased the visibility and saliency of veterans as a voting group, particularly to their traditional party. Second, it helped generate more demands for pension legislation and better claims-processing by the Pension Bureau.

Historical accounts suggest that pension demands and the pension issue reached their peak in 1888 with the Harrison-Cleveland battle, and such actions as Cleveland's pension bill vetoes and his return of Confederate battle flags. The experience of 1888 also suggests that the pension issue rarely had to stand alone. It was related to a series of sectional, economic, and social conflicts, from the cronyism of the Grand Army to the "waving of the bloody shirt." It is thus difficult to attribute a specific impact to pensions alone. There is, however, no question about partisan positions on pensions and related issues. The Republicans consistently cast themselves in the role of protector of veterans' interests. As a result, without regard to material incentives, pension questions were political issues.

One of the most outstanding characteristics of the history of pension legislation following the Civil War was the amount of time it involved. The first major postwar change, the arrears bill, came in 1879, fourteen years after the war. The Disability Pension Act, representing the first major

Table 6-6
Grand Army of the Republic Membership by Year

Year	Members
1878	31,016
1879	44,752
1880	60,634
1881	85,856
1882	134,701
1883	215,446
1884	273,168
1885	294,787
1886	323,571
1887	355,916
1888	372,960
1889	397,974
1890	409,781
1891	407,781
1892	399,880
1893	397,223
1894	369,083
1895	357,639
1896	340,610
1897	319,456

change in eligibility, came twenty-five years later. This twenty-five-year period was not characterized by a gradual and persistent movement for change, but by an irregular, episodic flow of proposals, pressures, and occasional legislation. The administrative arena was often the most salient to the individual veteran, concerned about claim and benefits. In this area the first breakthrough in the use of pensions for political purposes was the result of one man, Pension Commissioner Dudley.

That legislative developments came so slowly is even more remarkable in light of the environment of public policy making. While both parties generally supported distributive actions, the Republican party was wedded to a program of distribution. Tariffs were probably the best example. The congressional party would spend weeks haggling over the duties and restrictions on individual products from tar to hemp. Each good was bargained over individually, with the process designed to protect specific industrial and commercial interests.

Presumably the intense political competition of the era would stimulate Republican action on pensions, making their failure to move strongly even more difficult to understand. While the situation was complex, some initial answers can be suggested. The Republicans often lacked the political control of House, Senate, and presidency required for broad pension legislation. Although pensions policy divided the congressional Democrats and added opposition party to the Republicans' pro-pension proposals, they were often not enough. Another persistent issue in legislative consideration of pensions was *cost*. Pensions, particularly after arrears, represented a large budgetary outlay. Indeed, present evidence shows that the increase in spending caused by the liberal legislation of 1890 was striking. The Republicans were faced with two problems in the early postwar period. They might provide pensions at a cost or harm to some other useful distributive program; on the other hand, the expansion of the pension grant could raise Democratic cries of unwarranted expenditures and national bankruptcy. The major part of this dilemma was resolved by the tariff. As the Republicans solidified a protective tariff wall around the country, duties brought in unnecessary revenues that produced a surplus in the federal treasury. Pensions could then be provided with no cost to other programs, and with additional positive effects relating to the decrease of an embarrassing surplus.

Despite the generous platform position of the Republicans and their success in supporting new pension legislation, the strong tie between ex-soldiers and the Republican party might not have been cemented without partisan direction of the Bureau of Pensions. The success of a pension claim, the speed of review, and the generosity of payments were all subject to administrative discretion and partisan influence. Just as the Republican party needed to be assured of the loyal and enthusiastic support of the veterans as it sought new adherents, so the veteran needed the bias and favor of a Republican administration. This national machine could reward both its leaders and its followers.

Notes

1. U.S. Bureau of the Census, *Historical Statistics of the U.S., Part 2*, 1975, pp. 1106, 1149.

2. Richard Jensen, *The Winning of the Midwest* (Chicago: University of Chicago Press, 1975), p. 74.

3. Wallace Davies, *Patriotism on Parade* (Cambridge: Harvard University Press, 1955), p. 74.

4. The balance of this section relies on John Oliver, "History of Civil War Pensions, 1861-1885," *Bulletin of the University of Wisconsin* (History Series, 1, 1917) p. 4; and William Glasson, *Federal Military Pensions in the United States* (New York: Oxford University Press, 1918), pp. 124-421.

5. Edward McPherson, *A Handbook of Politics for 1880* (Washington: James Chapman, 1880), pp. 51-54, 74-76.

6. U.S. Bureau of Pensions, *Report of the Commissioner of Pensions for the Year Ending June 30, 1891*, pp. 72-73; Glasson, *Federal Military Pensions*, p. 203; Grand Army of the Republic, *Journal of the 31st National Encampment*, 1897, p. 92.

7. Kirk Porter and Donald Johnson, *National Party Platforms* (Urbana: University of Illinois Press, 1956), pp. 51, 54.

8. Ibid., p. 61.

9. Ibid., pp. 66, 73-74.

10. Ibid., pp. 77, 82.

11. Donald McMurray, "The Political Significance of the Pension Question," *Mississippi Valley Historical Review* 9(1922):28.

12. Ibid., p. 30.

13. Ibid., p. 32.

14. Edward McPherson, *A Handbook of Politics*, p. 69.

15. Ibid., pp. 119-127.

16. Grand Army of the Republic, *Journal of the 22nd National Encampment*, 1888, pp. 190-191.

17. Pensions Bureau, *1891 Report*, pp. 3-34.

18. Morton Keller, *Affairs of State* (Cambridge: Harvard University Press, 1977), p. 381.

19. Census Bureau, *Historical Statistics*, p. 1104.

20. Green Raum, "Pensions and Patriotism," *North American Review* 153(1891):211, in *The Republican Era* edited by Leonard White (New York: Free Press, 1958), p. 211.

21. Oliver, "History of Pensions," p. 106. The balance of this section relies on Oliver.

22. This increase of allowances for Indiana and Ohio came despite a decrease in the total number of invalid claims allowed.

23. Pensions Bureau, *1885 Report*, p. 111.

24. Pensions Bureau, *1892 Report*, pp. 90-91, 102-103.

25. Ibid., pp. 104-105. This particular statistical series was discontinued after 1892.

26. Pensions Bureau, *1889 Report*, p. 30.

27. Pensions Bureau, *1893 Report*, p. 43.

28. Pensions Bureau, *1897 Report*, p. 25.

29. McPherson, *1890 Handbook*, p. 126.

30. Glasson, *Federal Military Pensions*, p. 239.

31. Pensions Bureau, *1893 Report*, p. 6.

32. U.S. Bureau of Pensions, *Report . . . for the Year Ending June 30, 1895*, p. 7.

33. Census Bureau, *Historical Statistics*, pp. 1072, 1079.

34. Figures for pension recipients are taken from the annual *Report of the Commissioner of Pensions*. Figures for veterans are based on the 1890 Census and are taken from the Grand Army of the Republic, Department of Ohio, *Report of the Annual Encampment, 1891*, pp. 165-166. Population statistics are taken from the U.S. Bureau of the Census, *Census of Population* for 1890, *Census of Religious Bodies*, for 1890. The term *invalid* refers to pensions for physical disabilities.

35. Jensen, *Winning of the Midwest*, pp. 58-88; Paul Kleppner, *The Cross of Culture* (New York: Free Press, 1970), pp. 36-90. The religion variables are based on the number of church members by denomination and total church members reported in the 1890 *Census of Religious Bodies*.

36. An alternative procedure for eliminating the effects of traditional Republicanism would include an election relatively close in time to the date of dependent variable. Analyses run with the 1884 Republican vote rather than the 1868 vote continue to show a statistically significant effect for pensions on the 1892 vote division.

7 Fiscal Redistribution and State Spending Differentials: The United States from a Comparative Perspective

John M. Echols III

Introduction

It is no revelation to anyone that tremendous differentials exist in public spending levels across the American states. If you live in New York, you will enjoy much higher expenditures per capita on everything from education to highways than would be the case if you were in Mississippi. An entire literature has been built up around these differentials and the effort to explain them. Most of these studies have involved attempts to assess the impact of a variety of political factors on state or state and local expenditure levels. The first several attempts proved unsuccessful, as scholars discovered that by far the best variable that could differentiate state spending was, logically enough, the income of the state. Once that variable was controlled, relationships with such factors as the degree of party competition and the level of malapportionment fell to insignificance (see, for example, Dawson and Robinson, 1963; and Dye, 1966).

Since that time, several analyses have appeared that have uncovered some relationships between various political variables and expenditure levels. Scholars have found that, under certain conditions, political factors do seem to relate to certain expenditure patterns—for example, in a positive correlation between degree of party competition and welfare spending (see Cnudde and McCrone, 1969; Sharkansky and Hofferbert, 1969; and Carmines, 1974; for an exception to these findings, see Lewis-Beck, 1976). Yet even these studies have not substantially eroded the basic finding of a strong relationship between state expenditure levels and income, a relationship that these scholars explain, for the most part, by the imperatives of wealth: those that have, spend. New York is richer than Mississippi, thus it can raise and spend more.

A number of people have provided valuable comments on earlier drafts of this paper. I would like to thank Larry Cohen, Doris Graber, Gerry Strom, and, especially, Valerie Bunce and Barry Rundquist. I would also like to thank Kathleen Spoat and the Office of Social Science Research at Chicago Circle for typing assistance.

However, in this search for explanations, virtually all of these analysts have focused their attention solely on the state and local level. In doing so, they have neglected what some critics have been pointing out for several years now, that state and local policymaking does not take place in a vacuum. Rather, it occurs in the context of a national political system, and especially a federal government that, at least potentially, has a major say in what happens at subnational levels (Sachs and Harris, 1964; Osman, 1968; Fritschler and Segal, 1972; Rose, 1973; and Strouse and Jones, 1974). Several of these scholars have demonstrated, for example, the impact of federal aid on state spending. Given this impact, it is reasonable to ask whether the federal government may not be playing a role in the persistence of these spending differentials and their relationship to state income. That, in fact, is precisely what will be argued in this paper, that Washington does play a role, indeed the major role. Specifically, I will contend that the relationship between state spending and state income does not reflect state economic imperatives, as the present literature suggests, but rather decisions by federal government bodies to maintain that relationship by not redistributing funds through federal aid programs from richer to poorer states. In other words, the state income-spending relationship is highly dependent upon policy choices made in Washington concerning the distribution of federal aid.

I will attempt in this paper not only to set out this basic point concerning the federal government's impact on state expenditure differentials, but also to (1) demonstrate that Washington could rather easily break, or at least substantially reduce, the income-spending relationship if different policies were adopted; and (2) explain why this is not done; that is, why the federal government does not redistribute.

The Need for Comparative Analysis

In order to pursue these tasks, we will, of course examine the American case in some depth, analyzing the impact, both real and potential, of federal aid on state spending. However, in order to explain the American position on fiscal redistribution, as well as to further illustrate the American findings, it will be necessary to study patterns in other countries as well. Thus, in the latter part of the paper, we will present data and discuss intergovernmental fiscal redistribution in six other political systems: Australia, Canada, East Germany, Japan, Poland, and the Soviet Union. The selection of these particular systems necessarily reflects a consideration of the factors that might explain the American pattern—more generally, that might relate to whether or not a country redistributes aid from richer to poorer regions. Three variables were settled upon as plausibly important factors. Two of these center on important features of the American polity, its federal and democratic nature, while the third involves the impact of particular historical and environmental factors.

The Impact of Federalism

The argument concerning federalism is primarily that a system in which power is relatively dispersed will be less likely to redistribute than a system in which power is more concentrated. As J.R. Hicks puts it, the question of regional equality of public expenditures

> . . . is an issue that arises in unitary states as well as in federations; there is, however, a presumption that uniformity will be more easy to secure in a unitary state, where there are no "states rights" to be invoked in defense of a privileged position. . . . It is indeed arguable that the choice of a federal form of government is a prima facie indicator that the requisite degree of unity does not exist. (1961, pp. 72, 73)

David Cameron and Richard Hofferbert elaborate this point very well:

> Federalism ensures considerable variation in policy performance among the subnational units. Not only are there multiple layers of authority and numerous decision points, but decision makers at the subnational level have substantial autonomy. The effect of multiple levels and units of decision-making, each characterized by a degree of autonomy, is likely to be the perpetuation of policy diversity in federal systems. The overall effect would be wide territorial variation in the total funds allocated to education. . . . Centralization should encourage, in contrast to the situation in federal systems, uniformity and equality of output across the nation. (1974, p. 233)

James Buchanan even goes so far as to suggest that "if there were only one fiscal system, as there would be in a unitary form of government, regional differentiation in standards of public services and/or burdens of taxation would not exist" (1950, p. 585). While this is an extreme expectation, it does illustrate the feeling that the federal nature of the American system, with its relative emphasis on "states' rights" and, thus, greater acceptance of state diversity, goes a long way toward explaining the American federal aid distribution pattern.

The Impact of a Democracy

The other important aspect of the American polity that may relate to its distribution pattern is that it is a democratic state. Very simply, the expectation is that communist states will be much more redistributive than their western counterparts. Support for this hypothesis rests on the twin grounds of ideology and capacity, the desire to act and the ability to act. The first reflects the fact that equality is a fundamental Marxist concern—some say, in fact, it is its "basic principle" (Kernig, 1972, p. 213); and this principle, as several Marxist scholars have reiterated, clearly includes the dimension we are examining:

> (The Leninist) decision on the national problem called for the implementation of a whole system of measures toward the goal of equalizing the level of development of all the peoples of various nationalities and furthering the rise of their economy and culture. . . . In the distribution of both total budgetary resources and those for socio-cultural activities, it is obviously necessary to take into account the further equalization of the development of all union republics. (Kolomin and Shirkevich, 1972, pp. 23, 31)

This ideological concern is reinforced by a purportedly greater control on the part of the center over the means necessary for redistribution. As Z.L. Melnyk puts it for the Soviet Union,

> The almost complete centralization of economic planning and control in the U.S.S.R. permits the authorities in Moscow to impose their priorities and to demand total compliance with them in the fulfillment of the centrally-envisioned goals. This dominant position of the central government is further assured by a fiscal system that is strongly biased in favor of the central authorities. . . . As a result the central government can redistribute income and wealth within the U.S.S.R. according to its wishes and without respect to the desires and needs of the local population. (1973, p. 106)

The United States represents the other side of the coin. "States' rights" is a more important component of the political culture than regional equality, and power is not nearly as concentrated. Thus, Norton Long writes that "the program of the President cannot be a Gosplan because the nature of his institutional and group support gives him insufficient power" (1962, p. 56). One Soviet scholar, in fact, argues that regional inequality is "inherent" in capitalist systems, attributing it in large part to the "unplanned and spontaneous nature" of these systems (Pavlov, 1971).

The Impact of the Historical and Environmental Context

The final variable that we expect to play a role reflects factors peculiar to specific nations. Historical developments, in particular, will in all likelihood explain part of the American pattern; as Wallace Oates suggests, "the fiscal structure of a particular country is no doubt the result largely of the unique political and social history of that nation" (1972, p. vi; also see Willner and Nichols, 1973, p. 33; and Birch, 1955, p. 239). Historical events set certain precedents that are difficult to break out of, as patterns become routinized and accepted as natural. Thus, we shall examine these and other contextual variables after we have seen how much the two more general factors are able to explain.

The Methodology

The selection of countries, then, was made with an eye to obtaining a sampling of federal, unitary, democratic, and communist nations, all with varying historical and environmental contexts. The purpose, of course, is to provide several matching cases for each of the variables, or as Arend Lijphart calls them, "comparable cases," that is, similar in a large number of important characteristics (variables) which one wants to treat as a constant, but dissimilar as far as those variables are concerned which one wants to relate to each other (1971, p. 687). The sample provides several of these comparable cases for each variable.

The data and techniques of analysis employed are rather straightforward and will be explained as necessary. Generally, we wish to examine the extent to which fiscal aid from the center to subnational units in these countries is distributed in a progressive manner, and what impact that has on spending patterns. We will focus in each case on the highest subnational political units (provinces in Canada, republics in the Soviet Union, and so forth), and employ as our data base aid to, and expenditures by, all units within those regions. We begin with the American cause.

The Distribution of Federal Aid in the United States

The basic point, that the United States does not use federal aid as a redistributive tool, can be illustrated quite easily. In table 7-1, we present the correlations for several years between the personal income (per capita) of the American states, and the sum total, whether in the form of conditional grants, bloc grants, or revenue sharing, of federal aid (per capita) to all governments that the states receive. It is readily apparent that at no time in the last forty-odd years has there been a negative *and* significant relationship between aid and state income—no effort, in other words, to aid poorer states disproportionately. While there has been an undeniably large degree

Table 7-1

Correlations between Per Capita Federal Aid to State and Local Governments and Per Capita State Personal Income

Year	R
1932	.03
1942	.03
1957	− .16
1962	− .10
1967	− .22
1970	− .18
1973	− .06
N = 48	

Source: U.S. Bureau of the Census, *Statistical Abstract of the United States*, 1959:311; 1965:334; 1972:319, 418; 1974:730; *Census of Governments* 6:5 (56-107); 6:5 vol. 6 no. 5, pp. 56-107; 167: vol. 6 no. 5, pp. 63-114; 133 (63-114, 133, *Government Finances in 1972-1973*: 45; and *Financing Federal, State and Local Governments, 1941* (State and Local Special Study No. 20, 1942): 124-128.

of variation from state to state in the amount of aid that each receives (for instance, in 1973, per capita aid to Indiana was $130, while Vermont received $310 and Wyoming $346), this variation is not related to the wealth of a state.

If we examine specific areas and programs, we can occasionally locate high negative relationships, especially in recent years. Thus, for example, federal aid to education in 1970 correlated − .54 with state income (up from − .02 in 1962). However, though the correlation is high, the actual amounts involved are so small relative to total state and local expenditures on education that the impact of this redistribution is scarcely noticeable.

To examine that impact, or, more precisely, the lack of it, we present some additional data in table 7-2. The data show two clear patterns: (1) the correlations of revenues and expenditures with personal income remain as high as ever; yet, (2) the variation between rich and poor states, as measured by the coefficient of variation,[1] is declining over time. Though rich states continue to spend a great deal more than poor ones, equalization is, or perhaps more appropriately, was, taking place. However, as the coefficients in table 7-1 make clear, this trend cannot be attributed to federal aid policy. Rather, fiscal equalization is instead tied to the income equalization that has been going on. As the resource gap declines, logically enough, so does the expenditure gap—note particularly the striking changes during World War II, when federal grants were at their lowest levels in the last forty years—and federal aid cannot be credited with helping to close either of these.[2]

Table 7-2

Coefficients of Variation and Correlations with State Per Capita Income for All State Revenues and Education Expenditures, Per Capita

Variable	Year	Correlation Against Personal Income	Coefficient of Variation
Total revenues	1932	.78	.34
	1942	.59	.29
	1957	.48	.22
	1962	.64	.20
	1967	.45	.20
	1970	.57	.18
	1973	.63	.17
Education expenditures[a]	1930	.80	.35
	1940	.87	.36
	1950	.85	.25
	1957	.85	.22
	1962	.86	.22
	1967	.77	.19
	1970	.72	.19
	1973	.74	.21
Personal income	1929		.36
	1940		.35
	1950		.23
	1957		.23
	1962		.20
	1967		.17
	1970		.17
	1973		.14
	N = 48		

Sources: See table 7-1 and, in addition: Office of Education, *Statistics of State School Systems, 1961-1962*: 72; Office of Education, *Statistics of Public Elementary and Secondary Day Schools: Fall, 1967*: 26; Bureau of the Census, *U.S. Statistical Abstract, 1970*: 122; National Education Association Research Report, 1973 R-4, *Financial Status of the Public Schools, 1973*.

The point is, the federal government simply has not been willing to use the package of federal aid programs as a tool for redistribution. Instead, federal aid in the United States has been designed largely for other purposes, such as providing fiscal support to all state and local governments, encouraging new or expanded programs in certain functional areas, or ensuring minimum levels of program provision. Eradicating differences across states has never been a primary, or even secondary, goal. It is true that some programs do include in their formulas or regulations a stipulation that aid be distributed, at least in part, according to income. However, these provisions are invariably limited by, among other factors, the inclusion of additional elements in the formula (for instance, population or tax effort) that dilute the effect of the income provision, and the employment of ceilings and floors on the redistribution: every unit, no matter how well-off, receives something from formula grants.[3]

The formula for distributing revenue sharing funds provides an excellent example of these two limitations (for good discussions of the politics surrounding the revenue sharing formula, see Dommell, 1974, pp. 144-147, 155-164; and Beer, 1976). The wealth of a state, measured by per capita income, is one of the criteria for allocating revenue sharing funds: richer states are supposed to receive lesser amounts. However, the impact of that criterion is severely constrained by two other considerations in the formula. First of all, income is only one of several factors that are employed; tax effort, population, urban population, and income tax collection are all included, and compete with income for impact on the distribution pattern. In addition, the revenue sharing formula puts a floor and ceiling on the amounts a state (or other jurisdiction) may receive. Thus, every state—no matter how well-off—must receive something, while redistribution to poorer states is limited to a specified percentage. The result is that, though revenue sharing is redistributive, it is only mildly so. Considerations of need succumb to a desire to maximize benefits for the home state. On one public employment bill, funds were to have been targeted heavily according to the relative severity of unemployment. However, "when one of the house's leading liberal lights pointed out during floor debate that his amendment would increase the level of funding in fully thirty-seven states by diluting the relative severity criteria (thus making all unemployed workers count equally), the change was quickly agreed to without so much as a recorded vote" (Stockman, 1975, pp. 25-26).

When one adds to these restrictions on redistribution the fact that the majority of aid programs have no progressive features in them at all, the coefficients in table 7-1 become readily understandable. Time and again, decision-making bodies in Washington, primarily but not exclusively Congress, are faced with explicit decisions on how to distribute federal aid; in fact, on most bills the distribution formula is the primary concern of congressmen (Stockman, 1975, p. 25). Each time, those decisions reflect opposition to, or at best lukewarm support for, the use of income as the criterion. Regional fiscal redistribution is simply not a goal of this federal government. (For further discussion, see U.S. Advisory Commission on Intergovernmental Relations, 1964.)

What Impact Could the United States Have?

Perhaps, some might suggest, even if redistribution of federal aid monies did take place, it would have a great impact on the state spending differentials;

thus, it would not be worth the political effort to achieve it. This is an easy, but important, issue to dispose of. It is true that the federal government does not control a very high percentage of state and local revenues—currently, averaging around 20 to 25 percent. This figure would have to be increased substantially if every state were to be brought up to the spending level of the highest state; using 1972 data, this would have required an additional $36 billion on top of the $31 billion already allocated for aid that year, which would have meant a 16 percent increase in the budget or, alternatively, cuts from other programs.

While this is obviously too large a figure to contemplate congressional acceptance, if a lower standard were adopted, such as the average spending levels of the top ten states, or if the formula were based on revenue effort as well as ability to pay, the price of redistribution would be a good deal cheaper. For efforts to calculate some of these alternatives, see Thurow (1970); National Education Finance Project (1971); and Musgrave and Polinsky (1970). But, more important, simply by employing the amounts that are distributed now, the federal government could have a much greater redistributive impact than it currently has. As W. Norton Grubb and Stephan Michelson emphasize, "even a small amount of intergovernmental aid may produce a significant reduction in inequality *if* it is distributed appropriately" (1974, p. 59). The fact is, as table 7-1 demonstrates, what aid there is in the United States is not "distributed appropriately" to achieve this effect.

An Illustrative Contrast: The Six Other Systems

How much of an impact federal aid *could* have in the United States can be illustrated even more strongly by examining the distribution of fiscal transfers from the center in other systems, and it is to that task that we now turn. The relevant data are presented for all of the other countries in table 7-3, with the American coefficients repeated for easier comparison. Column 1 is the coefficient of variation for regional income in each system. Column 2 is the correlation of regional income with the fiscal aid from the center. Since, as we discussed above for the American case, this correlation by itself is not a sufficient indicator of the degree of redistribution, we also present (in columns 3 and 4 respectively) the coefficient of variation for the transfers and the percentage that these transfers constitute of total regional revenues. Finally, in columns 5, 6, 7, and 8, the correlations with income and coefficients of variation are given for total regional revenues and for education expenditures, as evidence for the impact, or lack of impact, of the transfers.

Perhaps the most striking aspect of the findings in table 7-3 is the tremendous amount of variation from country to country in transfer and

Table 7-3
Subnational Fiscal Patterns in Seven Countries, Per Capita

Country	Year[b]	Income[c] (1) CV	Transfers from the Center (2) R[d]	(3) CV	Percent of Central Transfers to Total Revenue (4)	Total Revenues (5) R	(6) CV	Education Expenditures[a] (7) R	(8) CV
Australia	1956	.08	−.74	.33	44	−.46	.15	.29[e]	.16
(n=6)	1970	.09	−.67	.33	57	−.67	.14	.69	.08
Canada[f]	1956	.27	−.69	.49	9	.57	.45		
(n=10)	1963	.24	−.90	.39	21	.80	.18	.74	.27
	1972	.20	−.93	.43	20	.59	.08	.74	.16
East Germany	1958	.37						−.63	.08
(n=15)	1969	.31						−.34	.04
Japan	1958	.19	−.70	.24	48	.10	.12	.18	.10
(n=46)	1968	.19	−.83	.34	51	−.59	.15	−.13	.11
Poland	1958	.20	−.02	.40	20	.24	.21	.09	.14
(n=17)	1971	.20	−.48	.42	62	−.48	.24	−.30	.09

Soviet Union (n = 15)								
1955	.30	−.02	.62	40	.60	.27	.45	.07
1970	.32	.05	.37	49	.70	.26	.76	.11
United States (n = 48)								
1957	.23	−.16	.52	16	.48	.22	.85	.22
1973	.14	−.06	.24	23	.63	.17	.74	.21

[a] Education expenditures, except for East Germany, are per pupil.

[b] The years that were chosen reflect data availability and the desire to obtain a reasonable time series, so that trends as well as cross-sectional data could be compared.

[c] The measure of income varies from country to country and is not strictly comparable.

[d] The correlations are against the respective measures of income for each country.

[e] The expenditure figures for Australia do not include expenditures made through conditional grants; the data are reported net of these transfers. Since the grants are redistributive, the data would look even more progressive than they are now if they were included.

[f] The 1956 data for Canada do not include municipalities, but tests for provincial only data for other years show that this makes little difference in the coefficients.

Sources: *Australia:* J. Dixon, "The Changing Role of the Australian Commonwealth Grants Commission," *Public Finance* 26 (1971):483; James Maxwell, "Revenue-Sharing in Canada and Australia: Some Implications for the United States," *National Tax Journal* 24 (June 1971):263; F. M. Archer, *Australian National Accounts, 1948-1949—1962-1963:* 40; *Yearbook of the Commonwealth,* 1958: 568, 812, 818, 1959: 690; 1971: 557, 588; 1972: 126, 586; *Canada:* M. C. Urquhart, *Historical Statistics of Canada* (Toronto, 1965):134; Nicholas Michas, "Variations in the Level of Provincial-Municipal Expenditures in Canada: An Econometric Analysis," *Public Finance* (1969):61-612; *Canada Yearbook,* 1957-1958: 119; 1973:209, 858; *Consolidated Public Finance,* 1962: 12-21; 1971: 18-21; *Provincial Government Finance,* 1962: 18-19; *East Germany: Statisiches Jarbuch der DDR,* 1956: 11, 41, 97-98; 1958: 243, 245; 1968: *Yearbook,* 1963: 85; 1972: 286; *Japanese Statistical Yearbook,* 1960: 15, 435-437; 1970: 14, 476-478, 567; *Poland: Rocznik Statstyczny,* 1959: 14-18, 78-79; *Union: Narodnoe khoziaistvo,* 1960: 627; 1964: 597; 1969: 587, 603; *Gosudarstvennii biudzhet SSSR i biudzheti soiuznikh respublik: Statisticheskii sbornik,* 1962: 35, 55, 100-214; 1966: 36, 57, 102-214; 1966-1970: 42, 62, 109-222; *United States:* See tables 7-1 and 7-2.

expenditure patterns. Yet out of this variation some patterns emerge. Most important, there are evident several clear and often very substantial efforts at redistribution: in the Australian, Canadian, Japanese, and Polish cases, the correlations between regional income and transfers from the center are strongly negative, in sharp contrast to the neutral U.S. coefficients. Moreover, in all but the Canadian case (and, as the data we have show, in East Germany as well), the redistribution is so great that the end result is for poorer areas to spend *more* than their richer counterparts. This is true even though, in most of these cases, income (resource) differences across regions are greater than they are in the United States.

A striking illustration of this phenomenon appears in a comparison of Tokyo, the richest region in Japan, with Kagoshima the southernmost and poorest prefecture. In 1968, Tokyo enjoyed over three times the per capita income of Kagoshima, yet its prefectural revenues were only 74,200 yen per capita, compared with 74,900 for Kagoshima. The reason is that central transfers accounted for 12,300 of the total for Tokyo, while Kagoshima received 53,400 yen, or over four times as much. One would have to imagine Mississippi receiving four times the federal aid California or New York receives, and spending more on public services than these states, in order to have a picture of a comparable situation in the United States.

It does seem, from some of the coefficients in table 7-3, as if there is at least one other nonredistributive country, and that is the Soviet Union. However, redistribution does in fact take place in that nation as well. It is simply masked by part of the data presented in table 7-3 because of some peculiar features of communist budgets. They include a substantial proportion, upwards of 50 percent of the entire budget, that goes to the national economy. These funds are allocated on a different basis than those intended for public services; the latter are clearly assigned with greater equalization in mind, and this is evidenced by the declining coefficients of variation for revenues and education expenditures in table 7-3. For Soviet confirmation of this point, see Diachenko and Sitarian, 1968, p. 158. Thus, redistribution is indeed occurring in the Soviet Union in several expenditure areas for which federal aid is not progressive in the United States.

Explaining the American Pattern

In spite of the variation among these seven states, then, the United States stands alone as the one nation that makes no significant effort to redistribute fiscal resources in order to help reduce public service spending differentials across its regions. The task in this section is to explain the unique American position.

To do this, we should examine the hypotheses set out earlier and see how well they fared. It is evident, first of all, that a strong impact by a communist regime is not readily apparent from these data. All of the communist states we analyzed are redistributive, but they are matched in this respect by several Western systems. While communism may be a sufficient condition for redistribution, then, it clearly is not a necessary one.

The other dichotomy, between unitary and federal polities, seems to be a much more promising distinction. The three unitary states in the sample all employ fiscal redistribution to such an extent as to result in greater expenditures on public services in poorer than in richer areas. There is only one federal state—Australia—out of the four we examined that redistributes this extensively, and even that performance is undermined somewhat by the fact that regional income disparities (see column 1 of table 7-3) are much smaller in that country than they are in the others. The distribution of much less aid is required to alter spending patterns in that manner in Australia than it would be in the others.

Therefore, there does seem to be a clear relationship between the extent of fiscal redistribution in a country and whether the political system is federal or unitary. This helps somewhat, then, in explaining the American pattern. It does not, however, tell the whole story. Australia and Canada are both federal systems, and yet they, though to varying degrees, redistribute resources from richer to poorer regions. How do we explain the difference between the United States and those nations? To do that, we shall have to turn to the third factor set out above, the impact of system-specific variables, especially historical developments, and the routines, cultural norms, and political forces that establish themselves around these developments to help lock in certain patterns.

Perhaps, for example, these differences in the degree of redistribution and equalization simply reflect fundamental variations among these three federal, democratic systems in the extent of local autonomy that is generally permitted. In other words, perhaps "states' rights" and "local control" are more pronounced in all areas in Canada and Australia than in the United States, and public expenditures is merely one, albeit an important, example of this difference. The problem with this argument is that many scholars would disagree with it strenuously, especially with respect to Canada. William Glaser, for instance, argues bluntly and persuasively that Canadian provinces are more powerful vis-à-vis Ottawa than American states are in relation to Washington (1977, pp. 3-4). At the least, one is very hard-pressed to make the case that Canadian provinces are less autonomous. As for Australia, scholars are generally less assured. However, in an area that we have been focusing upon—education—one expert is quite adamant about the power of the Australian states. He writes, "each of the six Australian states has sole constitutional responsibility for all education within its own boundaries and has jealously guarded this right against regular incursions into state powers by the Commonwealth, especially since

1939" (Sheehan, 1972, p. 133). The one area, obviously, where this right has not been guarded, either in Australia or Canada, is finances—at least with respect to overall levels of expenditures. So, it seems the primary difference in this area of "states' rights" between Canada and Australia on the one hand, and the United States on the other, is this issue of fiscal redistribution.

Thus, the fiscal issue seems to be an isolated aspect: we cannot explain the cross-national variation by citing varying general interpretations of "states' rights" and local autonomy. Instead, we shall have to look elsewhere, and the best place to turn is to historical developments, and the routines, norms, and political forces they create. Basically, I shall argue that it is in fact historical, and to some extent ecological, circumstances that are the primary factors in explaining why American federalism differs from the Canadian and Australian patterns.

The primary historical difference between the United States and the other two federations is that, at the time of national formation in these other systems, the rudiments, at least, of redistribution were established. Since it is from this base that redistribution evolved in Canada and Australia, we should first explain what happened at that time, and why: why did Canada and Australia establish a system of fiscal redistribution from the beginning, while the United States did not? The answer rests in large part on chronology. The United States was formed at a time when public finance, especially in relation to the provision of public services, such as education, was not at all well-developed. Thus, disparities across the states in what they could possibly raise to spend on services was not an issue. *Political* inequality among the states was very important, but few yet were aware of, much less concerned with, fiscal inequality. Thus, such early intergovernmental fiscal adjustments as the taking over of state debts did not involve the issue of relative inequality among the states, but rather vertical balance between them as a whole and the federal government. Moreover, the fiscal structure established by the new government left the states with a sufficient tax base to discharge their responsibilities without need of general grants from Washington (apart from the one-time takeover of the debts).

The patterns of formation in Canada and Australia differed sharply from the United States in two important respects. The first was that the federal government in both countries did take over major state taxes, leaving the subnational units with an insufficient tax base. This necessitated fiscal grants from the center to these units. The question naturally arose as to how these grants should be distributed, and this is where the other important difference comes in. At the time of the formation of these states, public finance was well-established, and thus "the financial position of the provinces played an important part in the discussions which led up to Confederation" (Birch, 1955, p. 52; also see Moore, et al., 1967; Maxwell, 1971 and 1974; and May, 1971). Regions were well aware of their expenditure needs and the resource disparities among them, and the poorer areas were extremely vocal in demanding a disproportionate share of the federal largesse. Why did they get it? It was not because they formed a majority of the units—rather, as one would logically expect, richer and poorer areas were balanced in number. Nor was the population in the poorer regions greater than in the richer areas—in fact, the opposite was true. Thus, other factors clearly were involved: (1) the refusal of the poorer states to join the federation, and their threats to secede in the first years after formation, unless some extra compensation was provided. Their demands were backed by evidence purporting to show how the poorer states would be hurt the most by the federal takeover of certain taxes and by the ending of trade barriers through the formation of the nation (see, for example, May, 1971, chapter 1). Thus, as James Maxwell notes, in both systems, "grants were the price of union" (1974, p. 64); (2) the fact that the poorer states were small. Therefore, the cost to the richer states was not very great and, they felt, a worthwhile price for a union they perceived to be beneficial to their interests; and, (3) the feeling on the part of everyone that these grants were only temporary adjustments necessary for a few years at most.

However, as every social scientist is fully aware, "temporary" programs have a habit of becoming fixed features of the system. Patterns established one year become the precedent, the base for the next; "even the most innovative creations are decisively shaped by the content of previous policy" (Heclo, 1974, p. 5). As resource disparities continued unabated, so did the demand for adjustments by the poorer states (accompanied often by threats of secession). Thus, the factors that underlay the original imposition of subsidies remained constant, and poorer states found, of course, that they could not do without this extra assistance. The justification for these grants changed gradually over the years, from disabilities caused by the union to the right of individuals to enjoy similar public services and tax burdens wherever they may live (see May's description of this metamorphosis, 1971, especially pp. 31-32). But with the other factors unchanged, and thus the pressure for subsidies unceasing, the programs became formalized and expanded, to the point where today debates no longer concern the fact of redistribution but merely its extent. A 1967 statement from the premier of Australia's richest state, New South Wales, exemplifies this point very well:

> Federation requires that the people of the more highly developed and financially stronger States contribute to the development of the other States and of Australia as a whole. This principle is accepted by my Government. But we feel that, as the financially weaker States improve their position, there should be some scaling down in the assistance they require and that there should be a narrowing of the gaps between the per capita grants to all States. (Quoted in May, 1971, p. 152).

The basic concept of fiscal redistribution thus has become an accepted part of the Australian and Canadian political culture, something that is not true in the United States. To paraphrase James Maxwell (replacing "unconditional grants" with "redistribution"), "in Canada and Australia (redistribution) became a part of the establishment; in the United States (it) did not and, for this reason alone, remained submerged as a public issue" (1971, p. 252). Fiscal redistribution, then, has been accepted as compatible with local control in Australia and Canada. In the United States, by contrast, efforts to equalize are contested by cries of local control, and this different stance seems logically attributable to variations in conceptions of what is proper in a federal state, conceptions that grew out of particular historical circumstances. As Lester Thurow stresses (1975, p. 193), citing the literature on relative deprivation, norms are extremely important in determining and preserving distributional patterns. In fact, he argues that "a necessary condition for the success of . . . (inequality-reducing) programs is a change in the norms of relative deprivation or economic justice." And these norms, he adds, are invariably established, and changed, only by extraordinary events, such as wars, social upheavals, and changes in the political order—events that disrupt routines and force, or at least strongly encourage new policy choices.

How else can we explain the fact that two decentralized federal states refuse to tolerate great regional disparities in public spending while another does tolerate them, or that poorer states in the other two systems press demands for subsidies, yet do not in the United States? As A.H. Birch argues, "These differences (in fiscal arrangements in Canada, Australia and the United States) which were accidental in the sense that they arose from the needs of the moment rather than from the application of thought-out principles, have had consequences of great importance" (1955, p. 239). The application of principles occurred ex post facto, yet these principles (local control in the one case, and greater equality of burdens and benefits in the other), both defensible yet in different ways, work to underly patterns that evolved primarily for other reasons.

We in the United States believe very strongly in local control, in the benefits of diversity, and in the existence of a trade-off between equality (especially equality imposed by a central government) and liberty. What is important is that we have come to consider fiscal control as an indispensable element of these concerns. The Australians and Canadians, on the other hand, may share these beliefs as strongly as do Americans, yet they have "grown up" with fiscal equalization and, not seeing their liberty or local control particularly threatened thereby, have come to accept it as a natural part of the system. There are good arguments (as well as coalitions) on both sides of the issue; thus, it is easy to see why the three countries are locked into the patterns they are in. It is simpler for decision makers to retain current policy when no compelling alternative or political force is present (on this point, see Sharkansky, 1970). Tinkering at the margins becomes the order of the day, and that is precisely what is taking place in each of these systems; in the process, the base, whether redistributive or nonredistributive, is unchanged.

This differing tradition in the United States, and its direct evolution from decisions made in 1787, is illustrated very nicely by Supreme Court decisions on the issue. These decisions have consistently upheld a nonredistributive reading of "states' rights." The issue, simply, has been that, as a Soviet scholar has aptly put it, "the Constitution of the U.S.A. does not forbid the federation to distribute resources unequally" (Krylov, 1968, p. 213). In the most recent case (Rodriguez), the Court held that the methods of financing education were not unconstitutional "merely because the burdens or benefits thereof fall unevenly, depending upon the relative wealth of the political subdivision in which citizens live." Justice Powell, in the majority opinion, wrote that the equal protection clause of the Constitution did not require "absolute equality or precisely equal advantages," and that the relative poverty of the poorer district's parents "has not occasioned an absolute deprivation of the desired (education) benefit" (Weaver, 1973, pp. 1, 32). Unlike race, then, wealth has not considered to be a "suspect" classification under the Constitution.[4]

Moreover, there is little evidence to believe that Congress will make wealth a suspect classification in the near future. Indeed, with the states in the Northeast and Midwest, many of which are relatively well-off, clamoring for more funds, the allocation of aid may in fact tilt away from a neutral pattern to one *in favor* of richer states. That, of course, would make the United States even more unique than it is now. At the least, it seems safe to suggest that redistribution is a long way off in this country.

Summary

I have tried to demonstrate several things in this paper: that the American federal government, in its aid programs, does not redistribute funds disproportionately in favor of poorer states; that the federal government, even without increasing the amount of funds it now hands out, *could* have a major redistributive impact; that the United States is rather unique in its reluctance to redistribute; and that the reasons for this reluctance primarily involve the federal nature of the American system and certain important historical events and circumstances.

I would like to conclude by returning to the issue that opened this paper—the problem of explaining the strong positive relationship between spending levels in the American states and the income of those states. What I hope has been made clear in this paper is that the primary reason that relationship exists is not because of the imperatives of differential state income, but rather because the federal government permits that relationship to persist. Washington has a tremendous impact on the income-spending correlation precisely by its refusal to upset that linkage. That it could do so has been amply illustrated by examples from several other countries, in all of which political decisions from the center concerning aid distribution patterns remove, to some extent at least, those imperatives supposedly provided by varying subnational resource levels. To put it simply, what states spend, to a great degree, is a direct function of what Washington decides on their behalf; that Washington has chosen to allow the rich states to enjoy the benefits of state resource disparities suggests no less of an impact than if the federal government instead redistributed enormous sums from the rich to the poor. As we have seen time and again in political science, failures to intervene, to decide, or to act, are as important as their positive counterparts. In this case, the U.S. government does not redistribute, while others do, for reasons that I have tried to elaborate. However, the impact of the central government is powerful in both cases, and it is very important that analysts of state and local policy making—in the United States or anywhere—keep that fact firmly in mind in future research.

Notes

1. The particular coefficient of variation (CV) used is an unweighted one, a choice that differs from most other analyses. Economists, in particular, use a weighted CV, with the weights for each regional deviation assigned according to the region's share in the total population. The coefficient of variation for national income is presented below as an example:

$$CV = \frac{\sqrt{\sum_i (y_i - y)^2 \frac{f_i}{n}}}{y}$$

where: f_i = population of region i

n = national population

y_i = income per capita of region i

y = mean regional per capita income

Thus, for example, California, having one-tenth of the total population, would have ten percent of the total effect on the coefficient. The unweighted CV, on the other hand, is simply the standard deviation over the mean, or:

$$CV = \frac{\sqrt{\sum_i \frac{(y_i - y)^2}{N}}}{y}$$

where: N = total number of regions

With this measure, California has the same impact on the coefficient as any other state. By using a weighted CV, economists want to avoid having the coefficient affected by arbitrary political definitions of regional units, which are often far from being demographically homogeneous. In this study, however, we *are* interested in looking at politically defined units, as these are what political decision makers use as their standard in allocating resources. Officials in Delaware are not going to feel that California should be given more consideration per capita simply because it is a larger region.

I chose the coefficient of variation primarily because it is generally employed as the measure of regional variation. Hubert Blalock calls it the technique to employ "to compare several groups with respect to their relative homogeneity in instances where the groups have very different means" (1972, p. 88). Generally, measures that focus on a standard or average (such as the CV) are better than those that look at an extreme. I should note that I did try the latter on some data, and produced the same results (as did Harrison, 1976, pp. 45-46, 50-51, also working with state data).

Though the CV has no upper limit, it will invariably range for the data in this study between .05 and 1.00. It has a fairly simple interpretation: if, for example, the CV is .10, then the standard deviation is 10 percent of the mean. Thus, if the mean of expenditures for states is $1000 per capita, then the standard deviation is $100 per capita. If the CV were .20 and the mean still $1000, the standard deviation for state expenditures would be $200.

2. Some might suggest that the distribution of other federal expenditures may have played a role, since the South benefits disproportionately from their distribution. However, that benefit to the South has existed since the early nineteenth century, and the income gap has only been closing in the last forty years.

3. Another important limitation on redistribution is the empirical reality that richer states, even in spite of the fact that the formula many times discriminates against them, often can still afford (because matching funds are required) to generate more federal funds than their poorer counterparts. The Medicaid program provides an excellent example of this problem. Even though richer states must pay a higher percentage than poorer states for every dollar they receive, the former still can afford to utilize more federal dollars than the latter. Thus, in 1970, the four wealthiest states, with 25 percent of the poverty population in the country, received 56 percent of all Medicaid funds, while the ten poorest states, with 15 percent of the poor people, only garnered 7 percent (see Porter and Warner, 1973, for a discussion of the related problem of grantsmanship and biases in aid distribution).

Even in instances, then, when the federal government is seemingly trying to aid the poorer states disproportionately, the attempt is thwarted by unforeseen consequences. For the most part, however, the lack of redistribution is intentional.

This example also helps illustrate the refutation of one possible argument for the lack of state-level redistribution, and that is that aid does not go to poorer states because poor individuals are concentrated in the richer states. Even though there often is a fairly high percentage of poor people in the wealthier states, overall, the poorer states have a substantially disproportionate share of the poor individuals (for data, see U.S. Department of Commerce, 1976, p. 419). Moreover, even if the poor were more evenly distributed, it is still the poorer states that would need more fiscal assistance in caring for them.

4. I should add, however, that some states have been under pressure to achieve greater within-state equality, with suits filed and won on the basis of the state constitution.

References

Beer, S.H. "The Adoption of General Revenue Sharing: A Case Study in Public Sector Politics." *Public Policy* 24(Spring 1976):127-195.

Birch, A.H. *Federalism, Finance, and Social Legislation in Canada, Australia and the United States.* Oxford: Clarendon, 1955.

Break, G. *Intergovernmental Fiscal Relationships in the United States.* Washington: Brookings Institution, 1967.

Browning, R.S., and D.C. Long. "School Finance Reform and the Courts after Rodriguez." In *School Finance in Transition: The Courts and Education Reform*, edited by J. Pincus. Cambridge: Ballinger, 1974, pp. 81-105.

Buchanan, J.M. "Federalism and Fiscal Equity." *American Economic Review* 40(September 1950):583-599.

Cameron, D.R., and R.J. Hofferbert. "The Impact of Federalism on Education Finance: A Comparative Analysis." *European Journal of Political Research* 2 (1974):225-258. Reprinted by permission of Elsevier Scientific Publishing Co.

Carmines, E.G. "The Mediating Influence of State Legislatures on the Linkage Between Interparty Competition and Welfare Policies." *American Political Science Review* 68(September 1974):1118-1124.

Cnudde, C.F., and D.J. McCrone. "Party Competition and Welfare Policies in the American States." *American Political Science Review* 63(September 1969):858-866.

Cuciti, P.L. "The Distribution of Grants to Local Governments: Equalization in the American Polity." Paper presented at the American Political Science Association Convention, Chicago, Ill., September 2-5, 1976.

Dawson, R.E., and J.A. Robinson. "Inter-Party Competition, Economic Variables and Welfare Policies in the American States." *Journal of Politics* 25(May 1963):265-289.

Diachenko, V.P., and S.A. Sitarian. "The Budget and the Inter-Territorial Distribution of National Income." *Public Finance* 23(1-2, 1968):146-163.

Dommel, P.R. *The Politics of Revenue Sharing*. Bloomington: Indiana University, 1974.

Dye, T.R. *Politics, Economics and the Public*. Chicago: Rand McNally, 1966.

Echols, J.M. "Politics, Budgets, and Regional Equality in Communist and Capitalist Systems." *Comparative Political Studies* 8(October 1975):259-292.

――――― . "Politics, Policy, and Equality Under Communism and Democracy." Ph.D. Dissertation, University of Michigan, 1976.

Fritschler, A.L., and M. Segal. "Intergovernmental Relations and Contemporary Political Science: Developing an Integrative Typology." *Publius* 1(Winter 1972):95-122.

Glaser, W.A. *Federalism in Canadian Health Services—Lessons for the United States*. New York: Center for the Social Sciences at Columbia University, 1977.

Grubb, W.N., and S. Michelson. *States and Schools: The Political Economy of Public School Finance*. Lexington, Mass.: Lexington Books, D.C. Heath and Company, 1974.

Heclo, H. *Modern Social Politics in Britain and Sweden*. New Haven: Yale University, 1974.

Hicks, J.R. "The Nature and Basis of Economic Growth." In *Federalism and Economic Growth in Underdeveloped Countries*, edited by U.K. Hicks, et al. London: George Allen and Unwin, 1961, pp. 70-85.

Kernig, L. "Equality—C. Critical Analysis." In *Marxism, Communism and Western Society*. Vol. 3, edited by C.D. Kernig. New York: Herder and Herder, 1972, pp. 212-214.

Kolomin, E., and N. Shirkevich. "Biudzhet SSSR: leninskaia natsional 'naia politika." *Finansy SSSR* (September 1972):23-31.

Krylov, B.S. *SShA: Federalizm, shtaty i mestnoe upravlenie*. Moscow: Nauka, 1968.

Lewis-Beck, M. "The Relative Importance of Socioeconomic and Political Variables for Public Policy." *American Political Science Review* 71(June 1976):559-566.

Lijphart, A. "Comparative Politics and the Comparative Method." *American Political Science Review* 65(September 1971):682-693.

Long, N. *The Polity*. Chicago: Rand McNally, 1962.

Maxwell, James A. *Commonwealth-State Financial Relations in Australia*. Melbourne: Melbourne University, 1967.

――――― . "Revenue-Sharing in Canada and Australia: Some Implications for the United States." *National Tax Journal* 24(June 1971):251-265.

――――― . "Federal Grants in Canada, Australia and the United States." *Publius* 4(Spring 1974):63-76.

May, R.J. *Federalism and Fiscal Adjustment*. London: Oxford University, 1969.

_____ . *Financing the Small States in Australian Federalism*. Melbourne: Oxford University, 1971.

Melnyk, Z.L. "Regional Contribution to Capital Formation in the USSR: The Case of the Ukranian Republic." In *The Soviet Economy in Regional Perspective*. Edited by V.N. Bandera and Z.L. Melnyk, New York: Praeger, 1973, pp. 104-131.

Ministry of Finance. *An Outline of Japanese Taxes*. Tokyo, 1966.

Moore, A.M.; J.H. Perry; and D.S. Beach. "The Financing of Canadian Federation," in Joint Economic Committee, *Revenue Sharing and Its Alternatives*. Washington: Government Printing Office, 1967.

Musgrave, R.M., and A.M. Polinsky. "Revenue Sharing: A Critical View." In *Proceedings of the Monetary Conference, Nantucket Island, Mass., June 14-16*. Boston: Federal Reserve Bank of Boston, 1970, pp. 17-51.

National Education Finance Project. *Alternative Programs for Financing Education*. Gainesville, 1971.

Oates, W. *Fiscal Federalism*. New York: Harcourt, Brace, Jovanovich, 1972.

Osman, J. "On the Use of Intergovernmental Aid as an Expenditure Determinant." *National Tax Journal* 21(December 1968):437-447.

Pavlov, IU.M. "The Bourgeois State and Regional Economic Development," trans. in *Problems of Economics* 14(May-June 1971):124-143.

Porter, D.O., and D.C. Warner. "How Effective are Grantor Controls? The Case of Federal Aid to Education." In *Transfers in an Urbanized Economy*. Edited by Kenneth E. Boulding, et al., Belmont: Wadsworth, 1973, pp. 276-302.

Rose, D.D. "National and Local Forces in State Politics: The Implications of Multi-Level Policy Analysis." *American Political Science Review* 67(December 1973):1162-1173.

Sachs, S., and R. Harris. "The Determinants of State and Local Government Expenditures and Intergovernmental Flow of Funds." *National Tax Journal* 17(March 1964):75-85.

Sharkansky, I. *The Routines of Politics*. New York: Van Nostrand Reinhold, 1970.

Sharkansky, I., and R.I. Hofferbert. "Dimensions of State Politics, Economics, and Public Policy." *American Political Science Review* 63(September 1969):867-879.

Sheehan, B. "The Organization and Financing of Education in Australia." *Comparative Education* 8(December 1972):133-146.

Sontheimer, K., and W. Bleek. *The Government and Politics of East Germany*. London: Hutchinson, 1975.

Stockman, D.A. "The Social Pork Barrel." *Public Interest* 39(Spring 1975):3-30.

Stonecash, J. "Local Policy Analysis and Autonomy: On Intergovernmental Relations and Theory Specification." Paper presented at the Midwest Political Science Association, April, 1977, Chicago, Illinois.

Strouse, J.C., and P. Jones. "Federal Aid: The Forgotten Variable in State Policy Research." *Journal of Politics* 36(February 1974):200-207.

Thurow, L. "Aid to State and Local Governments." *National Tax Journal* 23(March 1970):23-35.

———. *Generating Inequality*. New York: Basic Books, 1975.

U.S. Advisory Commission on Intergovernmental Relations. *The Role of Equalization in Federal Grants*. Washington: U.S. Government Printing Office, 1964.

U.S. Department of Commerce, Bureau of the Census. *U.S. Statistical Abstract*. Washington: U.S. Government Printing Office, 1976.

Weaver, W. "Court, 5-4 Backs Schools in Texas on Property Tax." *New York Times*, March 22, 1973, 1, 32.

Willner, W., and J.P. Nichols, *Revenue Sharing*. Washington: Pro-Plan International, 1973.

Wright, D.S. *Federal Grants-in-Aid: Perspectives and Alternatives*. Washington: American Enterprise Institute, 1968.

8 Taxes, Benefits, and Public Opinion

Susan B. Hansen

Introduction

Are government budgets too large or too small in democracies? The answer to this question depends to a great extent on the criteria one chooses to use for correct budget size. Amacher et al. (1975) suggest several: comparison with private markets, the effects of war and economic development, bureaucratic behavior, and the influence of risk factors on decision makers. Economists usually discount survey findings concerning preferences, because rationally self-interested actors would disguise their true preferences for collective goods so that they would not have to pay the cost. Buchanan and Tullock (1962) even advocate the use of economic criteria to determine constitutional arrangements for the aggregation of public preferences through voting rules.

For politicians, however, a highly relevant criteria for budget size is likely to be the preferences of taxpayers as these are channeled by the electoral system. Their chances for reelection are enhanced the more closely the balance between taxes and expenditures corresponds to the preferences of the majority of voters. Their problem, and ours as well, is to determine what voters prefer and what information they use in establishing that preference.

This chapter will explore some empirical evidence concerning public preferences for spending by the federal government, as indicated by responses to a Gallup Poll question concerning income taxes repeated nearly every year between 1947 and the present. The proportion of the public stating that their taxes are "about right," as opposed to "too high" or "too low," has varied considerably across time and among various political and social groups. A systematic evaluation of these fluctuations will be used to suggest decision rules people use in evaluating budget size. Of course federal spending has increased for many reasons (war, Cold War, the operations of bureaucracy) other than citizen preferences. But this

Data for this paper was made available through a grant from the Social Science Research Council Committee on Social Indicators and funds from the Research Board of the University of Illinois, which provided access to Gallup polls through the Roper Center for Public Opinion Research in Williamstown, Mass. My thanks to these agencies, to my research assistant John Carroll, and James C. Davis, Tom Smith, and Patrick Bova of the National Opinion Research Center, who gave me access to the tax questions on the 1976 NORC General Social Survey.

analysis finds considerable support for an expanded public sector, support which varies with spending patterns, party control of government, and the success of economic and foreign policy as well as tax burdens. With earmarked taxes, as Buchanan (1967) observed, people can evaluate tax burdens in terms of benefits received. Except for identifiable minorities, however, popular evaluation of general benefits and broad-based taxes depends on information costs and political values.

Taxes, Benefits, and Information Costs

Any analysis of the demand for public goods must consider the relationship between tax burdens and policy benefits. People who think they receive a net gain from governmental spending should be more willing to pay taxes than those who perceive a net loss. Individual utilities differ widely, however; a person who objectively receives more benefits than he pays in taxes may still think he is getting less than his fair share, compared to others, to his expectations, or to a previous state of affairs. Taxpayers may be unaware of benefits: Galbraith's analysis of the dependence effect suggests that demand for public goods is low because of the lack of advertising so prevalent in the private sector.[1] People may likewise be unaware of at least some of the taxes they pay, because of ignorance or the government's skill in devising fiscal illusions. Buchanan (1967) argues that people's preference for public goods depends on how these are financed.

Anthony Downs has suggested a parsimonious theory concerning popular preferences for the size of government budgets, based on the information costs involved in assessing benefits and tax burdens. His criterion for budget size is that of a state of perfect information, wherein citizens are aware of all items in the budget and the costs and benefits of each item. As he admits, this state is unlikely to occur in the real world; it is not to be used as a social-utility or welfare function, but simply as a benchmark to assess preferences based on less-than-perfect information.

Downs argues that the most common real-world condition is that of partial ignorance, whereby people have more information concerning tax burdens than they have concerning the benefits they receive from collective goods. Since the former are direct and obvious, while the latter are often remote or uncertain, politicians are reluctant to raise taxes because the votes lost thereby will be far more than the votes to be gained by providing additional services. Thus budgets in democracies tend to be smaller than they would be if citizens had better information concerning government spending.

Downs also considers a third situation, preponderant ignorance, where "each citizen's perception threshold is most likely to be crossed by minority-benefiting policies involving government spending that could raise his income" (1960, p. 92). This leads to a situation of logrolling among minorities, each seeking to enlarge the income they receive from government while spreading the taxes over the rest of the citizenry. Although each citizen ends up paying more in taxes to support others' benefits, he is more aware of his own income than of higher tax bills, and thus supports governments which expand public spending. The obvious result is budgets larger than would be the case if people were aware of the actual cost of this negative-sum game.

Downs assumes that partial ignorance is the prevalent condition, and that democratic budgets are too small. But such a conclusion requires evidence concerning people's awareness of taxes and government spending. If people's incomes come from the government, are they more or less willing to pay taxes? Are they indeed unaware of the social costs involved? Are taxes always more salient than benefits, or does their relative salience vary with changes in the national economy and the financial status of the individual? The problem is to discover the decision rules people actually use in calculating the benefits and costs to themselves of complex budgets.

An alternative theory is related to benefits and burdens in a more diffuse manner. According to Rogowski, political support is not simply a function of political outputs. Rather, Rogowski defines support as a citizen's willingness to accept as legitimate those constitutional arrangements which would maximize his or her probability of influencing (in his terms, "uniquely determining") the decision-making process, regardless of particular outcomes. This viewpoint suggests that, while outputs and tax rates certainly should not be ignored, people evaluate their tax burdens in a broader context than their own economic advantage. If they believe the government is legitimate, if they support the president or congressmen responsible for making tax policy, if the nation is at peace and the economy is flourishing, their tax bills may appear reasonable. But if the government is not functioning well, if the president is doing a poor job, if the nation is at war and the economy is in trouble, tax bills may appear onerous even if the dollar amount has not changed from earlier, happier times.

If Rogowski is right, people will evaluate general-purpose taxes such as the federal income tax in terms of political values. If Downs is right, most people's attitudes will depend on their tax bills, but persons who depend on the government for their income will consider benefits rather than taxes. It is more than likely that different people use different decision rules; the social-choice outcome in terms of preferred budget size would thus depend on the proportion of persons using various criteria for evaluation. Finally, as political and economic conditions change, public budgetary preferences may also change. Downs's assumptions should be restated as variables rather than constants.

Data and Methods

In order to explore public preferences concerning budget size, we need some indicator of people's attitudes toward taxes and some means of assessing the benefits people receive from the federal government. The first is readily available. Since 1947, the Gallup Poll has repeatedly asked the American public, "Do you think the federal income tax you (or your spouse) have to pay is too high, too low, or about right?" One might expect a universal response of "too high," but such is not the case; as figure 8-1 indicates, the proportion of "too high" responses has varied from a low of 43 percent in 1949 to highs of 72 percent in 1952 and 69 percent in 1973. These responses have also varied considerably among various political and social groups. If such variations represent only random fluctuation, we should find no relationship between taxes and benefits. But if the variation exhibits an identifiable pattern, changes in the perceived ratio of costs to benefits received constitute a possible explanation. If people say their income taxes are about right, we can plausibly assume that they are satisfied with the size of the federal budget.

Benefits are more difficult to assess. Collective goods are far more difficult to capitalize than are tax bills, and individual perceptions and utilities differ considerably. The Gallup polls which include the tax question do not include questions on benefits received or even on broad policy preferences. Cross-sectional analyses of individual surveys are thus of little help. The surveys do, however, include broad demographic categories, which have been defined fairly consistently over time. These will be used to identify groups in the population who are likely to be helped or hurt by particular spending programs. The unit of analysis will therefore be groups rather than individuals. Tax dissatisfaction across time and across these demographic categories should vary according to the tax burdens they face and to changes in benefits from federal spending accruing to a particular group.

Whether this series of Gallup surveys constitutes a reliable indicator of opinion shifts over time in the American population, depends on how problems of question wording, sampling, and no-opinion responses are resolved. Differences in wording of the tax question have been too slight to affect the analysis.[2] Gallup also changed from quota to stratified sampling after 1952; our analysis indicated that this had only a minor effect on trends in tax support, and we have followed the recommendations of a comprehensive NORC analysis in using unweighted samples (Newman, 1975). The surveys do underrepresent lower-status groups and blacks, but this bias has been reasonably consistent over time.

No-opinion responses have also varied little over time, and almost no one has ever complained that taxes are too low. The major dependent

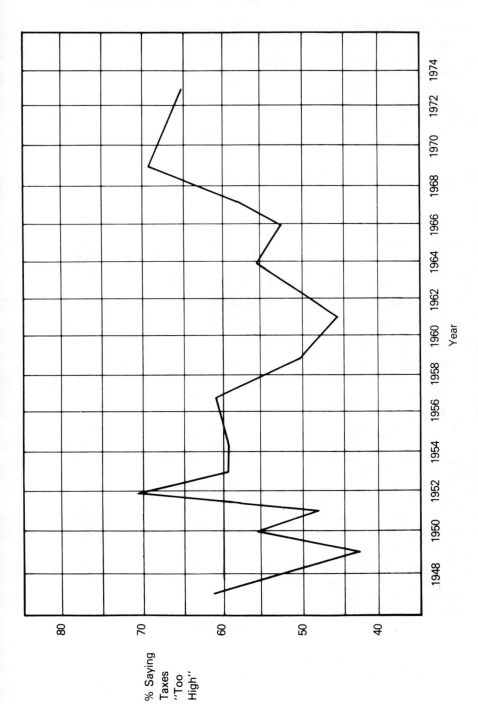

Figure 8-1. Responses to Gallup Questions on Support for Tax Levels, 1947-1973

variable for this analysis will therefore be the proportion of the sample responding that their income taxes were too high. The tax question was not asked for ten years in this twenty-eight-year period: the omission of several presidential election years is especially frustrating. Rather than interpolating data, we analyze only those years when the tax question was asked. Seasonal variation, however, is no problem: Gallup, concerned as always with the newsworthiness of his polls, kindly asked the tax question each year shortly before the March 15 (later, the April 15) filing deadline.[3]

Results

Tax Increases

Downs predicted that, if people were indeed rationally ignorant of most benefits from federal spending, their dissatisfaction with taxes should increase when taxes were raised. If Downs is right, changes in federal tax laws should account for most of the variation in "too high" responses to the Gallup tax question over the 1947-1976 period. But federal tax changes usually do not have an across-the-board impact; they vary widely depending on deductions, exemptions, and progressivity. Since the Gallup surveys seldom include usable data on respondents' incomes, we must concentrate on those years when people at most income levels did face increases or decreases in their tax bills. Such increases were enacted in 1952-1953 and 1968-1970, and general decreases from the previous year's rates occurred in 1954, 1964, 1972, and 1973.[4]

These changes did have a moderate impact on changes in tax dissatisfaction over time ($R = .43$), substantiating Downs's hypothesis. Examination of figure 8-1 shows that tax dissatisfaction peaked in 1952 and 1969, when war-related surcharges were enacted. Since we have had no peacetime income tax increases since 1947, however, one should not attribute increases in tax discontent only to tax hikes; tax discontent was high throughout the Korean and Vietnam wars, even before tax increases became necessary. Further, the 1964 tax cut had no appreciable impact on popular willingness to pay taxes.

We must also consider the effects of two other reasons for tax hikes: social security taxes and increases in real income. Payroll deductions for social security have increased geometrically since 1945, and thus are unlikely to account for fluctuations in tax support during that time. People seldom complain about social security tax increases because they see them as directly linked to benefits, and of course retirement and disability benefits have also increased substantially since 1945. As Buchanan argues, broad-based taxes, such as the federal income tax, are likely to be less popular than earmarked taxes for social security, but we lack the survey data to test this further.[5]

Even if the Internal Revenue Code is not changed, people may pay higher taxes as their real incomes rise or as inflation pushes them into higher tax brackets. Under our progressive tax system, we would expect to find upper-SES persons less willing to pay income taxes, and this is the case at the individual level. But the relationship (at least as far as we are able to determine, given Gallup's lack of precise income data) is quite weak; gammas between SES and tax discontent never exceed .05 over the entire set of surveys. Nor do aggregate indicators of rising income predict changes in tax support; both real and disposable income have risen at increasing rates since 1947, but their curves do not fit our pattern of changes in tax attitudes. Declines in real income, of course, might affect tax support, but such a decline occurred only once in this period (1954-1955). We thus cannot account for changes in income tax dissatisfacton on the basis of personal income.

Katona (1975) mentions another problem: tax increases are unlikely to change attitudes if people are unaware of such changes. His quarterly surveys of consumers found that a considerable number of people were aware of neither the imposition nor the removal of the Vietnam income tax surcharge. Politicians' fiscal illusions can decrease public awareness; Van Wagstaff (1975) found that people consistently underestimated their taxes when a system of withholding was introduced. Survey data is not available concerning changes over time in popular awareness of tax rates, but, given the complexities of the Internal Revenue code, we should not assume that knowledge of tax changes is universal.

Most people are undoubtedly aware of tax increases, however, and as Downs predicted, across-the-board tax increases are associated with increased tax dissatisfaction. The relationship is by no means perfect, however, suggesting that alternative explanations, such as unpopular wars, ignorance, and variations in personal incomes, must also be considered. Let us now examine the effects of changes in benefits on tax attitudes.

Benefits from Federal Programs

Benefits to individuals from federal spending are difficult to measure, even for economists. The Gallup polls do not ask respondents whether they think they benefit from particular programs. Nor is it possible to identify individual recipients of benefits (AFDC mothers, aerospace workers) from Gallup's broad demographic categories. Two sorts of indirect evidence are available, however, concerning the salience of benefits to individuals. The first makes quasi-experimental use of question ordering in a 1976 NORC survey which included the Gallup question on taxes. The second looks at changes over time in the attitudes of three demographic subgroups: blacks, farmers, and party identifiers.

No attempt will be made to predict a particular level of tax support as a function of benefits received at any given time. Rather, patterns of discontent with taxes will be viewed as a function of changes in governmental policies. The basic hypothesis, following Downs's analysis, is that the greater the salience of benefits accruing to a particular group, the more likely members of that group should be to state that their taxes are about right.

The relationship between perception of government benefits and tax attitudes was tested through questionnaire position of the Gallup Poll income tax question on the Spring 1976 NORC General Social Survey. In half of the interviews it preceded a question on federal spending; in the other half it followed that question. The prediction was that people who had just answered several questions on spending priorities would assess their tax burden differently than people who were not thus made aware of possible uses for their tax dollars.

The spending question was:

> We are faced with many problems in this country, none of which can be solved easily or inexpensively. I'm going to name some of these problems and for each one I'd like you to tell me whether you think we are spending too much money on it, too little, or about the right amount on . . . [space exploration, environment, health, big cities, crime, drugs, education, blacks, military and defense, foreign aid, welfare.]

When the spending question *followed* the tax question, 71 percent of the respondents said their taxes were too high. But when the spending question came first, only 57 percent of the respondents complained about high taxes, and the difference in responses between the two groups was statistically significant at the .05 level. This result supports Downs's hypothesis that the more aware people are of benefits received, the less likely they will be to complain about their tax bills.

Two additional tests of the relationship between benefits and tax dissatisfaction examined attitudes of blacks and farmers. Although there are many economic and social differences within each of these groups, both have reasonably well-defined and well-articulated sets of interests. Government policies which benefit either blacks or farmers, therefore, are likely to be (in Downs's terms) visible minority-benefiting policies which should cross their perceptual thresholds and affect their attitudes toward taxes along with their incomes.

Because their policy goals were seldom realized at state or local levels, blacks have turned to the federal government to support welfare, education, employment, and civil rights programs. Their willingness to pay federal taxes, therefore, should covary with federal initiatives in these areas. We would like to compare the tax attitudes of blacks who do and do not benefit from specific governmental policies, but cannot do so with the Gallup data. Neither can we examine trends over time for federal programs that benefit blacks disproportionately, since most such programs are of recent origin and benefit many whites as well. Therefore, we simply compare blacks' and whites' tax-support scores before, during, and after the War on Poverty impetus of the Kennedy and Johnson administrations.

As figure 8-2 shows, tax attitudes of black and white Americans moved in tandem until the mid-1950s.[6] Blacks' tax dissatisfaction decreased sharply about the time of Little Rock, but then moved considerably higher than whites' until the mid-1960s. This trend may have reflected a growing racial consciousness among blacks (heightened by events in Selma, Birmingham, the 1963 march on Washington, and the efforts of civil rights groups), plus discontent with the incremental and legalistic policy changes made by the federal government (Morris, 1975). Black tax scores declined sharply in 1965 and dipped below whites' in 1966, however, coinciding with federal efforts to provide direct and tangible benefits to blacks through the war on Poverty, Head Start, and other programs. By 1967, black scores marginally exceeded those of whites as Vietnam diverted national attention from domestic programs. Black dissatisfaction with taxes moved even higher under the Nixon administration's "benign neglect" and the economic downturn after 1972, which hurt blacks far more than whites.[7]

Policy changes, of course, are not the only explanations of blacks' tax attitudes. Blacks' incomes have risen somewhat, both in absolute terms and relative to whites, since 1947; this could account for the slight upward trend in blacks' tax scores from 1947 to 1973. But such a linear trend would not explain the sharp decline in blacks' dissatisfaction with taxes in the mid-1960s. Blacks are overwhelmingly Democratic in party preference, but their tax-dissatisfaction scores under Nixon and Eisenhower are considerably higher than those of white Democrats. While several studies have noted that blacks display lower levels of political trust than whites (Marvick, 1965), our evidence suggests considerable variability in blacks' attitudes and a reversal of the usual pattern in 1965. The hypothesis that blacks' tax attitudes depend partly on federal spending policies toward blacks, then, appears plausible. It merits further examination with more precise data on federal programs and on the attitudes of blacks toward those programs.

Farmers are of interest to us because they have the lowest tax dissatisfaction of any population group we examined. A few farmers even said their income taxes were too *low* (probably because they would much

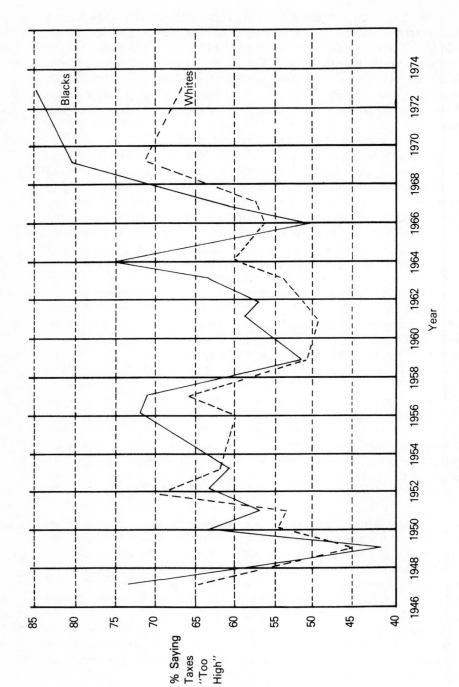

Figure 8-2. Tax Dissatisfaction Scores by Race, 1947-1973

prefer to pay income taxes than property taxes). But farmers have also been the recipients of largesse from the massive farm-subsidy program. We would therefore expect that variations in a government spending for agriculture would affect farmers' tax attitudes. On the benefit side, we should of course control for region and for the type of crop produced, but this was not feasible since farmers constitute such a small part of a Gallup survey. We must therefore assume that farmers as a group would be aware of an increase in federal spending on agriculture, and that their tax support would vary inversely with changes in federal spending.

In figure 8-3, farmers' tax-support scores are plotted against the percent change in federal spending on agriculture between the two fiscal years directly preceding the posing of the tax question. Some rough symmetry is evident, especially during the mid-1960s and during the Korean War; the fit is not as good before 1950 or in the late 1950s, when a huge, federally-financed agricultural surplus may have depressed farm prices. The overall relationship is a respectable Pearson's R of $-.41$. The greater the rate of increase in federal appropriations for agriculture and rural development, the greater the decrease in the proportion of farmers complaining their income taxes are too high.

Budget making, however, is not a zero-sum game. Downs (1960, p. 91) suggests the role of implicit logrolling among overlapping minorities in producing budget packages. Government decision makers seldom set an upper limit on the total size of a budget and then divide up the pie; instead, they seek to maximize returns at the polls per dollar spent. Benefits to farmers, therefore, are not necessarily granted at others' expense. Federal spending on agriculture may benefit many people, and farm appropriations can have a multiplier effect on the economy, especially since the Food Stamp program was initiated in 1961 under Agriculture Department auspices. To further test Downs's hypothesis about minority-benefiting policies, we computed Pearson correlations between changes in agricultural spending and tax-support scores of other occupational groups. None of the results (professionals, .03; white-collar, $-.07$; skilled workers, .11; unskilled workers, $-.11$) were statistically significant or very substantial. This would be expected, according to Downs's theory: although federal agricultural spending may ultimately benefit many people, few people other than farmers are likely to be aware of such benefits.

Tax Dissatisfaction and Political Values

Thus far, Downs's hypotheses concerning minority benefits and willingness to pay taxes have found some support based on an examination of blacks,

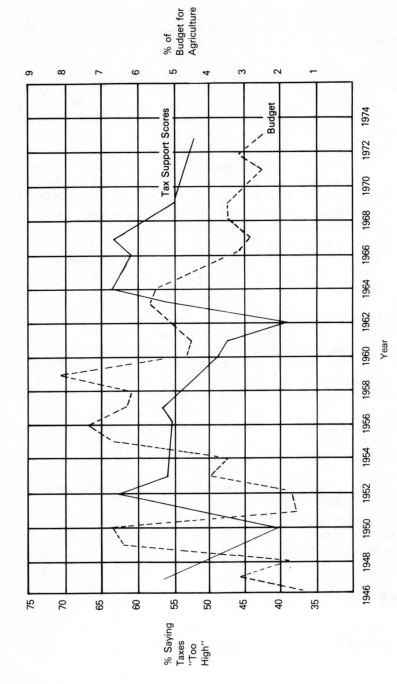

Figure 8-3. Tax Dissatisfaction among Farmers and Agriculture Appropriations as a Percent of Federal Budget, 1947-1973

farmers, and an NORC experiment with question ordering. We now return to the decision rules used by the general population to evaluate tax burdens and budget size. Tax increases have some effect, but cannot account for all of the variation in complaints about "too high" income taxes beween 1947 and 1978. As many studies of electoral behavior have found, party iden-tification provides a useful means of reducing information costs concerning government policies.

Most people are rationally ignorant of government policies and the size of budgets. Few may be able to describe party or administrative differences in these respects (Mosher and Poland, 1964, pp. 4-5). But, as Rogowski (1973, chapter 2) suggested, people who are rationally ignorant of policy outputs may judge them by the legitimacy of the procedures or the person-nel responsible for making decisions. Popular attitudes toward federal in-come should thus depend in part on political control of the government in Washington. A Democrat should be more likely to support the taxing and spending decisions of a Democratic than a Republican administration.

Democrats and Republicans generally differ in their evaluations of what governments should do and how collective goods should be financed. Democrats usually support increased spending by the federal government, progressive taxation, and active government intervention in the economy, while Republicans have traditionally opposed such measures. In general, one would therefore expect Republican party identifiers in the population to be less supportive of income taxes than Democratic identifiers, with political independents falling somewhere in between those two groups. But partisans' attitudes at any particular point should depend on what party in Washington is raising and spending their tax money.

To test these hypotheses, tax dissatisfaction was plotted separately (figure 8-4) for Democrats, Republicans, and Independents for the 1947-1973 period. Overall party differences are small and not statistically significant: Democrats average 57 percent, Independents 59 percent, and Republicans 60 percent "too high" responses. But in fourteen of the eigh-teen years in which Gallup posed the tax question, Democrats were less discontented with their income taxes than were Republicans, with In-dependents scoring in between the partisan groups. In general, however, party support scores show similar trends up until 1970.

Rogowski's legitimacy hypothesis also receives some support. In three of the four years in which Democrats' tax dissatisfaction exceeded Republicans' (1959, 1969, 1973), a Republican was President. And the fourth year (1948) was during one of the two Congresses controlled by Republicans since World War II. The 1973 difference of eighteen points is the largest in the series: the combined effects of Vietnam, a troubled economy, a Republican president, and the growing Watergate scandal

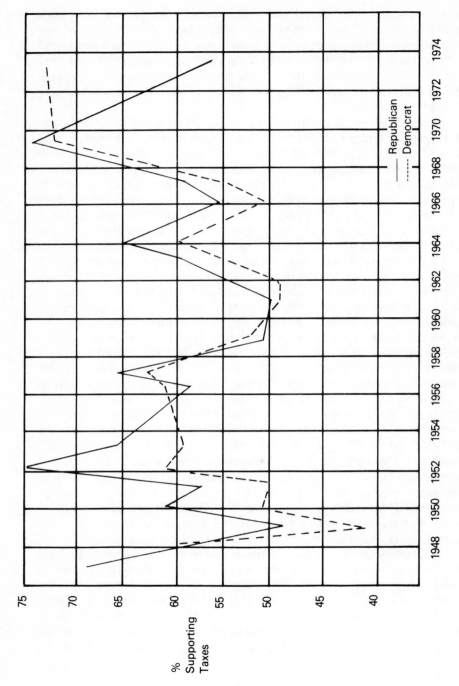

Figure 8-4. Partisan Trends in Support for Taxes, 1947-1973

dramatically reversed the usual propensity of Democrats to perceive their federal tax bill as about right.

To further test control of government on partisan evaluations of tax burdens, tax scores were computed separately for Democrats and Republicans during the periods when their party did and did not hold the presidency. The in-office party's average of 56 percent "too high" responses was lower than those for the out-of-office party (averaging 61 percent): the difference of means was statistically significant at the .06 level.

On closer examination, however, inparty-outparty differences proved to vary across administrations, and to be almost entirely due to shifts in the tax-support scores of *Democrats* (table 8-1). Under the Eisenhower and Kennedy administrations, tax dissatisfaction was low, and differences between Republicans and Democrats were small. Party differences were most dramatic during the Truman years and in 1973. Democratic tax scores averaged 54 under Democratic presidents and 64 under Eisenhower and Nixon. But Republicans averaged 60 under Democratic presidents and 61 under Republicans: their very high tax score of 74 in 1969, based on a Gallup survey fielded only a month after Nixon took office, was probably due to resentment over decisions (Vietnam, surtax, War on Poverty) of the Johnson years, not the actions of the new president.

It has been suggested that people's willingness to pay taxes may depend on a generalized trust in government and confidence in public officials. One index of such attitudes at the national level could be popular approval of the way a particular president is handling his job, Gallup's oft-repeated indicator of presidential popularity. This index does show some relationship to tax dissatisfaction ($R = .21$ overall, $R = .36$ if we exclude the furthest outlier on the trend line: Nixon's very high popularity immediately upon assuming office in 1969, at a time of considerable disgruntlement with taxes). This aggregate relationship is supported by data from individual

Table 8-1
Tax Discontent under Recent Presidential Administrations, Controlling for Party Identification

Percent Reporting Taxes "Too High"	Truman	Eisenhower	Kennedy	Johnson	Nixon
All	56.8	56.8	48.0	57.0	66.5
Democrats	54.2	59.8	51.0	55.3	73.5
Republicans	61.5	60.0	54.3	60.0	65.0
Independents	59.8	62.0	52.0	57.0	71.0

surveys: identifiers with both parties who approve of the president are less likely to feel their taxes are too high. But the relationship is not too strong, and we cannot determine whether presidential unpopularity produces discontent with taxes or vice versa.

For the general population, then, political ties and values are associated with attitudes toward taxes. Of course, party identifiers usually select their party on the basis of expected benefits from that party's policies, but socialization patterns, habit, ignorance, and regional differences in the meaning of party may produce considerable variations from an identity of party preferences and benefits received. Perceptions of party stands are what matters here; and these perceptions, accurate or not, are often the only low-cost political information many people have concerning the size of the federal budget.

Temporal Change in Preferences for Budget Size

The analysis thus far has tested several decision rules available to different population groups for evaluating their tax burdens. But what is the budgetary outcome of these separate group choices? One can hardly derive a social-choice function by summing across these individual utilities. We can, however, describe some changes in the relative influence of various population groups over the time period covered by the Gallup surveys, and suggest a temporal perspective on the question of budget size in democracies.

1. Since 1947, tax burdens have risen and government spending has increased, both in dollars and as a proportion of GNP. Net tax dissatisfaction is marginally higher over this period (Pearson R with time is .15), but has not increased in a steadily ascending curve as have spending and taxes. Instead, it has exhibited cyclical properties; the Taxpayers' Revolt of the late 1960s and 1970s parallels that of the late 1940s and early 1950s, and both are closely linked to American involvement in unpopular foreign wars. This suggests a modification of Peacock and Wiseman's (1961) theory: popular wars may indeed displace public tolerance of taxes to higher levels, but unpopular ones apparently do not (Hansen and Carroll, 1976). The tax burden (and by inference, the budget size) preferred by the public thus appears to be highly variable.

2. A dramatic change in federal spending has occurred since Downs concluded in 1960 that government budgets were too small. Transfer payments to individuals have increased from 18 percent of federal spending in 1955 to over 43 percent in 1976 (Leloup, 1977, p. 55). A much larger proportion of the public, therefore, is now dependent on federal spending for its income. In the aftermath of the Great Society and the War on Poverty,

many Americans may well have changed, in Downs's terms, from states of partial ignorance to preponderant ignorance. The result may well be considerable upward pressures on government budgets. Downs's conclusion about too-small budgets may well have been accurate for the Eisenhower era, but Buchanan and Tullock could be the prophets of the 1970s. The ongoing debate over budget size in democracies should consider Tufte's (1978, p. 151) rewording of Keynes: economic theory reflects political reality as least as much as politics is influenced by economic thought.

3. The proportion of persons identifying with a political party has decreased considerably since the early 1950s. This may dampen the cyclical swings in tax dissatisfaction which have corresponded to changes in party control of the presidency. Rogowski's analysis may be more appropriate for a highly partisan era. With the weakening of party ties as guides to the patterns of government spending, people must evaluate their tax burdens on other grounds.

4. Politicians must consider the size of budgets relative to the preferences of the median voter, not the median taxpayer. An irony of the present condition of low electoral turnout is that the persons (blacks, the poor, the elderly, and dependent children) most dependent on the government for their incomes are least likely to vote. As Verba and Nie (1972) noted, participation is much higher among upper-status Republicans, the population group least in favor of high taxes and spending. An electoral strategy advocating cuts in taxes and decreases in spending may thus curry political favor in the short run.

This could entail some political risk: if the cuts were deep enough, popular discontent could bring enough low-income people to the polls to bring about closer correspondence between median voter and median taxpayer, and to increase pressures for government spending. That possibility appears unlikely, however. Effective political support for federal spending depends not only on the number of persons favoring it, but on their strategic location. In Piven's (1974) analysis, the growth of federal spending for poverty programs in the 1960s was not a function of increases in numbers of blacks, or of poor persons (who actually declined). Rather, their concentration in northern cities became vital for Democratic presidential strategy. As Democratic votes shifted to the suburbs and the Sunbelt in the 1970s, however, urban black votes were no longer crucial to the party. Population shifts and low turnout among black and poor Americans have greatly diminished effective political support for increases in domestic spending.

Summary

In this chapter, time-series analysis of Gallup Poll data was used to examine the relationship between people's attitudes toward taxes and the benefits they receive from the federal government. The tests covered specific groups (blacks, farmers), party identifiers, and finally, the general population. In each case, the results were the same: the more visible the benefits, the more willing people were to feel their federal taxes were about right rather than too high. Such a result might be expected from analysis of individuals or groups who actually received benefits, but that approach has not been feasible because of the lack of appropriate survey data. These results are thus based more on inference than on direct evidence. Changes in tax attitudes have been noted to vary with changes in perceived benefits for the population as a whole as well as for the minority-benefiting policies which Downs's original theory suggested. But data on partisan evaluation of taxes suggests that factors other than costs and benefits account for attitudes toward taxes.

This evidence also suggests that Meltsner (1971) was on the right track when he suggested that local officials should emphasize the services they provide in order to obtain more revenue. Politicians do not simply respond to public preferences—they can also manipulate them. Political entrepreneurs who advertise the benefits to be gained from increased government spending in particular areas may gain the support not only of free riders, but of people who are willing to pay for services rendered in the public-goods arena, and who judge governmental programs in political as well as economic terms. An even more effective strategy may be to threaten cutbacks in popular programs, and thus increase the saliency of benefits. The threat of such cutbacks appears to have been an important reason for the failure of the Kemp-Roth proposals, and for the weak impact of the tax revolt of 1978.

Frohlich, Oppenheimer, and Young (1971) suggest a "leader's surplus"—excess of revenues over expenditures—as an incentive for political entrepreneurs to supply public-goods packages at attractive prices to citizen consumers (taxpayers). Political leaders therefore have incentives to increase the size of government revenues. On balance, analysts of public choice such as Buchanan and Wagner (1977) may well be right in saying that democracies tend toward a large gap between ideal (optimal or efficient) and actual budgets. Politicians must be far more concerned with the differences between present and preferred budgets than with the optimal or efficient budgets, however; large budgets that are preferred budgets can continue to grow and to win elections.

The size of preferred budgets, however, is highly variable. As this analysis has suggested, public preferences for government spending have varied considerably over time in the United States, and tax burdens account for only a portion of those preferences. As a result, budget size in democracies is self-correcting to some degree. The welfare state has indeed grown (Rose and Peters, 1978), but the result has been tax revolts in Denmark and the United

States, spending cuts in Britain, and a return to free-market practices in continental democracies previously inclined toward socialism. Whether these events will arrest the growth of the welfare state remains to be seen. Nevertheless, some democracies have managed to have balanced budgets, sound currency, and low inflation while providing considerably more public services than does the United States. Theories of budget size in democracy must consider changes in public preferences as well as the institutional arrangements which transform these preferences into collective outcomes. The budgets which result may be neither efficient nor optimal, but governments are unlikely to go bankrupt if citizens can be persuaded that the benefits gained thereby are worth their cost in taxes.

Notes

1. See Lindsay and Norman (1977) for an incisive critique of the logic of Galbraith's arguments and the liberal philosophy underlying them.

2. In some years, the order of the "too high, too low, or about right" responses was changed, but this had no apparent effect. Female respondents were asked about "the taxes your husband has to pay," but sex differences in responses were minimal and consistent. Between 1947 and 1952, Gallup included a filter question to eliminate persons who did not file income tax returns. The post-1952 surveys thus include responses of a small (less than 10 percent) portion of nonfilers, but we have no way of assessing differences in tax attitudes between filers and nonfilers.

3. Other factors in time-series analysis (secular trend, cyclical variation, and erratic or irregular fluctuation) will be considered below. See also Hansen and Carroll (1976) for more detailed discussion of these methodological issues.

4. Pechman (1977, pp. 288 ff.) has a concise discussion of changes in federal tax laws and tax incidence. For this correlational analysis, years with tax increases were coded +1; tax decreases, −1; and no across-the-board change, 0.

5. See Tufte (1978) for a discussion of the politics of Social Security; benefits have been increased before elections, while tax increases become effective months later.

6. Racial comparisons before 1952 are highly unreliable, since blacks were seriously underrepresented by Gallup's quota samples, and since "no opinion" responses were more frequently given by blacks than by whites.

7. An Urban League policy study found that "the recession of 1968-71 was so severe that it caused the number of black poor to rise for the first time since poverty statistics were instituted in the early 1960's." The economy may thus have augmented blacks' distrust of Nixon's policies.

References

Amacher, Ryan C., et al. "Budget Size in a Democracy: A Review of the Arguments." *Public Finance Quarterly* 3(April 1975):99-121.

Buchanan, James. *Public Finance in Democratic Process.* Chapel Hill: University of North Carolina Press, 1967.

Buchanan, James, and Gordon Tullock. *The Calculus of Consent.* Ann Arbor: University of Michigan Press, 1962.

Buchanan, James M., and Richard E. Wagner. *Democracy in Deficit: The Political Legacy of Lord Keynes.* New York: Academic Press, 1977.

Downs, Anthony. "Why the Government Budget is Too Small in a Democracy." *World Politics* 12(July 1960):76-95.

Frohlich, Norman; B. Oppenheimer; and O. Young. *Political Leadership and Collective Goods.* Princeton: Princeton University Press, 1971.

Galbraith, John Kenneth. *The Affluent Society.* Boston: Houghton Mifflin, 1958.

Hansen, Susan B., and John M. Carroll. "Changes in Popular Attitudes Toward Taxes, 1947-1973." Paper presented at the annual meeting of the American Political Science Association, Chicago, 1976.

Katona, George. *Psychological Economics.* New York: Atheneum, 1975.

Leloup, Lance T. *Budgetary Politics: Dollars, Deficits, Decisions.* Brunswick, Ohio: Kings Court, 1977.

Lindsay, Cotton M., and Don Norman. "Reopening the Questions of Government Spending." In *Budgets and Bureaucrats: The Sources of Economic Growth*, edited by Thomas Borcherding. Durham: Duke University Press, 1977.

Marvick, Duane. "The Political Socialization of the American Negro." *The Annals* 361(September 1965).

Meltsner, Andrew. *The Politics of City Revenue.* Berkeley: University of California Press, 1971.

Morris, Milton. *The Politics of Black America.* New York: Harper and Row, 1975.

Mosher, Frederick C., and Orville F. Poland. *The Costs of American Governments.* New York: Dodd, Mead, 1964.

Newman, Karen. "The Use of AIPO Surveys: to Weight or Not to Weight." Mimeo. Chicago: National Opinion Research Center, 1975.

Peacock, Alan T., and Jack Wiseman. *The Growth of Public Expenditures in the United Kingdom.* Princeton: Princeton University Press, 1961.

Pechman, Joseph A. *Federal Tax Policy.* 3rd ed. Washington: Brookings, 1977.

Piven, Frances Fox. "Who Got What and Why?" In *The Politics of Turmoil*, edited by Richard Cloward and Frances Fox Piven. New York: Pantheon Books, 1974.

Rogowski, Ronald. *Rational Legitimacy*. Princeton: Princeton University Press, 1973.

Rose, Richard, and Guy Peters. *Can Governments Go Bankrupt?* New York: Basic Books, 1978.

Tufte, Edward R. *Political Control of the Economy*. Princeton: Princeton University Press, 1978.

Van Wagstaff, Joseph. "Income Tax Consciousness Under Withholding." *Southern Economic Journal* 32(1965):73-80.

Verba, Sidney, and Norman H. Nie. *Participation in America: Political Democracy and Social Equality*. New York: Harper and Row, 1965.

9

Public Interest versus Private Benefit: An Empirical Test of Two Competing Theories of the Impact of the Oil Depletion Allowance

Jon R. Bond

Introduction

This chapter deals with the general question: "What are the effects of public policies?" It explicates two competing theories of the effects of the oil depletion allowance and tests the theories with time-series data.

The formation of policy is not the end of the policy-making process. To understand the total process, one must ask what, if anything, happens as a result of public policy. Impact analysis views public policies as one factor among many that influence behavior.

One of the greatest problems of impact analysis is to isolate the effects of policies from the effects of other factors. To make plausible causal inferences about policy impact, one must first think theoretically about what variables other than public policy are likely to influence the behavior in question and control or remove their possible effects.

This analysis seeks to discover the relationships between national oil policy and aggregate behavior of oil producers. Oil producers are primarily economic actors engaged in economic enterprise. Economic forces are major determinants (causes) of their behavior. In the evaluation of oil policy, the effects of economic forces must be controlled in order to separate out the effects of public policies. Thus, the question of the impact of oil policies becomes: "What effects do oil policies have on industry behavior in addition to the effects of economic variables?"

The literature analyzing the effects of the oil depletion allowance falls into two groups: (1) evaluations by and for the oil industry, and (2) evaluations by academic economists. The problem presented by these analyses is that they offer conflicting evaluations. This chapter views these conflicting evaluations as competing theories. This conceptualization helps explain the findings and understand why there are conflicting evaluations.

**Two Theories of the Effects of
the Oil Depletion Allowance**

Public Interest Theory: Oil Industry Evaluations

The common theme of oil industry justifications of the depletion allowance is that producing oil is a unique activity, so the special tax benefits that oil producers receive are in the public interest. The oil industry offers two related justifications for receiving the special tax benefits of the depletion allowance in addition to cost and depreciation deductions available to all taxpayers. First, the industry argues that the nation needs an abundant supply of domestic oil for national security, so public policy should encourage exploration for new reserves. The oil depletion allowance is a necessary and effective means to encourage exploration and discovery of new reserves to avoid shortages. This added incentive is necessary because discovery and development of new reserves is so risky and costly that the free market will not allocate sufficient resources to exploration. Second, the industry argues that the depletion allowance is in consumers' interest because it reduces the price of oil. The basis for this argument is that discovery and production of oil are so risky and costly, the price of oil to consumers must increase if new supplies are to be added. The oil depletion allowance helps offset the high costs of discovery and development which increases supply and reduces price (Davidson, 1970, p. 1; Davidson, 1963, p. 85; Freeman, 1955, pp. 416-417; Galvin, 1960, p. 1442; Gifford, 1960, pp. 211-212).

Private Benefit Theory

The alternative theory is based in part on the null hypothesis of the public interest theory; that is, the oil depletion allowance does not encourage exploration or keep prices low, so it does not serve the public interest. Failure to reject the null hypothesis implies that if the depletion allowance has an effect, it is to benefit private oil producers without benefiting the public. However, empirical support for a private benefit theory requires not only that one fail to reject the null hypothesis of the public interest theory, but also that one demonstrate the existence of a positive relationship between the oil depletion allowance and benefits received exclusively by oil producers.

A private benefit theory is implicit in economic analyses of the effects of the oil depletion allowance. Criticis question the validity of the oil industry's two major justifications for special treatment. First, economic critics argue that the oil depletion allowance is not an efficient means to encourage exploration and discovery of new reserves. Rather, the depletion allowance encourages production from existing wells. The greatest impetus for exploration is price (Kahn, 1964; Davidson, 1970; Davidson, 1963; Erickson, 1970). The reason the depletion allowance primarily affects producing land is because the depletion allowance is only a potential tax advantage for exploratory wells. However, the effects of price are more certain. Therefore, "the expectation of a stable, high price for output" is the greatest stimulus for exploration (Davidson, 1970, p. 6).

Second, economists argue that any price-depressing effects the depletion allowance might have are offset by market demand prorationing and import quotas (Mead, 1970, pp. 116-119). Because the depletion allowance has its greatest effect on already-producing property, it benefits only oil producers in the form of "windfall rents" (Davidson, 1963; Davidson, 1964).

These economic evaluations do not explain why the depletion policy fails to achieve its stated purpose. Nor do they explain why there are conflicting evaluations of the policy's effects. The private benefit theory can be expanded to explain why certain types of policy fail and why there are likely to be conflicting evaluations.

Public policy is governmental action (or inaction) intended to achieve a goal by influencing the behavior of individuals. The method of influencing behavior represents a choice to use the coercive power of government in one way rather than another. Thus, policies may be categorized on a continuum according to the level of governmental coercion associated with them. Government may attempt to achieve a goal directly by requiring or proscribing certain behavior with highly coercive sanctions, or it may attempt to achieve a goal indirectly with mildly coercive incentives or disincentives.

One assumes that policy recipients, those whose behavior a policy is attempting to influence, are rational actors who attempt to shape the impact of a policy to maximize their self-interest.[1] The form of a policy (indirect or direct) determines the ease with which policy recipients are able to manipulate policy impact to maximize self-interest. Policy recipients have a great deal of discretion to influence the impact of indirect policies.

If policy recipients are able to manipulate the impact of policy to maximize their private self-interest, then the stated goals of the policy are not likely to be achieved unless they coincide with the private self-interest. However, if public and private interests coincide, then indirect policies such as tax incentives create windfalls by paying policy recipients to do what they would do anyway (Surrey, 1970). Although such policies do not alter behavior, the interest receiving the benefits has an incentive to claim that the policy is working. A policy evaluation that claims that an ineffective policy is achieving its public purpose is not necessarily the result of an outright lie. Rather, the faulty evaluation may be related to what Gordon Tullock (1975) calls the "transitional gains trap." Tullock argues that some policies initially generate "transitional gains," or benefits, but these gains are "fully capitalized" over time. The result is that those who receive the benefits are not better off and do not behave any differently than they would if they had never received the policy benefits. However, termination of the policy would lead to large losses. Under these conditions, policy recipients will claim an ineffective policy is working, and they may even believe it.

The stated purposes of the oil depletion allowance are to encouarge exploration and keep the price of oil low. The depletion allowance is an indirect policy in that it attempts to achieve its public goals by providing incentives to private actors (oil companies) in the form of an additional tax deduction that is not available to other taxpayers. Oil companies receive the benefits of the oil depletion allowance whether it achieves its public goals or not, but economic forces in the free market are less generous. Therefore, the industry accepts the benefits of the public policy and provides evaluations of the policy indicating that it is achieving its public goals.

Hypotheses

Each theory generates a set of hypotheses that can be tested empirically with time-series data. The public interest theory suggests:

Hypothesis 1. Controlling for economic forces, there is a positive nonchance association between the level of the oil depletion allowance at time t-1 and exploration for crude oil at time t;

Hypothesis 2. Controlling for economic forces, there is a negative nonchance association between the level of the oil depletion allowance at time t-1 and the price of crude oil at time t.

The private benefit theory suggests:

Hypothesis 3. Controlling for economic forces, there is no relationship between the level of the oil depletion allowance at time t-1 and exploration for crude oil at time t (the null hypothesis of hypothesis 1);

Hypothesis 4. Controlling for economic forces, there is no relationship between the level of the oil depletion allowance at t-1 and the price of crude oil at time t (the null hypothesis of hypothesis 2);

Hypothesis 5. There is a positive nonchance relationship between the benefits of the oil depletion allowance at time t and the oil industry profit differential at time t.

Note that hypothesis 5 predicts that it is the benefits of the depletion deduction and not the level of the depletion allowance alone that explains variation in the difference between oil profits and all-industry profits (the profit differential). The rationale for this formulation is that oil producers receive the depletion allowance in addition to tax deductions received by all industries. Moreover, dollars saved from a given depletion rate increase as the tax increases. If either the depletion rate or the tax rate increases, the difference between oil industry taxes and all-industry taxes increases. If hypothesis 5 is correct, this additional tax saving (benefits) increases the difference between oil profits and all-industry profits. To test hypothesis 5, it is not necessary to include other economic variables as controls, because one is attempting to explain the profit *differential*, and the same factors affect the profits of oil companies and other industries.[2]

Data and Measurement of Variables

The Sample

The data are annual measures of the oil depletion allowance policy and the behavior of the oil-producing industry from 1900 through 1974. Four of the hypotheses predict a one-year time lag between the level of the depletion allowance and its effect, if any, on oil industry behavior. The decision to use annual measures with one-year lags is based on the recognition that income taxes are paid once annually. Therefore, the effects of the oil depletion allowance for a year will not be observable until the following year.

Policy Variables

For the test of hypotheses 1 through 4, the policy variable is measured as the percentage depletion rate each year from 1900 through 1974. One can obtain a percentage rate directly from the statutes for all years except ten (1917 through 1926).[3] For those years in which the statute did not provide a flat percentage deduction, one can estimate the empirical percentage being taken based on surveys of oil companies' practices in 1924 (Lichtblau and Spriggs, 1959, pp. 41-42), and knowledge of the percentage rates in the years immediately before and after this ten-year period.[4]

Hypothesis 5 requires a measure of depletion allowance benefits. Measuring the benefits of the oil depletion allowance is difficult. Individual tax returns are not available to the public, so there is no way to determine the number of dollars in taxes the depletion allowance saved oil companies each year in the policy's history. Moreover, because the tax rate is progressive, high-income companies benefit more from the depletion allowance in a given year than do low-income companies. These problems make direct measurement of benefits impossible, but an indirect measure can be constructed. From available data, one can compute an indicator of the effective tax rate for all corporations as follows:

$$\textit{Effective Tax Rate}_t \;=\; \frac{\textit{Corporate taxes}_t}{\textit{Corporate Net Income}_t}$$

This formula yields the proportion of all corporations' net income at time t paid in taxes. This figure is not the actual tax rate, but it does serve as an indicator of the overall *effective tax rate* for all corporations. The effective tax rate and the percentage depletion allowance at a given point in time determine the benefits of the depletion deduction. Therefore, an indicator of oil depletion allowance benefits may be calculated as follows:

$$\text{ODA Benefits}_t \;=\; \%\ ODA_t \cdot \text{Effective Tax Rate}_t$$

While this variable does not directly measure benefits, its behavior mimics the behavior depletion benefits—it increases if one or both of the components increases, and it decreases if one or both of these components decreases.

Economic Variables

The economic variables are yearly measures of exploration, price, production, and the oil industry profit differential. Exploration is measured as the total number of wells drilled each year from 1900 through 1974. Figure 9-1 is a plot of total wells drilled over time. Note that there are two trends present in the data, a *secular trend* and a *cyclical trend*. A secular trend is the "long-term tendency for a variable to change its value over time. It represents a regular progression in one direction or the other over time." (Kirkpatrick, 1974, p. 390). A cyclical trend is "a wavelike movement of data through time. They show no regularity as to when they recur or how long they last. . . ." (Simpson and Kafka, 1952, p. 252). In economic time-series data, these cycles are related to economic prosperity and depression and are commonly referred to as *business cycles*. While public policies often influence economic prosperity and business cycles, the changes in oil depletion policy alone are not likely to affect these cycles. The cycles in these data are more likely a function of nonpolicy economic variables. Hence, if one is interested in the impact of policy, one must control for the effects of these cycles, and focus on the relationship, if any, between the depletion policy and the secular trend.

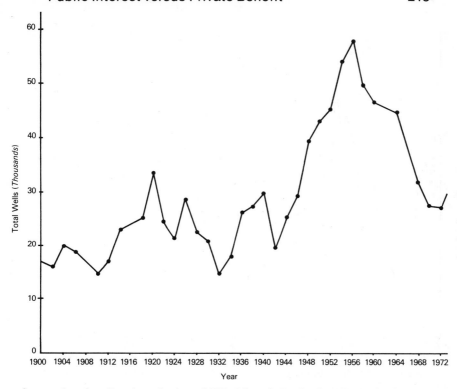

Source: American Petroleum Institute (1971), *Minerals Yearbook* (1973); Federal Energy Administration (1975).

Figure 9-1. Total Wells Drilled, 1900-1974

Price of crude oil is measured as the average yearly price per forty-two-gallon barrel of oil in constant 1967 dollars.[5] Figure 9-2 is a plot of the price of oil over time. With the effects of inflation removed, there is a notable absence of a secular trend in this variable, but there is a cyclical trend.

Production is measured as the total number of forty-two-gallon barrels of oil produced each year from 1900 through 1974. Figure 9-3 is a plot of oil production over time. The most striking characteristic of this measure is the strong secular trend. Closer inspection, however, reveals that cycles are also present, but they are much less pronounced than the cycles in exploration and price.

The oil industry profit differential is measured by the oil industry rate of return minus all-industry rate of return each year from 1925 through 1974.[6] Figure 9-4 is a plot of the profit differential over time. The data exhibit evidence of both a slight secular trend and a cyclical trend.

Source: American Petroleum Institute (1971), *Minerals Yearbook* (1973); Federal Energy Administration (1975).

Figure 9-2. Price per Barrel of Oil (1967 Dollars), 1900-1974

Data Limitations

These available measures do impose some limitations. First, the data are aggregate measures of behavior. Aggregate data present a problem because the oil industry is not a monolithic entity. Many small independents are involved only in domestic exploration and production. The major oil companies, on the other hand, are highly integrated. They are engaged in both domestic and foreign production as well as refining and distributing operations. Although the interests and policy preferences of independents and majors often diverge, there are many areas of convergence. The oil depletion allowance is an area of convergence. Until the law was changed in 1975, all producers, large and small alike, benefited from the depletion allowance.[7] Therefore, if the depletion allowance had an impact on the behavior of producers, its effects should show up in aggregate measures of domestic exploration, price, and profit differential.

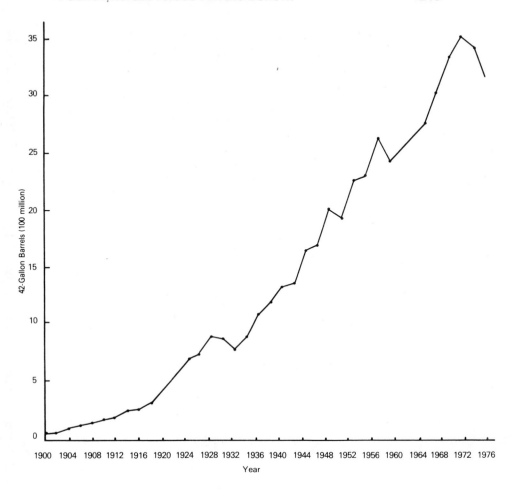

Source: American Petroleum Institute (1971), *Minerals Yearbook* (1973); Federal Energy Administration (1975).

Figure 9-3. Barrels of Oil, 1900-1974

Second, the available measure of exploration does not exactly capture *exploration for new reserves*. The only available measure of exploration for the entire time period is total wells drilled. Total wells include more than exploratory wells. However, if the depletion policy stimulated exploration, then its effects should be present in the total wells variable.[8] So long as their limitations are clear, analysis of these data should shed some light on the controversy over the effects of the oil depletion allowance.

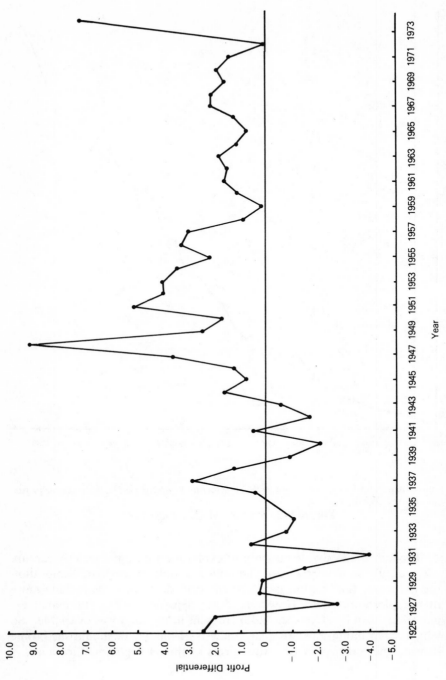

Source: American Petroleum Institute (1971, 1975).

Figure 9-4. Oil Profit Differential: Difference between Oil Profit Rate and All-Industry Profit Rate, 1925–1974

Methods

The Basic Models

Hypotheses 1 through 4 are tested with two multiple regression models to determine the effects of the oil depletion allowance on exploration and price. This approach permits one to control for economic forces that influence oil industry behavior and to account for the interrelationships among the different aspects of that behavior. The two models are:

$$W_t = a_0 + a_1 \text{ODA}_{t-1} + a_2 P_{t-1} + e_{1t}$$
$$P_t = b_0 + b_1 \text{ODA}_{t-1} + b_2 W_t + b_3 B_t + e_{2t}$$

where:

$$
\begin{aligned}
W_t &= \text{total wells drilled at time } t; \\
\text{ODA}_{t-1} &= \text{oil depletion allowance at time } t-1; \\
P_t \text{ or } t-1 &= \text{average yearly price per barrel of oil in constant 1967} \\
&\quad \text{dollars at time } t \text{ or } t-1; \\
B_t &= \text{total number of 42-gallon barrels of oil produced at} \\
&\quad \text{time } t; \\
e_{1t}, e_{2t} &= \text{random error in each equation.}
\end{aligned}
$$

The Autocorrelation Problem

Estimation of parameters from time-series data presents some special problems. One of the crucial assumptions of the basic regression model is that the error terms are nonautocorrelated (Kamenta, 1971, pp. 269-271; Johnston, 1972, pp. 243-246). This assumption is more frequently violated with time-series data than with cross-sectional data. Autocorrelated residuals may result from measurement error, an incorrectly specified model, and/or unmeasured variables (Johnston, 1972, pp. 243-244). These factors can cause autocorrelation in both cross-sectional and time-series data. However, autocorrelation is more likely to occur in time-series data because of the way they are generated. If time-series data represent a continuous process that is observed and measured at discrete points in time, then the value of a variable at one point in time will affect its own value in the next time period, and the effects of independent variables operating in one period will carry over into the next period. If autocorrelation is present, Ordinary Least Squares (OLS) parameter estimates are inefficient and standard tests of significance are not valid (Johnston, 1972, p. 246). Significant autocorrelation is present in the data used in this analysis. Visual inspection of the plots of the economic variables suggests that the autocorrelation problem is related to the cyclical trends in the data.

There are several methods available to deal with autocorrelation. One common method is Generalized Least Squares (GLS). This procedure transforms the data to force the residuals to behave consistently with the OLS assumption (Wonnacott and Wonnacott, 1970, pp. 328-332).

A second approach is to transform the variables into first differences and apply OLS. This approach predicts change in a dependent variable from change in the dependent variables. In many cases this procedure can solve the problem of autocorrelation because in some nonstationary time-series the first differences are stationary (Nelson, 1973, pp. 56-58).

A third approach is to detrend the data. Detrending usually involves estimating and removing a secular trend so that one can analyze cyclical variation. In this study, however, it is the secular trends that are of interest. The cycles create the statistical problem of autocorrelation, making least squares estimation inappropriate. In addition, the cycles are probably business cycles that are related to economic factors, making it difficult to isolate the effects of public policy on oil industry behavior. If policy has an impact on oil industry behavior, its effects are in the secular trend.

This third method of removing the business cycles from the economic variables involves accepting the fact that one year's value is related to the previous year's value. Thus, to remove the cycles, one regresses each variable as a function of itself lagged one year. The residuals from this lagged regression then become new variables with the business cycles removed. It is deviation from the previous year's value that is to be predicted. With the cycles removed, one can use Ordinary Least Squares regression to discover what impact public policies have on oil industry behavior independently of economic forces.[9]

Although these three techniques differ in their approach to solving the statistical problem of autocorrelation, substantively, each can be interpreted as a means to control or remove business cycles. Removing business cycles is essential because the public interest theory predicts that the oil depletion allowance affects industry behavior independently of economic forces. Failure to control for business cycles may produce erroneous findings. To demonstrate this point, the following section reports estimates of the basic model using OLS with no correction for autocorrelation, as well as estimates using the three techniques to remove autocorrelation. In each case, the unstandardized regression coefficient for the oil depletion variable indicates the effects of the policy on the relevant measure of industry behavior.

Public Interest Theory Results: The Effects of the Oil Depletion Allowance on Exploration and Price

Estimation by Ordinary Least Squares

Table 9-1 reports the OLS estimates. The estimates appear to support the public interest theory's prediction (hypotheses 1 and 2). The coefficients for the oil depletion allowance indicate that the policy had a positive, non-chance relationship with exploration and a negative nonchance relationship with price.[10] Based on these estimates, the model predicts that a 1 percent increase in the oil depletion allowance at time t-1 causes the total number of wells drilled in the following year to increase 550 wells ($a_1 = .550$) and the average yearly price in constant 1967 dollars to decrease about \$0.02 ($b_1 = -.02$). However, the Durbin-Watson statistics (d) indicate significant autocorrelation in each of the equations, so the estimates are inefficient and the significance tests (t) are not valid. If the argument in the present analysis is correct, autocorrelation in the model means that the effects of the policy on industry behavior have not been separated from the effects of business cycles. Therefore, a model with autocorrelation does not provide a valid test of the hypotheses of the public interest theory that the oil depletion allowance affects industry behavior independently of economic forces.

Estimation by Generalized Least Squares

Table 9-2 reports the GLS estimates. The Durbin-Watson statistics indicate that the procedure successfully removed the autocorrelation. The interpretation of the effects of the oil depletion allowance based on these efficient estimates is substantially different from the interpretation based on

Table 9-1
Estimates of the Effects of the Oil Depletion Allowance on Oil Industry Behavior Using Ordinary Least Squares

Dependent Variables	Independent Variables		Regression Coefficient	t-Test (One-Tail)	R^2	d
Wells$_t$	Intercept	(a_0)	-5.10		.43	.538
	ODA$_{t-1}$	(a_1)	.55	6.03 p < .0005		
	Price$_{t-1}$	(a_2)	8.05	4.81 p < .0005		
Price$_t$	Intercept	(b_0)	2.24		.40	.709
	ODA$_{t-1}$	(b_1)	$-.02$	-3.31 p < .005		
	Wells$_t$	(b_2)	.04	6.10 p < .0005		
	Barrels$_t$	(b_3)	$-.00007$	$-.73$ n.s.		

Table 9-2
Estimates of the Effects of the Oil Depletion Allowance on Oil Industry Behavior Using Generalized Least Squares

Dependent Variables	Independent Variables		Regression Coefficient	t-Test (One-Tail)	R^2	d
Wells$_t$	Intercept	(a_0)	31.09		.88[a]	1.848
	ODA$_{t-1}$	(a_1)	.08	.49 n.s.		
	Price$_{t-1}$	(a_2)	-1.44	-1.33 n.s.		
Price$_t$	Intercept	(b_0)	3.14		.70[a]	2.061
	ODA$_{t-1}$	(b_1)	-.005	-.31 n.s.		
	Wells$_t$	(b_2)	.08	8.13 p < .0005		
	Barrels$_t$	(b_3)	-.001	-2.72 p < .005		

[a]The interpretation of R^2 with GLS estimation is unclear.

the inefficient OLS estimates. With this correction for autocorrelation, the regression coefficients for the oil depletion allowance are not significant, so the null hypotheses that the oil depletion has no relationship to exploration or price cannot be rejected. Since hypotheses 3 and 4 are the null hypotheses of 1 and 2, this finding tends to support the private benefit theory.

Estimation of First Differences

Table 9-3 reports the OLS estimates of the model using first differences. In this case the original measures of oil industry behavior (wells drilled, barrels produced, and price in constant dollars) are transformed into measures of change from one year to the next: $\Delta X_t = X_t - X_{t-1}$; $\Delta X_{t-1} = X_{t-1} - X_{t-2}$. The Durbin-Watson statistics indicate that this procedure successfully removed autocorrelation. The substantive interpretation of the effects of

Table 9-3
Estimates of the Effects of the Oil Depletion Allowance on Oil Industry Behavior Using First Differences

Dependent Variables	Independent Variables		Regression Coefficient	t-Test	R^2	d
Wells$_t$	Intercept	(a_0)	.57		.02	1.929
	ODA$_{t-1}$	(a_1)	-.02	.42 n.s.		
	Price$_{t-1}$	(a_2)	-1.30	-1.22 n.s.		
Price$_t$	Intercept	(b_0)	-.052		.51	1.915
	ODA$_{t-1}$	(b_1)	.01	1.52 n.s.		
	Wells$_t$	(b_2)	.09	8.385 p < .0005		
	Barrels$_t$	(b_3)	-.19	-3.57 p < .0005		

the policy based on these estimates is identical to the interpretation based on the GLS estimates. There is no support for the hypotheses that the oil depletion allowance influences changes in exploration or price.

Estimation with Business Cycles Detrended

Table 9-4 reports the OLS estimates of the model with the business cycles detrended from the economic variables. The Durbin-Watson statistics indicate that this procedure also was successful in removing the autocorrelation. The results of this technique also lead to the same conclusion about the effects of the oil depletion allowance: with autocorrelation corrected, there is no evidence that the depletion policy encourages exploration or reduces prices.

This comparison of different estimation techniques demonstrates the importance of testing for and correcting autocorrelation. If autocorrelation is present, OLS estimates are inefficient and may lead to erroneous results. In the present case, the inefficient OLS estimates supported both hypotheses derived from the public interest theory. All three techniques which removed autocorrelation produced efficient estimates that failed to support the public interest theory. With all three techniques to correct autocorrelation, the model predicting total wells performs very badly. This finding suggests that exogenous economic forces which cause business cycles are also the major explanation of exploration. The model predicting price performs slightly better. Total wells and production are significantly related to price after correcting for autocorrelation.

Thus, the empirical evidence supports the private benefit theory that the oil depletion allowance did not cause oil producers to do anything that they would not have done anyway in response to economic forces in the free

Table 9-4
Estimates of the Effects of the Oil Depletion Allowance on Oil Industry Behavior with Business Cycles Detrended

Dependent Variables	Independent Variables	Regression Coefficient		t-Test (One Tail)	R^2	d
Wells$_t$	Intercept	(a_0)	.303		.002	1.869
	ODA$_{t-1}$	(a_1)	.016	.36 n.s.		
	Price$_{t-1}$	(a_2)	−1.386	−1.20 n.s.		
Price$_t$	Intercept	(b_0)	.019		.505	1.745
	ODA$_{t-1}$	(b_1)	− .0006	− .162 n.s.		
	Wells$_t$	(b_2)	.081	8.23 $p < .0005$		
	Barrels$_t$	(b_3)	− .002	−3.41 $p < .0005$		

market. However, the oil industry fought vigorously to protect and maintain the oil depletion allowance. If it did not encourage exploration or reduce price, what did it do? If the private benefit theory is correct, its effects should show up in the oil industry profit differential.

Private Benefit Theory Results: The Effects of the Oil Depletion Allowance on the Oil Industry Profit Differential

Hypothesis 5 predicts a positive nonchance relationship between oil depletion allowance benefits and the oil industry profit differential. Hypothesis 5 can be tested by a simple bivariate regression model:

$$\text{Pft. Diff.}_t = b_0 \pm b_1 \text{Dpl. Ben.}_t + e_t$$

where:

Pft. Diff._t	= the profit differential at time t;
Dpl. Ben._t	= depletion benefits at time t.
e_t	= random error

Table 9-5 reports the results of the regression using OLS and GLS. Although the Durbin-Watson statistic for the OLS estimate indicates that autocorrelation is present, the problem is not serious and the GLS correction does not alter the substantive interpretation. The empirical findings support hypothesis 5. The regression coefficient (from the GLS estimate)

Table 9-5

Estimates of the Effects of Oil Depletion Benefits on the Profit Differential Using OLS and GLS

Dependent Variable	Intercept b_0	Independent Variable Depletion Benefits b_1	R^2 b_0	d b_1
(OLS) Profit differential$_t$	-1.239 $(-1.818)^a$ $p < 05$	.347 $(4.357)^a$ $p < .0005$	.283	1.176
(GLS) Profit differential$_t$	-1.252 $(-1.254)^a$ n.s.	.360 $(3.095)^a$ $p < .005$	.388	1.767

[a]t-test, one-tailed

reveals that oil depletion benefits have a positive nonchance relationship with the profit differential (b_1 = .36). The model predicts that a one-unit increase in depletion benefits causes the oil industry profit differential to increase by slightly more than one-third of 1 percent. The intercept is negative (b_0 = -1.252), but it is not significantly different from zero. This result indicates that oil producers' profits would not have been significantly lower than all-industry profits if the depletion allowance had been zero during this period.

Summary

The findings of this study provide no empirical support for the public interest theory that the oil depletion allowance served the public interest by stimulating exploration and decreasing price. Rather, the empirical results are all consistent with a private benefit theory. There is no relationship between the oil depletion allowance and either exploration or price, but there is a statistically significant relationship between increases in depletion benefits and increases in the profit differential. These findings are consistent with the notion of transitional gains (Tullock, 1975). The initial benefits of the oil depletion allowance became fully capitalized over time. The result is that there is no evidence that the policy affected industry behavior, but termination of the benefits is costly to the industry. Therefore, the oil industry fought to protect and maintain the depletion allowance, and argued that it served the public interest.

Notes

1. The term "rationality" is used here and throughout this analysis in the objective, economic sense. An actor is rational if:

1. he is able to order preferences;
2. preferences are transitive;
3. more of a good is preferred to less; and
4. the action taken is the one that maximizes the probability that the preferred good is obtained.

2. The correlation between the oil industry profit rate and the all-industry profit rate over time (1925-1974) is .92.

3. The years for which the statutes indicate a percentage depletion rate are:

1900-1913 =   .0%   1927-1969 = 27.5%
1914-1916 = 5.0%   1970-1974 = 22.0%

4. The percentage rate in 1916 was 5 percent. Surveys indicate that the rate being deducted by the oil companies was around 28 to 31 percent in 1924. One can infer that the empirical percentage rate probably increasaed throughout the period until the 27.5 percent level was established in 1926. Therefore, a geometric progression with points fixed at 5 percent in 1916 and 29.5 percent in 1924 yields reasonable estimates of the empirical percentages for the remaining years. The estimates of the percentage depletion rate for 1917-1926 are as follows:

1917 =   6.2%   1922 = 18.9%
1918 =   7.8%   1923 = 23.6%
1919 =   9.7%   1924 = 29.5%
1920 = 12.1%   1925 = 36.8%
1921 = 15.1%   1926 = 46.0%

5. The actual price per barrel of oil each year was deflated using the Consumer Price Index (1967 = 100). This adjustment is necessary because a dollar in 1900 is not worth the same as a dollar in 1974. Thus: Price $(67\$_t)$

$$= \frac{\text{Price}_t}{\text{CPI}_t} \cdot 100.$$

6. The data for this measure were not available before 1925.

7. The Tax Reduction Act of 1975 (89 stat. 26) eliminated the depletion allowance for large integrated companies and provided for gradual reduction for the smaller independents.

8. The number of exploratory wells drilled each year is available only for 1938 to the present. Since there are no observations for the early years when the depletion policy was formulated, one cannot see the effects of the policy using this measure. Total wells is highly correlated with exploratory wells for the years when both measures are available $(r = .924)$.

9. This lagged regression presents a problem in that it removes the secular trends as well as the cycles. This problem and its solution are discussed in the Methodological Appendix.

10. A coefficient is considered statistically significant if it could occur by chance less than five times in one hundred (that is, at the .05 level or less).

References

American Petroleum Institute. *Petroleum Facts and Figures*. 1971 ed. Baltimore: Port City, 1971.

_____ . *Annual Statistical Review*. 1975.

Davidson, Paul. "Public Policy Problems of the Domestic Crude Oil Industry." *American Economic Review* 53(1963):83-108.

_____ . "Public Policy Problems of the Domestic Crude Oil Industry: A Reply." *American Economic Review* 54(1964):125-134.

_____ . "The Depletion Allowance Revisited." *Natural Resources Journal* 10(1970): 1-9.

Erickson, Edward. "Crude Oil Prices, Drilling Incentives and the Supply of New Discoveries." *Natural Resources Journal* 10(1970):27-52.

Federal Energy Administration. *Monthly Energy Review*. Washington: National Energy Information Center, 1975.

Freeman, Harrop A. "Percentage Depletion for Oil—A Policy Issue." *Indiana Law Journal* 30(1955):399-429.

Galvin, Charles O. "The 'Ought' and 'Is' of Oil and Gas Taxation." *Harvard Law Review*, 73(1960):1441-1509.

Gifford, Joseph E., ed. "Reduction in Percentage Depletion and Elimination of Production Payments Benefits Proposed by House of Representatives." *Oil and Gas Tax Quarterly* 18(1960):209-235.

Johnston, J. *Econometric Methods*. 2nd ed. New York: McGraw-Hill, 1972.

Kahn, Alfred E. "The Depletion Allowance in the Context of Cartelization." *American Economic Review* 54(1964):296-314.

Kirkpatrick, Samuel A. *Quantitative Analysis of Political Data*. Columbus: Charles E. Merril, 1974.

Kmenta, Jan. *Elements of Econometrics*. New York: Macmillan, 1971.

Lichtblau, John H., and Dillard P. Spriggs. *The Oil Depletion Issue*. New York: Petroleum Industry Research Foundation, 1959.

Mead, Walter J. "The System of Government Subsidies to the Oil Industry." *Natural Resources Journal* 10(1970):113-125.

Minerals Yearbook. Washington: Bureau of Mines, Government Printing Office, 1973.

Nelson, Charles R. *Applied Time Series Analysis for Managerial Forecasting*. San Francisco: Holden-Day, 1973.

Simpson, George, and Fritz Kafka. *Basic Statistics: A Textbook with Special Reference to Economics and Business*. New York: W.W. Norton, 1952.

Surrey, Stanley S. "Tax Incentives as a Device for Implementing Government Policy: A Comparison with Direct Government Expenditures." *Harvard Law Review* 83(1970):705-738.

Tullock, Gordon. "The Transitional Gains Trap." *Bell Journal of Economics* 6(1975):671-678.

Wonnacott, Ronald J., and Thomas H. Wonnacott. *Econometrics*. New York: John Wiley and Sons, 1970.

Appendix 9A
Methodology

Regressing a variable at time t as a function of itself at t-1 removes both secular and cyclical trends. To save ths secular trends in the data, first estimate the secular trends by regressing each dependent variable as a linear function of time ($1900 = 0$, $1901 = 1, \ldots, 1974 = 74$). The standardized regression coefficient squared (B^2) is the proportion of variance explained by time. The proportion not explained by time ($1 - B^2$) is due to effects of cycles. The value of the dependent variable at t-1 is weighted with the value ($1 - B^2$) to remove the effects of the secular trend and leave only the effects of cycles in the lagged variable. Thus, when the original dependent variable is expressed as a function of its weighted value in the previous year, only the cycles are removed.

The estimates of secular trends are:

$$\text{Total Wells}_t = 15.525 + .3749 \, (\text{year}_{00\text{-}74}) \qquad B^2 = .4545$$

$$\text{Price}_t = 2.79 + .0039 \, (\text{year}_{00\text{-}74}) \qquad B^2 = .0174$$

The dependent variables at t-1 are weighted as follows:

$$(\text{Total Wells}_{t\text{-}1}) \, (1 - .4545); \; (\text{Price}_{t\text{-}1}) \, (1 - .0174)$$

The results of lagged regression with these weighted variables are:

$$\text{Total Wells}_t = 2.220 + 1.702 \, (\text{Total Wells}_{t\text{-}1}) \qquad r^2 = .8744$$

$$\text{Price}_t = .985 + .677 \, (\text{Price}_{t\text{-}1}) \qquad r^2 = .4464$$

The residuals from this lagged regression are the new dependent variables with the cycles removed.

10 On the Theory of the Political Benefits in American Public Programs

Barry S. Rundquist

Introduction

Although the question of who benefits from government activity is a central one in political science, why and to what extent some people benefit more than others remains problematical. In part this reflects the great number and complexity of the activities performed by modern governments. But more fundamentally it results from the inadequacy of our current understanding of how complex policy making processes affect policy outcomes. That this is the case is suggested by the frequency with which hypotheses drawn from widely held theories of policy making fail to be supported by systematic studies at both national and subnational levels of American government. The purpose of this chapter is to reexamine principal elements of the theories upon which recent studies of the distribution of political benefits are based, and to suggest some modifications that seem more consistent with the findings of these studies.

The Problem

Recent research views the political benefits in a public program as the improvements in utility that individuals or groups derive from a program because of the influence of particular policy makers.[1] Some policy makers are thought to provide more benefits for certain individuals or groups because they have more political resources and a greater willingness to use their resources for this purpose than do other policy makers. However, because it is so difficult to distinguish between those parts of programs that are due to policy makers' efforts to benefit certain individuals or groups and those parts that are not, it remains unclear which policy makers have both enough resources and the ability to cause particular individuals or groups to benefit. It also remains unclear whether such policy makers are more prevalent in some programs than in others, and therefore whether

The present paper has benefited greatly from comments by Barry Ames, Gary Andres, Elinor Bowen, Andrea Friedman, Robert Lineberry, and Gerald Strom. Moreover, I am especially indebted to John Echols for several ideas developed together during a year's worth of discussions about political benefits.

some programs are more likely than others to evidence political benefits. Ultimately, because of these difficulties, it is unclear how much of American public policy actually consists of political benefits. Questions about political benefits have traditionally been left for journalists, political advocates, and an occasional academic case study to uncover. Recently, however, social scientists have conducted studies to test current generalizations about the nature of political benefits. This research calls into question much of our understanding of political benefits and the processes that are alleged to produce them. But it also suggests some new clues regarding these phenomena.

Stated most generally, political benefits research is concerned with identifying the conditions under which particular policy makers use some process, such as logrolling or coercion, to get other policy makers to allow units (people, places, or things) they favor to benefit in some way. In order to conduct such research, one must start from theoretical assumptions about the conditions, actors, processes, units, and form of benefit that one expects to occur in the real world. So far the hypotheses that have guided political benefits research have been drawn from reasoning like the following about Congress:

1. Congressmen seek reelection and view the provisions of political benefits to their constituents as a way of increasing their likelihood of reelection.
2. Congressmen can affect the content of programs either directly through the authorizing or appropriations processes or by getting bureaucrats to implement programs in ways they desire.
3. Some congressmen have more resources than others and are better able to obtain political benefits for their constituencies.
4. The congressmen with the most resources for controlling a given program are those on a committee with jurisdiction over the program.
5. Therefore, the constituencies of members of these committees should benefit to a greater extent than other congressmen from a program under their jurisdiction.

This argument takes a variety of different forms. Lowi, for example, argues that the committees, bureaus, and interest groups are able to form programs in the interest of their members rather than the broader public interest because other constitutionally empowered policy makers (such as, presidents and legislative majorities) acquiesce in their decisions.[2] In alternative versions, the argument is built on a premise that being president or a member of the majority party in Congress, or being both a member of the majority party and on a relevant committee, is a source of influence and, hence, of political benefits.

The general theory underlying all such arguments, however, is that people in the society who have more political resources are able to get more of what there is to get from government, and that this power effect should be treated as a political benefit. This theory, which I will call the power theory, assumes that policy makers with direct authority over government programs have the greatest ability to affect the content of those programs. It also assumes that some government policy makers regularly exercise more influence over particular policy decisions than do others. Hence, to the extent that potential beneficiaries can get powerful policy makers to favor their interests, they should end up benefiting from government allocations.

Some versions of the power theory further postulate that policy makers seek to remain in or advance from their current office, and that elected policy makers' incentive to survive gives citizens the leverage to constrain their allocative behavior. Citizens must simply threaten the policy makers' ability to get reelected or promoted to a higher administrative or elected position. Indeed, most researchers have assumed the primacy of the electoral constraint.[3] They posit that legislators and executives seek reelection, and that nonelected officials, especially budget-constrained bureaucrats, comply with the electoral needs of powerful legislators by benefiting their constituents.

These assumptions about the nature of the constraints on government officials imply three conclusions. (1) The people who succeed in benefiting from government policy should be those who can threaten the survival of a powerful elected official. Most researchers have assumed that these people are voters or political activists in legislators' constituencies. (2) The constituents of officials with the greatest amount of influence over a particular policy should benefit relative to the constituencies of other officials. (3) Influence in policy-making processes is a stable structure anchored in institutional rules and positions that should be reflected in a stable pattern of government outputs—namely, political benefits.

Recent studies suggest, however, that many programs evidence no political benefits at all, or more precisely, that they do not evidence the political benefits that researchers have been looking for. For example, several scholars have found no tendency for the expenditures of executive departments to benefit constituencies represented on the standing committees in Congress that are responsible for authorizing and funding the departments' programs.[4] Similarly, studies find that the constituencies of representatives and senators voting for an agency's legislation often do not benefit from the implementation of that legislation, or from other activities in which the agency is engaged.[5] Important studies at the state and local levels also find little or no such influence.[6] Such studies suggest that a biased structure of policy-making influence need not be associated with a corresponding pattern of political benefits.

Secondly, research indicates that if they *are* apparent, political benefits seldom comprise very much of a program. Several multivariate analyses have revealed statistically significant tendencies in the hypothesized direction; in other studies the small tendencies discovered are statistically insignificant.[7] Moreover, how much of a political benefit is found in a program depends on how the researcher has defined what he or she is looking for, and this varies considerably from study to study.[8] In other words, political benefits may be part of a program, but much of the program is apparently caused by considerations (equity, technical feasibility, efficiency) other than policy makers' influence.

Third, in some programs political benefits are narrowly distributed, to one key congressman, for example, and in other programs they are widely distributed. Some studies report chairman-centered and/or committee-centered biases in the geographic distribution of programmatic expenditures; others report partisan biases, and still others report universalism—that is, no bias at all.[9] Thus, the recipients of political benefits seem to range along a continuum from the constituencies of one to the constituencies of all legislators.

Such a pattern of findings may indicate one of two things. Either the assumptions guiding the studies need revision, or the studies themselves were poorly designed or analyzed and need replication.[10] There is little doubt that further theoretical and methodological work on political benefits is appropriate. However, since a number of methodological improvements have been attempted (witness the replications and methodological innovations in the present volume) without fully clarifying either the extent of political benefits in various programs or the conditions under which they occur, a reexamination of theoretical assumptions seems in order.

Some Theory

So far we have seen that the most common versions of the power theory are only inconsistently upheld by the empirical studies designed to test them. This implies either that aspects of policy-making processes commonly thought to serve as power resources for certain members of society are not in fact used as power resources at all, or else that they do serve as power resources but in different ways than is assumed in the version of the power theory we have been considering. In this section I suggest that there is some truth in both of these implications. Specifically, I argue that the power theory itself should be modified somewhat, first by dropping the assumption that policy makers generally perceived as influential in particular policy processes will invariably affect the allocation of the benefits of such policies, and second by deemphasizing the importance of electoral survival in explaining the allocative behavior of legislative, and especially bureaucratic, policy makers. In place of these assumptions I argue that influentials should only be assumed to affect allocative decisions when some other policy maker needs their support, that this occurs only at particular times during the policy cycle, that bureaucrats and legislators employ different decision rules in allocating political benefits, and that the net effect of these different political benefit decisions may better be viewed in terms of which income classes are served rather than which geographic constituencies are benefited.

A prime candidate for reevaluation is the assumption that stable patterns of policy influence are necessarily associated with stable patterns of political benefits. The studies which test hypotheses based on this assumption suggest that these two things are at best only sometimes, and even then only marginally, associated. This may mean that policy makers thought to be influential are not influential after all, or that influential policy makers choose not to bestow political benefits on whomever the researcher is looking at.[11] More interesting, however, is the possibility that even though policy makers are influential in forming and/or implementing a program, and want to benefit somebody, they are only sometimes able to do so. In these cases, something must intervene between the influentials and political benefits. In what follows, I suggest that this intervening something is the decision by another influential policy maker (or policy makers) that he needs the support of the influential policy maker(s). Accordingly, we should expect political benefits to occur in a program when a policy maker who wants the program needs an influential policy maker's support in order to get it. An influential policy maker in this case is anyone who has the resources to help or hinder the enactment, implementation, or continuation of the program.[12]

Unfortunately, the analyst's problem is complicated by the assumption that between influence and benefits lies another actor's decision regarding whether or not to seek political support. In addition to asking who has the resources and predisposition to influence the formation or implementation of a program, what targets these influentials favor, and whether these targets benefit disproportionately from the program, analysts must answer questions about who needs whose support, when they need it, and whether targets favored by the latter policy makers benefit at these times. I here review one set of answers to the questions of when political benefits will be provided, by and to whom they will be provided, and what form they will take.[13]

1. To begin with, I assume that a policy maker will benefit another policy maker when the following conditions obtain: (a) he believes the program he favors faces serious opposition; (b) he sees that an actor's support is needed to overcome this opposition; (c) he perceives that this actor is

either indifferent to or opposed to the program and that, without some kind of inducement, the actor is unlikely to support it; (d) he believes that benefiting the actor or someone the actor favors will win his support. In other words, without opposition, advocates of a program have no need to provide political benefits. But once opposition is present, the other three conditions must also be satisfied before they will include political benefits in the program.

Note that the opposition that concerns us here is the original amount of opposition implied by an intended program before it is modified to build political support. This analytical distinction between original and subsequent opposition may be difficult to work with empirically, but it is the logical starting place in discussing the occurrence and scope of political benefits. Among other things, it leads to the conclusion that any adjustment in a program to obtain support, before a program is either proposed, legislated, implemented, or reviewed, is a political benefit, and the total of political benefits in a program is the sum of all such adjustments.[14]

When should we expect opposition to a program? Since it is reasonable for people to oppose a program when it hurts them in some way, we should expect that programs that deprive people will generate opposition. Moreover, the more people a program deprives, and/or the greater the extent of their deprivation, the more the program will be opposed. Of course, if too many people are deprived too much, the amount of political benefits required to induce support will exceed the value of the program and a program advocate will drop it. But within this limit, the political benefits in a program should be related to the extent of the deprivations it imposes, and therefore the opposition it generates.

The foregoing suggests a simple conclusion: among the whole set of programs that a government may or may not conduct in a given time period, those depriving few people only a little and those depriving too many people too much will include few political benefits, whereas those depriving significant numbers of people will include more political benefits.

2. Who will receive political benefits? Although political benefits are a response to programmatic opposition and indifference, they need not go directly to the opponents of a program. Rather, if we assume that those seeking political support also want to conserve their pool of potential political benefits, it follows that they would, if possible, provide political benefits to a few actors who are both among the least opposed to the program and who have more influence than anybody else over its content. For example, if the support of one actor is sufficient, he would be the beneficiary; alternatively, if the support of many actors is necessary, then they would benefit. Since political benefits can be depleted either by providing a lot to a few or a little to many, the program advocate's general rule will be to provide as few political benefits as possible to as few actors as possible.

Finally, it is important to acknowledge that program advocates may value a program strongly or weakly. If they value it strongly, we should expect that they will be more likely to use political benefits to induce support than if they value it weakly. Moreover, strong advocates should be more attentive to determining the extent of the deprivations the program will inflict and whose support will be sufficient to overcome the resultant opposition. Therefore, we should expect more political benefits in programs that are strongly preferred by program advocates.

3. Who will provide political benefits? The providers of political benefits may be anybody with jurisdiction over a program who wants it enacted, continued, implemented, expanded, or renewed. For present purposes, it is useful to restrict the potential providers of political benefits to government officials—legislators, bureaucrats, executives. Moreover, a distinction between two types of government officials, policy generalists and policy specialists, can help here.[15] Policy generalists are policy makers who have authority over a wide range of programs; policy specialists have authority over either a single or a narrow range of programs. The importance of this difference lies in its implications for the nature of the political benefits each can provide. Policy generalists can trade benefits in different programs in return for a policy maker's support of a given program. Policy specialists can trade benefits in one or a few programs in return for a policy maker's support for that program. Thus, if a program advocate is a policy generalist, the political benefits he may use to induce policy maker X's support may cover a wide range of the things X values. If a program advocate is a policy specialist, the political benefits he or she can provide to X consist only of the things X values that the specialist has control over. Thus, ceteris paribus, we should expect policy generalists like presidents and legislative party leaders to use a wider range of programs as sources of political benefits than policy specialists like bureaucrats and legislative committee members.

4. What form will political benefits take? I have already suggested that generalists and specialists will provide different kinds of political benefits. To go beyond this it is necessary to specify the conditions under which specialists or generalists will tend to be the providers of political benefits. Two things seem to determine this. The first is the distribution of policy preferences in the government. Policy makers may want about the same thing, or they may be indifferent or opposed to one anothers' preferences. The problem, as I noted above, is that the more indifference or opposition there is in a group of policy makers, the more political benefits it takes to induce cooperation in the group. Now, other things being equal, generalists and specialists would be equally sensitive to such direct costs and would provide political benefits in similar amounts per each unit of cost. Thus, the specialist would induce support by building political benefits into programs

he recommends; the generalist, by trading or brokering trades across different programs under his purview. And both would include political benefits in programs as long as the value of the program they got as a result outweighed the direct costs of supplying political benefits.

The difference between policy generalists and policy specialists is in the nature of their transaction costs. For generalists, transaction costs tend to come from arranging explicit logrolls on a variety of programs. In explicit logrolling, opponents, indifferents, and the programs they care about must be identified, and reciprocal support must be negotiated and enforced.[16] The problem is, such transaction costs tend to increase with the number of separate trades that must be negotiated. Therefore, since the number of separate trades needed increases with the number of opponents or indifferents who must be appealed to with different provisions of political benefits, policy generalists should be more likely to provide political benefits when only a few policy makers or groups of policy makers need be appealed to. But, as I indicated earlier, the more consensus there is among policy makers, the less need there is to use political benefits to induce support. Thus, generally, except when nearly but not quite enough policy makers are likely to support their program, the marginal utility of political benefits to policy specialists will exceed that to policy generalists, and policy specialists will be more likely to offer them. Indeed, the only limit on the number of implicit trades that specialists can make is the extent to which the deprivations (in the form of taxes, for example) imposed by the program either (1) exceed the benefits provided to the targeted recipient, or (2) exceed the point at which each additional unit of benefits provided to induce one policy maker's support is offset by an increase in the number and/or intensity of opposition from other policy makers.

From this consideration of the costs of providing political benefits it follows that, where opposition or indifference to a program is widespread, policy specialists will be more likely to use political benefits to induce support than will policy generalists. Since, in American government, programs tend to be pursued by a few and ignored or opposed by most other actors, it follows that except for a few programs each year (such as a Panama Canal or SALT treaty), generalists will shy away from using political benefits in inducing political support. On most programs where political benefits might make a difference, they will be provided by policy specialists. Therefore, to the extent that policy specialists only have jurisdiction over the program for which support is being sought, political benefits will be built into that program.[17]

Two clarifications and an extension of the foregoing are noteworthy. First, specialists are as constrained as generalists by the information and transaction costs associated with explicit logrolling. Therefore, if they have jurisdiction over more than one program, they should generally refrain from using these programs as a source of political benefits. Second, not all programs *can* include political benefits. The limiting case is a program that, regardless of how it is disaggregated or adorned, cannot be made attractive to enough policy makers who are initially disposed to ignore or oppose it.

Third, a characteristic of the governmental environment that also may affect the nature of political benefits is the budget level. So far the argument proceeds as if the budget level is the sum of all program budgets. When, instead, the amount that can be spent for a given program is limited by the amount that can be spent for all programs, two effects are consistent with the argument. First, the number of programs that are susceptible to passage or implementation using political benefits should decrease to the extent that scarcity increases conflict over available funds among the actors favoring different programs. Second, the proportion of political benefits in programs that are enacted or are ongoing should increase because specialists would move to protect their program by giving all actors relevant to supporting it a material stake in its continuation.

Finally, the argument can be elaborated to identify in a general way which elements in society will be targeted for political benefits by legislators and bureaucrats. To do this it is useful to introduce some assumptions about the constraints on these decision makers. Assume first that legislators seek support from both recruiters in their constituency and a majority in their chamber of the legislature. Both of these incentives derive from constitutional specifications—on the one hand, that legislators must win a plurality of votes in one's constituency, and on the other, that at a minimum a majority of the legislators in one's chamber must support one's policy preferences if they are to become law. Unlike some electoral theories, however, this one assumes that the electoral constraint works indirectly through recruiters, whether they be party leaders, local business and labor leaders, major campaign contributors, or whoever from constituency-to-constituency, rather than directly through voters.[18] Thus it can be argued that legislators are constrained to satisfy recruiters; that if they do so better than alternative candidates they receive the recruiters' support, and that with their support the likelihood of being elected is enhanced.[19]

The majority voting constraint builds on Riker's idea that under certain legislative conditions legislators seek to develop minimum winning coalitions.[20] I assume that one thing recruiters want from their legislator is satisfaction of their most intensely-held policy preferences. Since legislators cannot be certain of obtaining majority support, they may seek support from a somewhat larger-than-minimum winning majority, or a minimum winning majority of the total number of legislators in the chamber—rather than of those present—or a majority that can reasonably be expected to endure over a relatively long period of time (such as a legislative party or the conservative coalition).[21] But whatever is the case, they will try to obtain passage of recruiter-constrained policy preferences by less than an unanimous vote.

Now, without elaborating on the nature of the constituency and majoritarian constraints any further, it can be argued that legislators subject to them would allocate political benefits so as to satisfy the recruiter-constrained policy preferences of majorities of legislators. They can do this by simply creating the programs or parts of programs that these recruiters prefer. Or they might create an "unlimited program" for local recruiters in the constituencies of enough legislators to assure programmatic support.

By an unlimited program I mean a program that can fully satisfy the designated beneficiaries because they determine how much of the service, or whatever, they obtain. In other words, such legislation specifies that the supply of program benefits will be determined by the claimants to the program. In contrast, for a limited program, legislation would specify not only who would be eligible to participate in the program but how much of their preference for the program would be satisfied. There are two basic ways that unlimited programs can be used to build an exclusionary or, in some sense, minimum winning coalition. One is to write legislation that is so complex that the costs of obtaining useful information on the program are high enough to exclude nonrecruiters. The other is to stimulate favored recruiters to make claims on the program. If these tactics work and recruiters are benefited, presumably legislators will be elected or reelected.

The rule of benefiting local recruiters suggests another hypothesis about the nature of political benefits. Thus, when majorities like parliamentary parties replace one another, we should expect at least some shift in the allocation of political benefits. Specifically, to the extent that local recruiters for the two parties have different policy preferences, the programs created to benefit them should differ. But to the extent that the preferences of local recruiters remain similar, the change in who benefits should be minimal. Additional hypotheses follow here, but it is useful to consider bureaucratic decision makers before discussing them.

To constrain the behavior of bureaucrats I assume that the incentive of bureaucrats is to get promoted, or at least maintain their current position.[22] I also assume that the ambitions of bureaucrats in bureaus that receive their operating budgets from the legislature, and those in bureaus that are funded in proportion to the usage of their services, may be affected by decisions of elected officials to reorganize the programs they administer. Moreover, a major cause of a political reorganization is the complaint that people eligible for the program are denied its services for political reasons; consider, for example, the complaint during the Chicago snow disaster of 1979 that the mass transit service was closed down for black communities on the south and west sides but kept open on the white north side. Thus, bureaucrats should not be expected to distribute programmatic services to some claimants and not others. Rather, the strategy that is most consistent with minimizing opposition to their program and position is to follow the rule: serve all claimants equally.[23]

The principal implication of this argument is that, contrary to the democratic version of the power theory, bureaucrats should not be expected to benefit claimants in the constituencies of powerful policy makers at the expense of claimants in other constituencies. And to the extent that bureaucrats seek to reward all claimants in order to maintain support, we should expect the political benefits in bureaucratic programs—most ongoing programs and new ones authorized by vague legislation—to be widespread to all claimants, whereas those asociated with legislature-dominated programs—many new programs—will not be. Of course, like legislators, bureaucratic policy makers will design new programs so that they include political benefits for those whose support they need to get them authorized and implemented. Indeed, they only need some version of minimum winning support at this stage. More important, since opposition is likely to stress the opportunity costs of the new program, if spreading political benefits more widely would further increase the absolute costs of the program, to do so would be strategically suicidal. But once the program is in effect, the "satisfy all claimants" rule should become the preferred bureaucratic rule for allocating political benefits. Interestingly, it also seems to be the rule by which legislators allocate their more bureaucratic services. For example, there is no indication that congressmen ask constituents their party or voting records before handling their requests for casework.

Some Implications

So far I have argued that political benefits are programs or parts of programs that are used by program advocates to induce the support of others, that they are only used for this purpose under special circumstances, that recipients vary in number and position, that program advocates may be policy generalists or specialists but political benefits tend to take the form of implicit logrolls arranged by policy specialists, and that bureaucrats and legislators allocate political benefits differently. What does this imply?

Are Political Benefits Marginal or Central to Public Programs?

To begin with, the above perspective suggests that whether political benefits constitute much or little of a program will vary from program to program.

As we have seen, some programs need include no political benefits; some will include enough to, for instance, induce swing members to support the program or induce strong opponents to soften their attacks on it; and some—one thinks of the federal buildings that were authorized during the Eisenhower administration and received their first appropriations during the Nixon administration—consist mainly of political benefits. Moreover, different decisions affecting the same program may include different amounts of political benefits depending on their perceived effectiveness in building or retaining political support under the immediate circumstances of those decisions. Thus the question of whether political benefits are marginal or central to public programs is not easily answered in general—even for particular kinds of programs.

The foregoing considerations help in explaining why empirical studies tend to find marginal and/or negligible political benefit effects. Most tests for political benefits have been against output data produced by a number of separate policy decisions, often decisions made over a period of years. The assumptions implicit in such tests include the following: (1) an influential policy maker's influence is constant over the span of decisions producing the outputs; (2) this policy maker (X) has a preference regarding all or many of these decisions; (3) the sum of all benefits from policy decisions regarding which actor X is indifferent is smaller than the sum of those resulting from decisions regarding which he has preferences; (4) if the policy decisions involve programs that may vary in size and one's indicators of political benefits are size-sensitive (dollars, employment rates, and so on), either the programs do not in fact vary very much, or, if they do vary, those programs regarding which the influential policy maker has preferences tend to be larger than those regarding which he is indifferent.[24] The political support argument suggests that the reason empirical studies based on these assumptions have yielded small or negligible evidence of political benefits is either that one or more of the assumptions are false, or else, (1) political benefits were unneeded or pointless, (2) political benefits included to induce support from one set of policy makers for one decision were offset by political benefits included in another decision to induce support from different policy makers, or (3) the set of policy makers hypothesized to be the targets of political benefits was too large or too small. Accordingly, the political benefit studies to date probably underestimate the occurrence of political benefits in real world programs.

Crass versus Justified Political Benefits

One fairly general implication of the foregoing is that policy makers will attempt to justify the political benefits they allocate. The advantages of justifying a political benefit are fairly obvious. For example, if policy maker X simply pursues a project for his hometown, the result will either be resentment or a request for similar projects by everyone else of X's status. Indeed, X would prefer to avoid both results, for the one would mean direct frustration, and the other, indirect frustration in the form of providing revenue to fund a set of projects of which his possibly constituents but a small fraction. Accordingly, X would have an incentive to justify his project in some terms that preclude having to provide the same project to other actors of his status. Hence, one would expect more political benefits to be justified than unjustified. Among legislators, for example, justifying political benefits in terms of equity, efficiency, or some other common value is an elementary political skill. Indeed, from this perspective, what made Mendel Rivers so notorious in the late 1960s was less that so many military facilities were located in Charleston than that he did not justify them adequately.

Indeed, in regards to bureaucratic policy makers we have seen that the political benefit strategy of rewarding all claimants is perfectly consistent with justifying one's allocations in terms of objective criteria, specified in legislative formulae or whatever. But that it can be justified in this way does not necessarily make it less of a political benefit.

This may seem obvious to many political observers, but a failure to recognize it has probably been a source of error in empirical studies of political benefits. The problem is, analysts have tended to accept the politicians' justifications of their political benefits. Hence they tend to treat political benefits as the amount of variance in an output indicator—programmatic expenditures, for example—that is not accounted for by some objective or nonpolitical causal variable, such as real need, efficiency, and so on. In effect, therefore, scholars have been examining mainly "crass" political benefits, whereas, as I have just argued, we should expect crass political benefits to be exceptional. Rather, it seems sensible to treat as political benefits programmatic activities that are justified in some terms but would not exist in the absence of a policy maker's influence as well as unjustified programmatic activities. Of course, distinguishing these two types of programmatic activities from those that are justified and would exist in the absence of a policy maker's influence is a difficult research problem, but one that probably should not be ignored.[25]

The Few and Many as Beneficiaries

Consider next the situation in which programs initiated by bureaucrats and/or committee members include political benefits for one another. The political support argument suggests that not all committee members would benefit from a bureaucratically administered program, for those already in complete agreement with the program, as well as those totally opposed to it, could be ignored. And to the extent that congressmen seek and obtain membership on committees that oversee agencies whose programs they generally favor, they should not be targeted for political benefits. However, to the extent that committee members do disagree or are indifferent, the assumption that bureaucrats would start building support with those who are most likely to support them suggests that at least those committee members would benefit. Thus, to begin with we can conclude that, if a bureaucratic specialist's program is widely opposed, committee members who are indifferent or only mildly opposed to it should receive political benefits. Conversely, if a committee-favored program is widely opposed, committee members should target relevant bureaucrats for political benefits, perhaps by including in the program more budget or administrative positions than they originally intended, in return for support during the legislative and subsequent implementation process.

However, political benefits will be distributed more widely than specialists if the support specialists can provide is insufficient. Therefore, if the program entails enough deprivations and generates enough opposition, specialists will include political benefits for other policy makers as well. These may stop with a simple majority of members, or perhaps members of the majority party, or they may include almost everybody—again depending on the deprivations the program entails. Thus, the conclusion that committee members benefit need not imply that they benefit relative to nonmembers. Indeed, committee members should only benefit relative to nonmembers when the opposition to the program is so weak that their support is sufficient to enact and/or implement the program.

New and Old Programs

Thirdly, if we adhere to the view that political benefits are included in programs to induce political support, the question of whether new or old programs will include more political benefits becomes rather tricky. On the one hand, an old program that has faced opposition in the past should include inducements sufficient to have overcome opposition encountered at different stages of the policy cycle, perhaps on a number of different turns of the cycle. Thus the old program should have more political benefits overall. But at any point in time, the old program will encounter less opposition and therefore be less likely to have new political benefits included in it. This is because the old political benefits provide a wide range of people with incentives to either favor or be indifferent to the program. A new program, however, is more dependent on including new political benefits to overcome opposition at each step in its development. Thus, when first enacted, a program should include enough political benefits to provide at least minimum winning support. In its first years of implementation it should be expanded to include enough political benefits to make it uncontroversial and after that it should include no new political benefits. For example, what we may be witnessing as a program like the National Endowment for the Arts advances from benefiting majority members disproportionately to not doing so, is an aggregate effect of including new political benefits to induce state and local governments (such as educational bureaucracies) to implement the program and Congress to provide continuing budgetary support for the program.[26]

Large and Small Programs

The foregoing conception of the nature of political benefits can also be used to explain the following puzzle. On the one hand, several studies have found that the distribution of funds under the Corps of Engineers Civil Works Program, the military construction program, the sewerage treatment construction grant program, and others, follows the pattern predicted by the so-called distributive theory: districts or states on relevant standing committees in Congress seem to benefit more than constituencies of other congressmen.[27] On the other hand, studies have shown that the distribution of military procurement expenditures does not conform to the expectations of the distributive theory.[28] Thus, the distributive theory seems to hold for relatively small programs that involve funds that can be distributed in piecemeal fashion, but not for the largest program of this type.

Several explanations of this situation have been offered, but the one suggested by the foregoing is that committee members' constituencies benefit from small programs because the support of these committees is sufficient to provide program administrators with political support, whereas larger programs like military procurement require a broader base of political support. According to this reasoning, committee support is sufficient for smaller programs because of intercommittee reciprocity in Congress. A majority of congressmen will accept a committee's recommendations regarding a program so long as the benefits are small, and as long as they know those members will in turn support similar recommendations from their own committees. As long as such intercommittee reciprocity is in effect, program adminstrators can obtain full support for their program and budget requests by inducing committee members to recommend properly in regard to them. But intercommittee reciprocity can only be counted on to generate legislative majorities as long as the programs being recommended do not deprive nonmembers too much. Specifically, the costs of recommended programs must not exceed the costs of programs the nonmember's committee

can recommend. If it does, the net utility to the nonmember of recip-
rocating with members of the recommending committee is negative,
and he will rationally oppose the committee's recommendation. In such
cases, the agency's program will be opposed in Congress regardless of
whether it has distributed its expenditures so that committee members' constituencies are benefited. Accordingly, the agency will distribute its benefits
more widely than the committee so as to induce nonmembers to support the
committees' recommendations. Specifically, such inducements to nonmembers should be large enough to make up the difference between the cost to
the nonmember of the recommended program and the value of programs
his own committee would recommend. Under most circumstances one
would expect such extracommittee trading to stop at a simple majority of
the chamber, for that would be sufficient to enact the agency's program.
But even in this situation, committee members should beneift more than
other members, for their recommendation is still central to getting congressional approval for the agency's recommendation. Thus benefits should
favor committee members' constituencies more than those of enough other
members to produce majority support for their program, and both these
groups should benefit more than the remaining congressmen.

Military procurement is a case in point. The size of the program is such
that the military committees cannot rely on intercommittee reciprocity to
obtain House and Senate support. Therefore, procurement expenditures are
distributed more broadly than committee members' constituencies, and
committee members' constituencies do not appear to benefit relative to
nonmembers' constituencies. Most studies find that committee members'
constituencies average somewhat more than nonmembers' constituencies,
but the difference is not statistically significant.[29] There is, however, some
evidence of a partisan bias to the distribution on military procurement expenditures. Thus, when Eisenhower and the Republicans assumed control
of Congress and the presidency in the Eighty-third Congress, states that had
only elected Republican congressmen for the preceding four years showed a
significant increase in the prime military contract awards they received.
Conversely, states only electing Democratic congressmen showed a proportionate decrease. This pattern is consistent with the expectation that support
for a large program would center on legislative majorities.[30]

But the military procurement program has a characteristic in addition to
its size that would lead the Department of Defense (DOD) to spread military
contracts among many constituencies. This is the uncertainty regarding how
large the procurement budget will be each year. To be able to implement
changing national security policies, DOD must be assured that Congress
will support a procurement budget that may be three or four times larger
next year than it is this year. To do this, it cannot rely on even a sim-

ple majority, for majorities are famous for cycling over time and there is no guarantee that a majority that is benefited today will be intact in the next Congress, and, even if it is, that it will support a larger or even the same request.[31] Therefore, DOD should be expected to pursue a strategy designed to give all or most congressmen an incentive to support its procurement requests. One such strategy is the simple one of trying the amount of procurement expenditures each constituency receives to the overall size of the defense budget. Thus, if the budget increases twofold, the amount each constituency receives will increase proportionately. Indeed, if this did not occur, and large increases benefited only, for example, Democratic constituencies, legislators from other constituencies would have an incentive to coalesce, bribe marginal Democrats, and defeat the procurement request. This could be disastrous, particularly in wartime. By tying the procurement request to a proportionate increase of procurement spending in each state, most congressmen would have a similar benefit-based incentive to support any level of procurement.[32] Of course, if that state's benefits could be negated by increases in the income tax or war deaths, other methods of inducing their support would also be required.[33]

In sum, the differences between military procurement and several other expenditure programs seem attributable to differences in the support needed to gain approval of their programs in Congress. Note how this explanation differs from the major alternative line of explanation, which starts from the assumption that policy makers simply use their influence to get benefits for their constituencies. In that view, if legislators' constituencies do not benefit, then either the legislator did not really want to benefit his constituency or else a more influential official was opposed to his constituency benefiting from the program. The support explanation, in contrast, assumes that, if a constituency did not benefit, the support of its representative was not needed by someone—regardless of how much influence he was known to have.

The Possible Redistributive Impact of Political Benefits

The final implication of the modified theory under consideration is that the targets of political benefits may not be powerful legislators' constituencies, and therefore tests comparing constituencies may be inappropriate. But if this is true, what are the appropriate units of analysis for political benefits studies? A priori, they may be anything. However, the argument about legislative and bureaucratic decision rules implies the tentative answer that these political benefit strategies affect the way government services are distributed among income classes, and that it is among such units rather than geographic ones that we should look for political benefits. Moreover, the income class effects should differ at different times in the policy cycle. Specifically, if legislators create unlimited programs to benefit local recruiters, we should expect that at least some new programs will be open programs designed to satisfy recruiters' preferences. Furthermore, the recruiters so benefited should be those in the constituencies of members of the majority passing the bill. Therefore, given that recruiters are likely to be wealthier than other citizens, as long as they are paid out of general revenues these programs should have the effect of transferring income from low- and middle-income citizens to citizens with higher incomes. However, it need not follow that recruiters in the constituencies of members voting with the minority will be deprived. On the contrary, as long as the program is unlimited and bureaucrats observe the "serve all claimants" rule, recruiters in minority members' constituencies can also subscribe to it. And to the extent they do, the regressive impact on low- and middle-income groups will increase. Finally, participation in the program by lower-income individuals is restricted by either taste (they value other things more highly than the activities provided by the program) or information costs.

Of course not all programs are designed to serve local recruiters, and some programs are in fact redistributive from high- to middle- and low-income groups. But, as LeGrande concludes from a study of selected British and American programs,

> Expenditures . . . on health care, higher education, housing, defense, transport and libraries, all have an unequal distribution with the rich getting 'more,' however defined, than the poor. Only compulsory education, protection, and social services and parks do not have an obviously pro-rich impact, and even with these the distribution is not necessarily pro-poor.[34]

Moreover, LeGrande observes that the programs with a pro-rich bias are those whose distribution depends on user decisions: ". . . the pro-rich services are those whose use is largely discretionary, the remainder, largely undiscretionary."[35] The argument suggested here is that at least some part of these income class effects are political benefits.

Summary

This chapter has dealt with the theoretical expectations underlying political benefit studies and to a lesser extent some of the methodological problems associated with these expectations. I began by suggesting that the hodgepodge of findings regarding the extent of political benefits in different programs suggests that the democratic power theory that underlies most political benefits research may be misleading. Accordingly, it seemed useful to trudge through our understanding of how political benefits are produced to see if a modified democratic power theory might provide a more reasonable basis for additional empirical work.

The suggested modification of the democratic power theory emphasizes the role of the need for political support in the production of political benefits. Contrary to the original theory, the modified theory suggests that a policy maker's ability to provide political benefits is contingent on whether some other policy maker needs his support and is willing to trade political benefits to get it. From this perspective it is clear that political benefits researchers should not assume that the political benefits in programs reflect a stable pattern of power among policy makers, but rather that they are produced at different times in the policy cycle when different policy makers need political support from different quarters. Most of the paper concerns the implications of thinking about political benefits this way, but the principal implication is that identifying political benefits requires specifying time-bound structures of support dependence among policy makers.

In concluding, however, it should be noted that this argument is an attempt to account for the provision of political benefits in public programs under conditions like those characterizing American governments in the postwar period, that is, when most of the studies have been done (see the chapter by Heywood Sanders for an exception).[36] Therefore it assumes the existence of a complex government and a relatively weak governing coalition. The democratic power theory also assumes this situation, but it implies that, when the governing coalition is weak, policy specialists (committee and bureaucratic leaders) will dominate policy making, with the effect that their favorite targets will obtain political benefits. The modified power theory stresses that it is precisely under these circumstances that whether such powerful members of the process succeed in producing political benefits depends on whether other policy makers need their political support. Hence, in the absence of assumptions about who needs political support from whom, and when, there is no reason to predict that policy specialists will necessarily succeed in producing political benefits under these conditions. I have proposed some tentative answers to these questions. But regardless of the usefulness of these answers, it is clear that some set of assumptions about the over-time structure of support among policy makers is needed before predictions can be made about which apparently influential policy makers will succeed in allocating political benefits to units they favor.

Of course governing coalitions are not always weak, and when they are strong we should not expect that the provision of political benefits will depend on political support considerations. In this situation, powerful actors in the policy-making process should produce political benefits straightaway. For example, we should find that committee leaders were better able to produce political benefits for their constituents when the New Deal governing coalition was strong than after it weakened.

At several points in the paper I have suggested partial explanations of benefit patterns, but so far I can think of few general, across-program benefit hypotheses that follow from the political support perspective. This may indicate that the theory needs further work, or it may be an indication that the pattern of political benefits produced by weak governing coalitions is quite unpredictable. Or it may mean, as I have begun to argue, that programs are structured so that in the aggregate they satisfy income classes about equally: the middle and lower classes with supplier-determined programs, the wealthier classes with demand-determined programs (including special tax exemption programs). And it may be that this latter pattern affects the size, scope, and rate of change in government activity, and impacts most directly on the economy.

Notes

1. The definition of a political benefit is a major problem. The approach discussed here assumes that not all of the positive utility that people derive from a program is a political benefit. It is not a political benefit as long as it would occur without the expenditure of political resources by some policy maker. In other words, I am distinguishing the utility that individuals experience for reasons that have nothing to do with a program and the utility they experience from a program that was not intended by a policy maker to benefit them, from the utility they experience from a program (or part of a program) for which they were the intended target. By political resources I mean such things as control of sanctions, information, and so on, that allow one policy maker to induce others to accept his decision to benefit someone. Given this definition, political benefit hypotheses are to the effect that some characteristic of a policy maker causes him to have more political influence and therefore allows him to benefit whomever he wants to benefit to a greater extent than policy makers without that characteristic.

The generality of this definition is purposeful. For reasons that will become apparent, it leaves open questions of the units that receive political benefits, such as individuals, firms, congressional districts, income classes; the policy makers who produce them, such as legislators, judges, bureaucrats, and so on; and whether a political benefit is all or part of a program, or a gross or net benefit in the sense that individuals discount taxes paid in assessing whether a program benefits them or an expenditure or nonexpenditure (such as regulatory programs) phenomenon. Finally, no effort is made to distinguish political benefits from government activities that can be justified in terms of need, efficiency, justice, or whatever. If such programs fit the definition of political benefits, they are treated as such, regardless of the accounting perspective (government, society) and/or normative criteria (pareto optimality, for example) that others may use in evaluating the program.

2. Theodore J. Lowi, *The End of Liberalism*, 2nd ed. (New York: Norton, 1979).

3. See, for example, David R. Mayhew, *Congress: The Electoral Connection* (New Haven: Yale University Press, 1979); and Morris Fiorina, *Congress: Keystone of the Washington Establishment* (New Haven: Yale University Press, 1977).

4. See, for example, Bruce A. Ray, "Congressional Promotion of District Interests: Does Power on the Hill Really Make a Difference," in this volume; and Leonard Ritt, "Committee Position, Seniority, and the Distribution of Government Exenditures," *Public Policy* 24(Fall 1976).

5. See, for example, Stephen Cobb, "Defense Spending and Defense Voting in the House: An Empirical Study of an Aspect of the Military Industrial Complex," *American Journal of Sociology* 82(1976):163-182.

6. See, for example, Robert L. Lineberry, *Equality and Urban Policy: The Distribution of Municipal Services* (Beverly Hills: Sage, 1977); Frank Levy, Arnold J. Meltsner, and Aaron Wildavsky, *Urban Outcomes: Schools, Streets, and Libraries* (Berkeley: University of California Press, 1974); and Kenneth Mladenka, "The Urban Bureaucracy and the Political Machine: Who Gets What and the Limits of Political Control," paper presented at the Annual Meetings of the American Political Science Association, Washington, D.C., 1979.

7. For example, see Ray, "Congressional Promotion." Other papers reporting negligible political benefits relationships include Anne Permaloff and Carl Grafton, "The Distribution of Highway Construction Projects in Alabama: A Test of the Conventional Wisdom," paper presented at the Annual Meeting of the Midwest Political Science Association, Chicago, Illinois, 1977; Jon Bond, "Oil State Representation on the Tax Committees in the House and Senate and the Oil Depletion Allowance, 1900-1974," paper presented at the Annual Meeting of the Midwest Political Science Association, Chicago, 1978, a revised version of which is forthcoming in the *American Journal of Political Science*; R.J. Johnston, "Congressional Committees and the Inter-State Distribution of Military Spending," unpublished paper, University of Sheffield, England, 1978; J. Clark Archer, "Congressional Incumbent Reelection Success and Federal Outlays Distribution: A Test of the Electoral Connection," unpublished paper, Dartmouth College, 1979; and Cary R. Covington, "Congressmen, Constituencies, and Committees: The House Committee on Science and Astronautics and a Distributive Theory," unpublished paper, University of Illinois, 1975.

8. For example, in a study conducted by Pamela Hurley, Karen Makate, and Barbara Rubenstein, "The Variables of Successful Military

Contracting,'' University of Illinois, Spring 1977), the military sales of manufacturers located in areas electing mainly Democrats to Congress (Boeing, Lockheed, McDonnell-Douglas) were found to average 1.4 percent less in contract awards following Nixon's ascension to the presidency; firms located in predominantly Republican areas (Grumman, North American Rockwell) averaged 1.5 percent more in sales. Manufacturers in mixed Republican/Democratic areas (General Dynamics, Ling-Temco-Vought, and Northrop) averaged .45 percent more. The comparisons here are between the amount areas averaged in the period 1969-1975. The same pattern obtains for particular types of aircraft sales. In only one of nine types of military aircraft sales (reconnaissance aircraft) did firms in Republican areas not experience an increase in market share. The gains ranged from .6 percent for observation aircraft to 5.3 percent for bomber, early warning, and antisubmarine aircraft. Conversely, firms in Democratic areas evidence a loss in all nine categories. The losses range from —2.2 percent for early warnings to —.2 percent for antisubmarine, utility, observation, and bomber aircraft. These data, obtained from *Aviation Week and Space Technology's* annual issue on military systems from 1960 through 1976, suggest a small but consistent political benefit favoring firms in areas which support the president's party.

9. See, for example, John A. Ferejohn, *Porkbarrel Politics* (Stanford: Stanford University Press, 1974); and J. Theodore Anagnoson, ''Politics in the Distribution of Federal Grants,'' in this volume.

10. See Edward T. Jennings, Jr., ''Competition, Constituencies, and Welfare Policies in American States,'' *American Political Science Review* 72(June 1979):414-429.

11. Of course, by this definition of political benefits, if policy makers are not influential or choose not to exercise their influence, no aspect of the program over which they have jurisdiction can be considered political benefits.

12. Or, more precisely, he both has the resources and is likely to use them to affect the program.

13. For related discussions see the concluding chapter of John A. Ferejohn, *Porkbarrel Politics;* Susan Rose-Ackerman, *Corruption: A Study in Political Economy* (New York: Academic, 1978); and R. Douglas Arnold, *Congress and the Bureaucracy: A Theory of Influence* (New Haven: Yale University Press, 1979), chapters 3 and 4.

14. Note that this approach to political benefits requires a distinction between two things that fit my definition of political benefits. The first are those programs and/or parts of programs that increase some unit's utility because a policy maker's influence is needed for political support. The second is those programs or parts of programs that increase some unit's utility because of some actor's influence, but despite the fact that his or her support is unneeded.

The political support perspective assumes that this second type of political benefit seldom occurs. The effect of this distinction is to limit our attention to programs over which there is a likelihood of conflict. This purely instrumental approach to political benefits allows for an analytical clarity that gets lost in attempts to link output patterns to the simultaneous, symbiotic, or coincidental preferences of policy makers. I am not denying the existence of programs that result from such distributions of preferences, although I suspect that strict adherence to the distinction between a policy preference before it is modified to obtain support and a policy preference after it has been so modified would lead one to conclude that few programs result from the coincidental preferences of policy makers. For present purposes, however, the assumption that political benefits are instrumental vis-a-vis gaining political support in policy processes is heuristic.

15. For a related distinction see E. E. Schattschneider, *Semisovereign People* (New York: Holt, Rhinehart, and Winston, 1960).

16. James M. Buchanan and Gordon Tullock, *The Calculus of Consent: Logical Foundations of Constitutional Democracy* (Ann Arbor: University of Michigan Press, 1962), pp. 134-135. Regarding implicit logrolling, they say:

> Here there is *no* formal trading of votes, but an analogous process takes place. The political "entrepreneurs" who offer candidates or programs to the voters make up a complex mixture of policies designed to attract support.

17. Note that the set of programs that I say should evidence political benefits is precisely the set that we should expect to be the subject of the norm of universalism—that is, the tendency to satisfy the preferences of every policy maker who has a preference. For it is in these marginal cases, where enough policy makers may form either in support of or in opposition to one's favored program (that is, the probability of being a winner or a loser approaches 50-50), that all would opt to form universalistic rather than zero-sum coalitions. The pivotal condition here is that a policy maker believes that coalitions opposed to his or her position are just as likely to form as are coalitions for his or her position. When this condition obtains, every member's policy preference, or at least intense policy preference, should be satisfied, and the programs that result should be considered political benefits in their entirety because they satisfy the definition of political benefits. But although a priori such programs would be as likely or more likely to be explicit, cross-policy logrolls either brokered by policy generalists or bartered in an open market, the transaction costs associated with such extensive trading would result in an emphasis on implicit, specialist-centered logrolls favoring everybody with an intense preference for things under the specialist's jurisdiction.

But it should also be clear that if members believe that a coalition favoring their position has a much greater than 50-50 chance of forming, universalism should not be expected. Rather, some policy preferrers, specifically, those whose positions conflict with one's own position, plus those whose policy preference is nonconflictual but who do not share with oneself the characteristic that leads him or her to expect support for his or her preference, should win and others should lose. Under these circumstances logrolls should still be specialist-centered, but because the number of potential traders is decreased, the transaction costs to generalists should also be decreased, and therefore more generalist-centered, explicit logrolls should be possible. On the general condition for universalism, see Barry R. Weingast, "A Rational Choice Perspective on Congressional Norms," *American Journal of Political Science* 23 (May 1979):245-262. For a discussion of conditions under which actors in a legislative process would abandon universalism in favor of a zero-sum strategy, see Barry S. Rundquist and Gerald S. Strom, *A Theory of Legislative Organization and Output* (forthcoming).

18. The concept of recruiters is meant to denote any individual or group that can affect a candidate's likelihood of winning an election. In recent years the apparent weakening of party organizations both in the national government and locally has led many observers to stress the independence of legislative candidates from partisan limits on their constituency-relevant behavior. But that party leaders have less control over candidates, especially incumbents, need not imply the absence of other recruiter constraints. Thus, for example, some combination of political action committees and local newspaper writers may provide backing that is necessary and sufficient to elect or unseat an incumbent. And, if so, they would constitute his recruiters. It is possible for candidates to be independent of any such recruiters, to be, in effect, their own recruiters, and if so they would not be recruiter-constrained at all. However, the assumption here is that few are independent.

19. This argument is elaborated in Rundquist and Strom, *Legislative Organization*.

20. William Riker, *A Theory of Political Coalitions* (New Haven: Yale University Press, 1962).

21. David Koehler, "Legislative Coalition Formation: The Meaning of Minimum Winning Size With Uncertain Participation," *American Journal of Political Science* 27-39.

The nature of enduring majority coalitions is discussed in Rundquist and Strom, *Legislative Organization*.

22. On different approaches to characterizing bureaucratic incentives, see Graham Allison, *The Essence of Decision* (Boston: Little Brown, 1971); and William A. Niskanen, *Bureaucracy and Representative Government* (Chicago: Aldine, 1971).

23. I am grateful to Robert Lineberry for this idea.

24. These assumptions may be inappropriate for particular spans of policy decisions, such as those reflected in all dollar expenditures for a program enacted twenty years ago but funded annually when party control of the agency involved has changed three times and the leadership of the relevant appropriations subcommittees has changed several times. No doubt one source of the discrepancy between anecdotal discussions of policy-making processes (such as Mendel Rivers stories) and systematic analyses of those processes is that the purveyors of anecdotes are more sensitive than the analysts to the accuracy of these assumptions. But the more stable the pattern of influence, and either the larger the program on which the influential has a preference or the larger the proportion of all decisions on which the influential is influential, the more one is justified in using aggregated output data to test for political benefits. For a methodological critique of some political benefit studies, see Arnold, *Congress and the Bureaucracy.*

25. This section was written in collaboration with John Echols. It may also be that treating justified allocations in some way as political benefits will reveal stronger and more consistent support for hypotheses drawn from the straight democratic power theory rather than the modified version of that theory being advanced here.

26. Also see Arnold's argument (in *Congress and the Bureaucracy*) that in new programs benefits are more likely to be distributed so as to benefit the program's opponents as well as its proponents.

27. For example, see Carol F. Goss, "Military Committee Membership and Defense Related Benefits in the House of Representatives," *Western Political Quarterly* 25(June 1972):215-233.

28. For example, see Barry S. Rundquist, "On Testing a Military Industrial Complex Theory," *American Politics Quarterly* 6(January 1978):29.53.

29. Ibid.

30. This analysis was performed by the author and Richard Fleisher. A description is available on request. Also see footnote 8 above, where a test of the same hypothesis in the context of the Johnson/Nixon turnover is discussed.

31. For a recent discussion of the Condorcet and Arrow paradoxes, see Norman Frolich and Joe A. Oppenheimer, *Modern Political Economy* (Englewood Cliffs: Prentice Hall, 1978).

32. An analysis David Griffith and I have performed shows that, during the period 1952 to 1972, only three states did not average more prime military contract awards when the overall level of expenditures was increased. A partial report of this study is "The Parochial Constraint on Foreign Policymaking," *Policy Studies Journal* 3(Winter 1974):142-146. A description of the larger study is available on request.

33. See Marion Anderson, "The Empty Pork Barrel: Unemployment

and the Pentagon Budget" (Lansing, Michigan: Public Interest Research Group in Michigan, 1975), for a study of the *negative* impact of military spending on some local economies.

34. Julian LeGrande, "The Distributional Impact of Public Expenditures: A Review of the Evidence," London School of Economics, June 1979.

35. Ibid.

36. See "Paying for the 'Bloody Shirt': the Politics of Civil War Pensions," in this volume.

Index

255

About the Contributors

J. Theodore Anagnoson received the Ph.D. in political science from The University of Rochester in 1977, after working for the Defense Intelligence Agency and the Economic Development Agency in Washington, D.C. In 1975 Dr. Anagnoson was a Research Fellow in governmental studies at the Brookings Institution, and is currently an assistant professor at the University of California at Santa Barbara.

Jon R. Bond received the Ph.D. degree from the University of Illinois in 1978. Dr. Bond is now an assistant professor at Texas A and M University, where he specializes in public law and policy studies.

Ralph K. Carlton is a 1977 graduate of Dartmouth College and a 1978 graduate of the Amos Tuck School of Business Administration at Dartmouth. He is currently employed by Booz-Allen and Hamilton in New York City.

John M. Echols III received the Ph.D. degree from the University of Michigan in 1977 and is an assistant professor at The University of Illinois at Chicago Circle. Dr. Echols specializes in comparative public policy and Soviet and East European politics.

Susan B. Hansen received the Ph.D. degree from Stanford University in 1972, taught political science at Washington State University and The University of Illinois, and is currently a lecturer at the University of Michigan and a faculty research associate at the Institute for Social Research. Dr. Hansen's published work concerns political participation and public opinion about taxes.

Bruce A. Ray received the Ph.D. in political science from Washington University in 1977 and has taught at Buffalo College and the University of Nebraska. Dr. Ray is currently an assistant professor of political science at Northern Illinois University.

J. Norman Reid received the Ph.D. in political science from The University of Illinois in 1975. Dr. Reid has worked for the Illinois Commission on Intergovernmental Cooperation and is currently conducting social science research for the Economics, Statistics, and Cooperative Service of the U.S. Department of Agriculture.

Timothy J. Russell is a 1978 graduate of Dartmouth College and is in private business in Marshfield, Massachusetts.

Heywood T. Sanders received the Ph.D. degree from Harvard University in 1978. Dr. Sanders is currently an assistant professor of political science and is associated with the Institute of Governmental Studies at The University of Illinois. His principal work concerns American housing policy.

Richard T. Sylves received the Ph.D. in political science in 1978 from The University of Illinois. Dr. Sylves has worked as a staff researcher for the New York State Senate Finance Committee and has taught at The University of Cincinnati. He is currently an assistant professor at The University of Delaware, where he specializes in energy and environmental policy.

Richard Winters received the Ph.D. degree from Stanford University in 1973 and is currently an associate professor at Dartmouth College. His published work includes papers on state legislative processes and policy outputs.

About the Editor

Barry S. Rundquist did his graduate work at Stanford University, was a Congressional Fellow of the American Political Science Association, and now teaches political science at the University of Illinois at Chicago Circle. Most of his research has dealt with legislative policy making—primarily in the U.S. Congress. Professor Rundquist's published work includes studies of the operation of conference committees, the selection of committee chairmen, the relationship between committee membership and the distribution of military procurement expenditures, informal interaction between House and Senate committees in reaching policy decisions, and the reasons corrupt legislators get reelected. He is coauthor with Gerald S. Strom of *A Theory of Legislative Organization and Output* (forthcoming). He is also beginning a study of the changing pattern of business relations with the Congress focusing on the Illinois congressional delegation.